Also by Eddy L. Harris:
Mississippi Solo (1988)
Native Stranger (1992)

Eddy L. Harris

SIMON & SCHUSTER

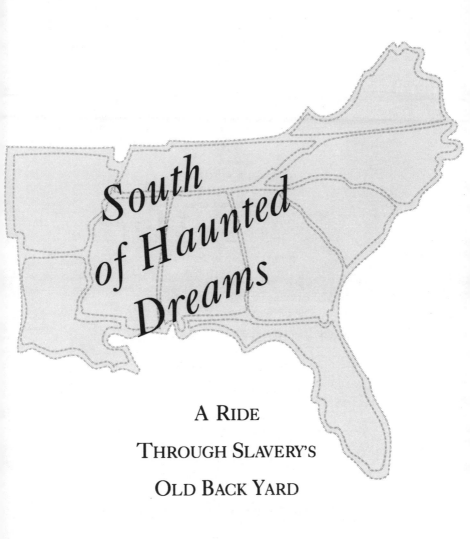

South
of Haunted
Dreams

A RIDE

THROUGH SLAVERY'S

OLD BACK YARD

New York London Toronto Sydney Tokyo Singapore

SIMON & SCHUSTER
Simon & Schuster Building
Rockefeller Center
1230 Avenue of the Americas
New York, New York 10020

SIMON & SCHUSTER and colophon are registered
trademarks
of Simon & Schuster Inc.

Designed by Deirdre C. Amthor

Manufactured in the United States of America

1   3   5   7   9   10   8   6   4   2

Library of Congress Cataloging-in-Publication Data
Harris, Eddy L.
South of haunted dreams : a ride through slavery's old back
yard / Eddy L. Harris.
p.   cm.
1. Southern States—Race relations.   2. Southern States—
Description and travel—1981–   3. Racism—Southern States.
4. Harris, Eddy L.—Journeys—Southern States.   I. Title.
E185.92.H37 1993
818′.5403—dc20   93-6558
                                                       CIP

ISBN: 0-671-74896-3

Some names have been changed to protect the identities of
some of the people portrayed herein.

TO HARRY JAMES CARGAS

BECAUSE HIS LIGHT SHINES LIKE A BEACON
BECAUSE HE KNOWS THE VALUE OF SELF-DISCOVERY
BECAUSE HE IS MY FRIEND

*A most special thanks
to Marie Arana-Ward,
whose patience and understanding
guided me through this effort*

I am your brother Joseph, whom
you once sold into Egypt.

&

—*Genesis 45, 4*

Philosophy has informed us that
the most difficult thing in the world
is to know ourselves.

&

—*Marcus Tullius Cicero*

I

*I wish I was in the land of cotton, Old times there are
not forgotten.*

—"Dixie"

South of Owensboro, Kentucky, a wooden sign hangs from a
rusted post. DAVIESS COUNTY COON HUNTERS' CLUB, the sign says,
and as I ride past, a cold hand touches the small of my back. A
shiver runs up my spine. The road I am on, Highway 231, goes
over the Ohio River at Owensboro. I have crossed into the South.

Instinctively my hand locks tighter around the grip of my
motorcycle and twists open the throttle. The engine roars. The
bike—a blue BMW—quickens. I hold on tight. I crouch forward
on the bike and hurry past the sign, hurry past the evil spirits
that hold the thing upright and steady. These many years later,
the South still owns my nightmares and haunts my memory. Like
links in the heavy chains dragged by ghosts, the images form one
by one and rattle round me, weighing me down, terrifying me.

Coon, Ape, Pickaninny, Darkie, Nigra, Nigger, Boy: these are a few of the names blacks were once and not so long ago called in the Deep South, and when a white man said, "We're going coon huntin' tonight, boy," a colored man in those days never knew quite how to take it. I imagine the white man's voice menacing, perhaps teasing a little, or even sporting and jocular. The knife edge of terror would slice into the backbone of even the bravest black man, as indeed now it slices into mine.

Those were the nightmare days of our history, a time not long enough ago when killing a nigger in the South was no more an offense than jaywalking. That era has passed us now, times do change (I hope), but the memory of those days has not died.

Incredibly those old times are remembered now as gentler than today, somehow looked upon fondly by many southern whites longing for the glory that has been lost and the simplicity that went with it, the chivalry, the courtesy, the gallantry, and of course the southern hospitality.

"*The South shall rise again,*" they say, hoping once more, I suppose, for a time when white supremacy was the rule, a time when life seemed simple and easy. The lines were clearly drawn, the boundaries set: blacks and whites, Indians, Asians, Hispanics, and Jews all knew their places in society, where they could and could not go, what they could and could not do, who they could and could not be. It was a white man's country, all right, a white man's world, and if you were lucky enough to have been born white, all was right with the world. The land was prosperous and generous, peaceful for all, the bounty trickling down supposedly from rich to poor, from white to black. As long as no one upset the delicate balance, the world seemed to spin in a greased groove.

But behind the storefront of gentility hid, and perhaps still hides, an edifice of white supremacy and segregation so rigid and so codified that in 1949 the racist society of South Africa could have turned to the American South to learn the system of apartheid. Beneath the myth of chivalry and gallantry lay a reality of paternalism and repression that lent shame to the miracle of human justice and equality upon which this country was founded. Beneath the veneer of largess lurked a poverty that would rival the worst conditions of the poorest Third World nations. And beneath it all lay a core of hatred and commingled violence, and the politics of injustice.

Perhaps in a way, then, the kindly old South is responsible for the violent present we have inherited. Since the founding of the republic the South has dictated and defined us. Perhaps the South, more even than the wild wild West, more in fact than any other region, is responsible for who we are as a people and as a nation. Since the very beginning the South has compromised us.

This is the South into which I had crossed, the South of mythic reality:

In 1945, on his way home after serving his country during the Second World War, a black veteran named Isaac Woodward was attacked by a gang of angry whites at a bus station. He had used the wrong men's room. There was no men's room for coloreds and the one he had used was reserved for whites only. The white mob gouged out his eyes. He was still in uniform.

In 1955, a black male named Emmett Till went from Chicago to Money, Mississippi, to visit relatives in the South. He didn't know any better, whistled at a white woman, and that night two men dragged him from his bed and beat him savagely. They shot him, then pitched his body into the Tallahatchie River. An all-white jury found the two men innocent of murder. Emmett Till was fourteen years old.

In 1958, Jimmy Wilson was tried in an Alabama court and convicted of stealing $1.95 from Estelle Barker, a white woman. Wilson was black. He was sentenced to die. The Alabama Supreme Court upheld the conviction.

In 1955, while trying to organize blacks to vote in an upcoming election, Lamar Smith was shot dead in front of the courthouse— in broad daylight, by a white man. His assassin was never indicted. No one would admit to seeing a white man kill a black man.

There's more. There's Medgar Evers. There's Virgil Lamar Ware. There's Herbert Lee and Louis Allen.

And these are only the most notable ones.

There's the Groveland Four, the four black men in Groveland, Florida, accused of raping a white woman. They were beaten and tortured by the police until finally they confessed. And then they were sentenced to die.

There's Addie Mae Collins, Denise McNair, Carole Robertson, and Cynthia Wesley—four young children blown up when their Birmingham, Alabama, church was bombed one Sunday morning in September 1963.

The list goes on and on. And on.

Their crimes, the real crimes of all these men, women, and little children? That they were born black, already damned by the color of their skin, born nonwhite in a white man's world, a country where being black has always been the greatest curse, has always been the greatest crime, such an offense, in fact, such a heinous and damaging insult that in 1957 the South Carolina Supreme Court ruled that it was indeed a grave error to confuse a white person with a black one, and a libelous act to call the white person a Negro by mistake. Even without proof of actual harm, the injured white party could sue for damages—and win.

Being black was considered such a crime that white persons keeping company with blacks were as guilty as spies caught consorting with the enemy. In 1958 an ordinance was passed in Montgomery, Alabama, forbidding even the friendly association of blacks and whites. "It shall be unlawful," the statute read, "for white and colored persons to play together . . . in any game of cards, dice, dominoes, checkers, pool, billiards, softball, basketball, football, golf, track, and at swimming pools or in any athletic contest."

Being black determined where you could live, where your kids went to school, who you could sit next to on a bus, whom you could love and marry. It was against the law in twenty-nine states (not just in the South) for whites and blacks to marry. The law in Alabama: *"The legislature shall never pass any law to legalize marriage between any white person and a negro, or a descendant of a negro."*

White women making love with blacks in Florida, $1,000 fine. (No penalty for white men with black women.)

Ministers performing marriage ceremonies between blacks and whites in South Carolina—$500 fine, twelve months in jail.

Texas: *"If any white person and negro shall knowingly intermarry with each other in this state, or having so intermarried in or out of the state shall continue to live together as man and wife within this state, they shall be confined in the penitentiary not less than two nor more than five years."*

Georgia: *"It shall be unlawful for a white person to marry anyone except a white person."*

Being black was limitation, and one drop of black blood was enough; one African ancestor three, four, five generations ago, and you were legally shit.

Alabama: *"The term 'negro' includes mulatto . . . a person of mixed blood, descended on the part of the father or mother from negro ancestors, without reference to or limit of time or number of generations."*

Arkansas: *"The words 'person of negro race' shall be held to apply to and include any person who has in his or her veins any negro blood whatever."*

Louisiana classified blacks more carefully. Negroes, 3/4 or more Negro blood; Griffe, 1/2 Negro, 1/2 mulatto; Mulatto, 1/2 Negro, 1/2 white; Quadroon, 1/4 Negro, 3/4 white; Octoroon, 1/8 Negro, 7/8 white.

This is the South I had entered and had chosen to motorcycle across, where Governor George Wallace of Alabama had the battle flag of the old Confederacy raised as a symbol of hate, a symbol of segregation and white supremacy to fly above the dome of the capitol.

"Segregation now, segregation forever," he declared during his inauguration address. Later, for all the world to see and hear, he stood in the doorway of the University of Alabama and announced that he would defy even the authority of the U.S. Supreme Court. He would not allow the public schools in Alabama to be integrated.

In Oxford, Mississippi, riots broke out when James Meredith went to register for classes at the university there. The police refused to protect him from the armed and angry crowds shouting invectives, hurling insults and stones, threatening his life. Federal marshals had to escort him. The National Guard had to be summoned. Just so a lone black man could go to college. And not a single white voice to offer him support nor lend him courage. It was 1962. I was six years old.

I cannot remember the details of my birthday party that same year, but I have heard the stories of those angry days too many times, have seen the images often enough that I cannot forget them. I remember as if I had been there. I remember as if it had happened to me.

I remember the signs—WE CATER TO WHITE ONLY. NIGGERS MEXICANS PUERTO RICANS NOT ALLOWED—and I know the shame and the fear. I burn with the same rage, feel the degradation that generations of black men have had to endure, men like my father, a strong and arrogant man who is a hero to me and yet who had to walk lightly in the shadow of white men, sleeping in his car at the side of the road because unless he was lucky enough to find a colored hotel when he traveled, he would not have been given a room for the night, nor allowed to eat when hungry, drink when thirsty, or ever enter by the front door. He would have had to call the lowest white man "sir," would have had to remove his hat and bow his head whenever a white woman passed. Afraid of a lynching, fearing for his life, he would never have sassed back, would never have hit back, would have put up with every indignity. He knew the boundaries, as all black men did. He would not have crossed over.

As a young man during the Great Depression he hoboed around the country, as many did—no matter the color of skin. He hitchhiked. He hopped freight trains. He slept out in the rain. He tried to find a little work wherever he could, following the promise, even the rumor of a job. Eventually he found himself in the South.

"It wasn't too good for black folks up north," he used to say. "But down south! Hell, no northern black man ever wanted to spend too much time in the South."

But he went there anyway, tempting fate, testing his limits.

"It would have been about 1934 or '35," he said, repeating a story he had told many times. He would take a deep breath each time and pucker his lips to help him remember. And each time he would wince. From somewhere within a tangle of wistful melancholy, pain and shame, the memory would awaken.

"I was just a boy," he said. "Barely twenty years old. Brother . . ." (He often calls me brother.) "Brother, it's so long ago I can't even remember the name of that little town. But it was somewhere on the Ohio River, not too far from Louisville, Kentucky. And what I was doing there, I'm only guessing. Passing through, mostly."

Passing through until he met a young woman who was lovely to look at, he said, and very nice to talk to. He decided to hang around awhile.

"Yeah, she was pretty," he said. "She was very pretty."

He might not remember the name of the town, might not really want to, but this woman he will never forget.

"Her hair was shiny black, soft and wavy," he said. "Her skin was smooth and tight. She was black, but her complexion was light enough that she could have passed for white. They called them high yellow in those days. I don't know what they call them now."

My father, very light-skinned himself, and this pretty young woman started keeping company. He said they made a handsome couple.

But then one day an old black man with a limp came to warn my father to stay away from her. The old man raised the stick he used for a cane and shook it, but he never said why, and my father just ignored him.

"I must have thought he was jealous or something," said my father. "But man! That wasn't it at all."

One night as my father was walking alone down a dark road near the river, a car pulled up. Four angry white men dressed in sheets jumped out, surrounded my father, trapped him. There was nowhere to run, no way to attempt to get away without giving them an excuse to shoot. Two of the men pulled out shotguns. One man had a pistol, another carried a big stick. All they needed was half an excuse.

"Boy, didn't you get word to stop fooling around up there on that hill?"

That's what they said to him. Then they grabbed him and started shoving him back and forth.

"Ain't you just been told to stop hanging around that girl Sally Ann?"

"But, mister, that girl's colored," my father said.

"That don't mean she spends her time with nigger men. Don't

you know whose colored girl that is? Don't you know who she belongs to?"

"No, sir, I sure don't."

"Then, boy, you need to find out. And you're going to find out tonight."

"Nigger, you think you could drink all the water in this here Ohio River? We're going to throw your coon ass off this damned bridge and find out."

"Naw, let's don't kill him tonight. Let's have a little sport. Let's see how fast he can skedaddle."

"Let's light a fire under his black ass and watch him squirm."

"Okay, nigger, did you hear that? We ain't going to kill you tonight. We're going give you until noontime tomorrow to get the hell out of town. If we see you around here after that, we're going to hunt you down like a dog and then we're going to drown your black ass. You got that?"

"Yes, sir," my father said. He must have said "yes, sir" ten hundred times that night.

"We're going to bind your ass with barbed wire and tie you to something that ain't going to float. Then we're going to dump you in the river. You understand?"

"Yes, sir."

"Tomorrow noon. Now you be gone."

"Mister," my father said, cowering. "Mister, I don't need that much time."

The way he said it, imitating himself so many years after, was hilarious. His eyes crinkled with shameless fear, his bowed head cocked to one side, his voice humble, trembling.

He went to the station that very night and that arrogant young man, my father, suddenly a coward, was on the next bus to anywhere.

It used to be a story we laughed about. It isn't so funny anymore.

The Black Codes of the old South defined how blacks were to act. These guidelines of etiquette between the races were established during slavery days, but they were still the order of the day a hundred years after. Louisiana's: *Free persons of color ought never to insult or strike white people, nor pressure to con-*

ceive themselves equal to the white; but on the contrary they ought
to yield to them in every occasion, and never speak or answer to
them but with respect, under penalty of imprisonment according
to the nature of the offense." To act otherwise was to risk a
lynching, have your home burned, your family driven out into
the street. And no one, black or white, would lift a finger to
help.

Jesse Brooks was raised in the South, in Eads, Tennessee. He
should have known better. But he had relatives in St. Louis, not
quite the North and not quite the South either, and poor Jesse
spent too much time there one summer. He learned from his
young cousins that it was all right to fight the white boys from
the next neighborhood over.

On the corner of Ashland and Lambden was a vacant lot where
the boys, black and white, played ball. When the games were
over, the boys would fight—simple as that—and then go home.
It was, in a way, friendly fighting, the kind of crazy thing young
boys do, playing one minute, fighting the next, with some sem-
blance of fairness, equality even. Poor Jesse. He went back to
Eads, Tennessee, and thought he could expect blacks and whites
to get along the way they did in St. Louis. He got too arrogant.
He fought with the white boys in Tennessee, and they didn't like
it. He went too far when, like the other boys, he tried to buy
candy on credit at the local grocer's.

"What makes you think you can buy candy on credit, boy?
You sure you got your daddy's permission?"

"Of course I do," he said. "He's my daddy, ain't he? I can
buy what I want. Just like the other boys."

They didn't like his attitude.

"You ain't like the other boys," he was told. They said he was
a sassy little nigger and they chased him that day through the
town.

The black folks in Eads were afraid to help him. Every door
he passed was suddenly shut to him. The black folks said, "God
help you, son, but please don't stop here." They were that afraid.

When the white folks caught up with Jesse they threw one end
of a rope over the limb of an apple tree, the other end they tied
around his neck. Maybe they just wanted to scare him. Maybe

they wanted to warn him what happens to smart niggers. Maybe they hadn't intended to and went a bit too far, but they lynched him just the same and left him hanging there. He was sixteen years old. He was my father's cousin. And this was another story, not so funny, my father used to tell.

No wonder my father drinks as much whiskey as he does.

No wonder black men fear the South.

I too am afraid, for I too carry the curse of dark skin, but my fear is different.

Can you imagine how it is to waken every morning and know your father and relatives had to act the coward, had to act the "good Negro" instead of the "bad nigger," had to adopt attitudes of subservience? When Blackamericans look at themselves and at their history, this in part is what we see: this violence, these constant reminders of being unwanted and unloved, of being treated as if we were less than human, these shadows of indignation, indignity and shame. Black men and women have had to bear them like crosses and there have been too few Simons (from Cyrene) to help with the load.

Forgive me if I rant, but you cannot know how I have cried and despaired and nearly given myself over to the dark gods of bitterness and frustration. You cannot know, unless I now tell you, how the anger often wells up in me lately and I am driven to the edges of violence and hate and I want insanely to fight men bigger than myself and burn buildings down, set fire to their homes, their happiness, their way of life. They and I alike pretend not to know whence comes this anger, for it seems in my case to be especially unfounded, to make little sense. I was not born into slavery or into abject circumstance. Luckily, for me and for those around me, the gods in whose laps we sit saw fit that I should not be so cursed, for then surely I would have been a murderer, indeed a butcher.

Instead, I travel to the South to confront the source of my anger. I am half hoping to hurt someone. At the same time I am longing to find a new South, a new America, hoping with heart and soul that all is not hopelessness and despair. For if nothing has changed in these thirty years, then we as a people are living a great lie and are no different from other nations that now are crumbling in the crucible of disunity and ethnic discord. Then we are not a nation wholly joined by a common culture, but instead are separated by color and class and religion and judged by them and by them alone. How easy then it will be to surrender to the viler angels of my nature. How easy it will be to break the arm of anyone calling me "boy," or the neck of someone who calls me "nigger."

Afraid? Yes. And my fear is indeed different from my father's fear, different perhaps from the fears of other black men too, for I am afraid not only for the things that might happen to me as I wander south. I fear as well for the things I might do.

I am not my father, not of my father's generation. I was not tempered in the kiln of Jim Crow. I was instead forged in a new furnace, hammered out of a new tradition—wholly connected to the old, as all tradition must be, but so utterly different. I do not come to the South with hat in hand, head bowed, timid and humble. I stand tall and firmly planted. I am not small. I take up plenty of space. I am proud of who and what I am, as arrogant as my father ever was. And I burn with an anger that is rightfully his, but that is anger nonetheless. And I am afraid, am almost certain in fact, that before this trip ends someone will have died.

Slowly I come to realize that I am not the man I once was, not the man who once believed he was who he was from the inside out, that the blackness of my skin is merely a physical attribute like being bearded or being tall.

No. I am different now. I have awakened from my slumber.

DAVIESS COUNTY COON HUNTERS' CLUB. The sign helps to awaken me. The sign helps me remember. I am black, and being black matters.

I turn the bike around and go back—slowly this time—back to the sign and to the arrow pointing down a narrow lane that disappears around a sharp bend.

The sign is wooden, its painted letters fading in the hot sun, its post rusting. The arrow painted on it shows the way, and down this road I ride.

The countryside smells faintly of tobacco, the scent borne on a gentle wind that riffles over the fields. Kentucky is tobacco country, just about the northernmost edge, but corn country too,

and the fields are green with tall stalks. The corn tops are rip-
ening. Their tassels once flowing gold have dried and turned to
brown, dangling now, swaying in the delicate breeze that blows
a hush across the valley and leads the eye from wave to wave of
stalks bending. Deep into the distance the eye floats over an
endless sea of meadows in bloom and corn fields that change
color beneath sun and cloud-shadow from gold and green to
amber and orange.

The road winds through these fields on one side; trees, shrubs,
and vines on the other. Beyond the trees a creek courses in the
valley below. A dilapidated footbridge tries to cross the creek
but has rotted with age and is ready to collapse halfway across.
On the near edge of these trees there is a small white frame
house for sale. Nearby, a shed with a corrugated metal roof waits
to fall over. Next to the shed a small greenhouse decays. The
roof has caved in, the windows are broken out, not yet boarded
up. The house, now a shack, is overgrown with weeds and consumed by the undergrowth. Saplings and vines creep through the
walls and climb through the gaps in the roof. Nature has staked
its claim on all that once seemed it would last forever. But nothing
is permanent. All eventually passes away.

When the road bends, the trees end. Cultivation runs on from
there, the fields owning lines of sight from here to the horizon.

There ought to be a huge plantation house up on the hill, these
fields of corn should be fields of cotton perhaps; old Negro laborers stooped over their hoes and baking in the hot sun should
be happily singing their woes in these fields, for this is the South
and that is the image, and down this road is the Coon Hunters'
Club.

I expect that when I arrive there I will find a bunch of big-
bellied rednecks sitting around an old wood-burning stove. They
will be chewing tobacco and wearing caps advertising seed corn,
tractors, and transmission companies. And they will be drinking
beer, of course, telling stories and dreaming about the good old
days, dreaming about lynching niggers.

Up on a hill a farmhouse does rise, but a modern one. Big
metal silos glimmer in the sunlight. At the foot of the hill there
is a sign for a school bus stop.

A car approaches and passes. The driver throws up a wave, does not stop, but goes on. From the yard surrounding a house on another hill, a child, awed, I suppose, by this big blue bike I ride, waves and runs down to the edge of the street. And I, not knowing how to take this waving, these friendly gestures, toss up my hand and continue on.

A couple of miles farther on, there is a right turn. One sign on the corner says GOD IS THE ANSWER, another sign promises GOD ANSWERS PRAYER. Just beyond the signs, the Coon Hunters' Club. Not much of a clubhouse, just a concrete box made of cinder blocks, a squat building only one story tall, four small windows on the front. But there is indeed a wood-burning stove inside, revealed by an exhaust pipe coming through a hole in the wall. An air-conditioner unit sticks out of the opposite wall and promises relief from the intense autumn heat. And perhaps there is beer inside to help with the same relief, but at this I can only guess, for the place is deserted. No one answers my knocking at the door. I will not this day get to see the inside of the Coon Hunters' Club, nor talk to any of the coon hunters. I will have to wait until some other time to be glared at, threatened, turned away, called names, and made afraid.

Some other time, of course, will be soon enough.

The motorcycle revs to its highest-pitched whine and continues on, following the road over these rolling hills and around every bend, leading me on. I have no idea where the road will go.

II

I . . . turning about in my saddle took a farewell look in the direction from which we came, conscious of having reached the dividing line.

—William Johnston

I too turned around in my saddle and long I looked in the direction from which I had come, not knowing then that my backward glance, like William Johnston's so long before me, also would be a farewell one.

The road behind bent in the distance and disappeared in the trees; ahead it ran straight like a time-line into the haze of future. It ran to the horizon and got lost in the glare, shrank near the faraway limits of my sight and was gone. I faced forward on the machine, toward tomorrow, toward the unknown. I put the bike in gear. Spurning the fear and apprehension that vibrated through me, I rode on, into the labyrinth of time, the ultimate purpose of my mission and its final significance as hidden from me as the future, as unknown to me then as William Johnston's was to him.

William Johnston was an overlander with the Lewis and Clark

expedition who in 1804 left St. Louis to explore the upper reaches of the Missouri River and the newly purchased Louisiana Territory. Their mission was to learn about the land, to make peace with the native tribes they encountered, and to add still one more jigsaw section that would help make this puzzle one indivisible nation from sea to shining sea.

Perhaps William Johnston and the others saw their lives as insignificant compared to the task before them. Perhaps they surrendered their fates to Providence, the same as I surrendered mine, to chance, to Providence, to the wind.

They went west; I left my home in St. Louis and headed south.

For William Johnston and for the other explorers with him the dividing line was a range of mountains that split the nation and the continent east and west. On one side of the great divide the rivers all flow into the Pacific Ocean; on the other side they run ultimately down to the Gulf of Mexico, out to the Atlantic.

But there are other partitions, not all of them physical, other continental divides, and one of them, just an imaginary line— as imaginary and arbitrary as all man-made boundaries are— has divided the land as no physical barrier could ever have done.

Originally it was no more than the southern border of Pennsylvania, a line named for the two surveyors who had laid it out, Jeremiah Dixon and Charles Mason, a mere marking on a map, a red line on some engineer's drawing. But not for long. The line began to grow and soon it stretched across the eastern half of the nation, which at that time was nearly the entire nation, and as the line grew it gained in significance both actual and symbolic. It extended west following the very real line of the Ohio River and itself became as real as a river, as plain and obvious as any rail fence of the day, separating neighbor from neighbor along a thousand-mile frontier reaching from the Atlantic Ocean to the Mississippi River, as formidable in many ways and as insurmountable as any mountain range. Mason and Dixon's line separated the slave states to the south from the free states to the north. And that has made all the difference.

To the north of this not-so-imaginary line and to the south of it men and women speak the same language. They share a common history, and for the most part they claim the same heroes, ancestors, lands of origin. But the perception, upon crossing the Mason-Dixon, is of entering another country, a land whose customs, whose pace, whose traditions make it altogether different from the land next-door. And the one tradition that sets the South cleanly apart has always been, and remains to this day, slavery and its lingering legacy. Its shadow still hangs over the South, hangs still over us all. And we are all complicit.

The southern climate is temperate, mild winters, searing summers, the heat lending itself to laze, to slow movement and long naps in the afternoon, to sipping iced tea in the shade, to long visits and great hospitality, to the romantic images of the South that naturally spring to mind. Lives of leisure and of indolence.

But still the work had to be done, fields had to be plowed, cows milked, crops harvested. And the work was done by hand.

Bent backs, straining sinew, sweat and song.

The Industrial Revolution came late to the South. There were no factories, no mills. The economy was all in the soil. Cheap labor was a necessity. A way of life hinged on it.

The South did not invent slavery. But as with God, had slavery not existed, the South would have had to create it. The South needed it. The South worshipped it. The South insisted on it. Without it there would have been no union—nor disunion—no thirteen original states, no Manifest Destiny, no Civil War. It was acceptance of slavery that kept the country whole. Yet it was slavery, its absence on one side of the line, its existence on the other, that divided this nation into North and South, slavery that turned the one country into two.

When the war forced slavery's end, the South clung to its racist ways, its separateness. The Civil War in spirit went on. The ways of the South continued to divide.

Among Blackamericans who have not forgotten old times in the land of cotton, crossing into the South revisits upon them the shadows of a culture that regarded their forebears as second-class citizens at best, certainly as inferior, often as less than human.

When I left my home, when I loaded my motorcycle and hit the road that wet August morning, I had no desire, no intention whatsoever, to travel the Deep South.

It was ten o'clock on a cloudy Tuesday morning. The air was

electric with rumbled threats of thunder and rain and with the unspoken promise of excitement. The smell of moisture crowded the air. It was one of those heavily humid summer days when the moisture hangs like haze in the air, denser than fog but not quite a drizzle. Already the day was hot and steamy, the sky overcast, and the sun less than a hint in the tops of the trees. Rain was on the way. A light wind gathered. Fallen leaves drifted in the yard, paper danced in the street, but little else was moved by the wind. Overhead, a jet plane glided across the sky. Far behind, the plane's rumble got lost in the clouds and was swallowed up by the thunderstorm stirring in the southwest, growling like a grizzly bear and lumbering toward me. Soft rain like tears began to fall.

I had in mind to spend some time on the road, aiming perhaps for Alaska—the long way round, of course: via New England and the Canadian maritime provinces. Winter would catch up with me somewhere along the way and force me toward the southwest, toward California. Then the following spring I would go up the coast and on to the frozen north. If it took me a year, what did it matter? I just wanted to hit the road and go.

In Africa, where I spent nearly a year traversing that continent, I promised myself I would do just that: come home, hit the road, and go.

In Africa I came face to face with the bitterest suffering. The hunger and starvation are relentless. The bribery, the corruption and suspicion so widespread they are a way of life. The simple act of getting from one place to another was so complicated with roadblock after roadblock and checkpoint after checkpoint that even a minor journey was an ordeal. Getting enough to eat was a miracle. I hungered for things easy and American, for cheeseburgers and fried chicken, for well-paved roads, for a comfortable bed. So much, in fact, that at the bottom of a letter to a friend I wrote that when I returned home I was going to head for the open road and ride as far as my imagination would take me.

I'm going to buy for myself a car, a convertible, of course, or a motorcycle, and head for the open road where I will eat greasy roadside food and think for some crazy reason that I'm in heaven. It will be impossible, I know, because nobody in this world makes a coconut cream pie like my mother's, meringue piled high and golden and slightly chewy, sweet and creamy and always more coconut than any recipe ever called for, but I'm going to search and search until I find the best coconut cream pie in the country, and with it, the best cheeseburger. And thick strawberry milkshakes to wash the taste of dust and loneliness from my mouth. I will celebrate the joys of freedom and plenty. With the wind in my face and bugs in my teeth I will fly down that open road going everywhere and nowhere in particular, with thoughts all my own and— wonder of wonders—no roadblocks, no checkpoints, no bribes to pay.

Why? Hell! Why not? Or better still: because I wanted to and because I could. No golden fleece, apart from the coconut pie, no grand yearnings except to travel freely and easily in this land where I was born, my real homeland, and to rediscover it, to take to the road for no real reason but to go.

It was wanderlust that took me to Africa.

I did not travel to Africa to find my roots. My roots are here. The thinnest tips that branch deep deep deep into the earth to suck sustenance from the soil might indeed extend all the way to Africa, but those are the roots of my blackness. They affect the color of my skin, the texture of my hair. But I am not African. The soil from which I draw my strength, my pride, and my happiness is American soil.

I cannot speak for those of French descent, or Irish or Lithuanian or Chinese—or even other blacks—but here is the land I love, the land I long for. Here is where I belong. Because here is where I am.

So much of a Blackamerican's Africanness was stolen away or lost that a new breed has been born, of African stock but not

African, a new race almost, born out of warm love, roiling passions, and long suffering. Born out of the jungle rhythms of Africa but even more out of the pains of slavery and persecution, we are a people bred in fear and with freedom always out of reach, schooled in long-term denial and everlasting patience. A new race born of the blues, a hybrid strain, resilient, resistant, forgiving. And strong.

The sturdiest shafts of my roots are anchored solidly here in this land of my creation, this place whose history and various cultures are mine. And mine is its heritage. Its dreams and broken promises, its lies and its defeats. Each fulfillment is mine and every achievement. Every failing likewise belongs to me. And with each failure and broken promise I die a little.

Slowly the mist recedes from a steamed-up bathroom mirror. The mission becomes clearer.

I would travel this country for the first time in my life as a racist, with color and race always on my mind. Spoken or merely implied, my battle cry to every black person I meet would be: "How are the white folks treating you?"—because I have seen what the white folks, the Europeans, have done to Africa, to black folks like me. And I know what the white folks, the Americans, have felt about black folks here. I wanted to experience it myself, as a way of connection.

How could I not have been drawn to the South, magnetized as my bones were, the dreaded South? The South which defines us, the South which has done so much to make black people who they are, the South that has been the cause of so much suffering. The South that has been saturated in fear and in monumental hatefulness white toward black.

White people have never suffered the brunt of such hatred. They have never known it. Nor can they ever know it.

In 1959 a white man named John Howard Griffin tried to know it. He chemically treated his skin so it would darken enough to pass as the skin of a black man. He shaved his head. He traveled the South to taste the fear and the degradation for a time, and to know what it was to be black. He told about it in his book *Black Like Me.* But he could never really know it. He could never be black like me. His heart might have been heroic and in the right place, but always in the back of his mind was the safety net. He could always go home. He could be white once more— as if he weren't always white anyway, white in his thinking, white in his outlook, white in the range of his possibilities. When the chemicals and the sunlamp treatments wore off, there was a way out. He could awaken from the nightmare.

For black people there is no escape, no way out for me, I know that now and know it perhaps for the very first time in my life, no way to shun this blackness. Not by being ashamed of my race and color, not with skin bleaches and lighteners, not with hair straighteners and not with plastic surgery. Not by immersion in things white and European, nor by education, nor by pretending. Not even by wishing that when you see me you see first of all who I am, that you see above all a person and not a black person, for that wish too is denial.

When you look at me, you see before anything else the color of my skin. That, I have decided, is not a bad thing. It is how you react to the color that offends me. If what you see is someone—some-*thing*—strange and terrible, utterly different from yourself, something inferior, something criminal and evil, something to be avoided, then that is what pisses me off, what brings me to the point of rage and violence.

On the road from New England I stopped to spend the afternoon and maybe a few days in Saratoga Springs, New York. I was coming down the Hudson River valley from Canada, had ridden along the edge of Lake Champlain. I had been on the bike for too many hours without stopping and my legs were stiff. Before finding a place to have lunch, I took a stroll through town.

It was a chilly late summer afternoon. I wore a puffy red riding suit to cut the wind and keep me warm. When I got off the bike I did not remove the suit. If anything, I must have looked ridiculous, certainly not dangerous, certainly not like someone about to commit a crime, certainly not grabbing a purse and trying to run with it.

"Can you identify the man, lady?"

"Well, he was wearing a big red snowsuit, and he walked kind of stiff-legged like Frankenstein's monster."

"Shouldn't be too hard to find."

A man in a big red snowsuit, carrying a motorcycle helmet. In broad daylight. In plain view. Walking slow and stiff. I would have to have been an idiot to even think about snatching some lady's purse.

And yet . . .

I turned off the main road and took a short tour among the turn-of-the-century homes that had been restored. A woman came toward me. She looked up. When she saw me coming toward her she panicked. Either she saw Frankenstein's monster, or else she saw something much much worse.

We were walking toward each other on the same side of the street. She strolled casually, her dress swaying in the slight breeze, her handbag swinging as she moved her arms. She saw me when she was still a good distance away. She stumbled and nearly froze. Then she clutched her purse and quickened her pace. She crossed the street and hurried away almost running.

Certainly there could have been other reasons for the fear in her face, the sudden panic. But the most obvious one was this: she had seen a black man and had been alone on a street with him. Alone on a deserted street. A white woman with a purse. Even a white woman without a purse. A black man coming toward her. Someone to be feared. Someone to be avoided. A drug addict. A thief. A rapist.

I wanted to laugh but suddenly could not. I wanted to take a deep breath and feel this sudden new power, wanted to be proud like a bully, proud of this ability to have people notice me, fear me, run from me. But I found no pride.

I have never before had a chip on my shoulder. I wonder now why I didn't. It doesn't take much reflection to figure out that something is very wrong.

Can you possibly know what it is to stand at a street corner and be made to feel so instantly and so absolutely vile, to be categorized at a glance and found guilty of some atrocity?

You're waiting for the light to change so you can cross the street. A car pulls up and stops. The white lady at the wheel looks over. She sees you there. Click! She flips the switch and all the car doors lock. You want to laugh, but you can't. You want to make a face at her, but she won't even look at you. She stares straight ahead, anxious, doesn't want to know you are still there.

How different things were in Africa, how easy to be black, how comfortable! No one was afraid of me because of my blackness. No one hated me.

Traveling Africa altered my vision, made me acutely aware of being black, surrounded as I was by black, and made me possibly even more at ease with being black, for I had ignored it so long. For the longest time in my life I quite strangely and honestly didn't know what it meant to be black or even in some weird sense that I was black, or that the color of my skin should make a difference. I thought I simply was. Simply me. Just a tall guy with dark skin. A peculiar misfortune, this lack of awareness, from the perspective of good fortune.

When I, in a more innocent age, was a little squirt surrounded by blacks in my childhood neighborhood, there was nothing special, nothing different about being black, nothing different about me, not much reason for a kid to give deep thought to the color of his skin.

Not deep thought, but some, for the big insult in those days was to comment on the shade of someone else's skin; degrees of darkness mattered. To call someone black was almost worse than using the word *nigger,* which among black people was perversely and still is a bantering term of familiarity and even endearment. So when the neighbor boy Charles Reynolds hollered in anger at me that I was stupid and ugly and black, I ignored the stupid and ugly and dwelt on the black. I shouted back an insult of my own based on color.

"Oh yeah? Oh yeah?" I stammered, trying to think of something to counter with. "Well, you're white," I said because his skin was very light, so almost white that his eyelids were like old paintings cracking with blue veins. "And white people stink," I screamed. I was eight years old.

There was a family that lived in our parish and went to our school. They were white and poor and lacking in common standards of personal hygiene. No one ever wanted to play with them. They were the butt of our jokes. Their house was a dilapidated shack and their front yard a clutter of two rusted stoves and an old wringer washing machine. Clothes and diapers hung on a line from the porch to a sapling dying in the middle of the yard. The tree was surrounded by a mound of trash that had killed all the grass and left only a bare patch of clay and dust. Their clothes were always dirty. They never combed their hair. They never bathed. They stank. To us who made jokes about them, it stood to reason that all white people stank. Our exposure to whites was limited, our derision not very deep-seated. Our prejudices were shallow. But we had our stereotypes too.

Yes, but nothing so bitter as crossing the street just because a white person happened to be on the same sidewalk. No, nothing so bitter as that, nothing so permanent, nothing so ingrained or filled with hatred and disdain.

For along with my deep love for Lisa Thomas, along with what I thought was a budding romance with Sherril Douglas, along with my silent and unrequited yearning for Vicki Foxwell, I harbored as well a warm and secret kindergarten crush on Cheryl Neroda, and she was white. My crush on her was color-blind and lasted, along with all those other youthful affairs of my heart, until I was ten. Then we moved away.

Away from the city, away from the neighborhood, away from so many black people. The neighborhood had changed. Crime was on the increase. Property was falling into disrepair. The whites by then had all moved out. And then, as if we too felt there were something wrong with being stuck in a community that was all black, something dangerous, more isolated and limiting, something not quite as good as living in a white or mixed neighborhood, my family moved out too, caught in the swelling tide of flight from inner city to suburb—escape for those who could afford to, abandonment for those who could not—and to the sudden realization that white, if not better, was certainly richer and certainly smarter.

At my former school I had been the brightest kid in class, so smart in fact that one of the nuns, Sister Deckland, to shame her eighth-grade class, would send for me, haul me out of fifth grade to solve problems on the blackboard in front of her math class and explain the solutions to them. Suddenly, in my new school—and I noticed it—I was the only black kid in the smart kids' class, put there because of my record but light-years behind the rest of that class and struggling to keep up. Tim Casselli was assigned to help me. He would turn his desk around to face mine, the same as I used to do in second grade with Charles Reynolds, but instead of playing games as Charles and I had done, sword-fighting with our pencils, Tim tried over and over to explain math concepts and solutions to problems I had trouble grasping. For the first time in my life I felt this racial difference and knew inadequacy. When no one was with me and no one was looking I would sit in the back of the class and acid tears would fill my eyes and spill down my cheeks. My skin burned with shame. I would turn away and stare out the window, dreamily recalling big-fish days in a small pond.

After a year and a half the crying stopped. I caught up and moved beyond that class, beyond that school. White wasn't better, it turned out, or smarter. Just richer. Still richer. Always richer.

There is a difference between richer and better. I was lucky enough to learn early. But somewhere in the deep recesses of Blackamerican memory, built on a history of inhuman treatment that turned into shame and into guilt, the opposite lesson has been learned: that richer *is* better, and that white means richer *and* better. And conversely that black means poor and inferior. It is from this almost bottomless well that are drawn such feelings of inferiority on the one hand, superiority on the other hand, and resentment on both hands.

And so I headed south.

I did not travel across Africa to find my roots. I traveled the South to find them. For the South, not Africa, is home to Black-americans, and Blackamericans as a race are essentially south-erners. Only in the South could I discover where my beginnings as a Blackamerican have gone. Without realizing it at the time, I was going home.

Alaska would have to wait.

I crossed into the South and looked back. I knew without knowing that I would never be the same again. I had crossed the divide.

III

You show me a black man who isn't an extremist and
I'll show you one who needs a psychiatrist.

—Malcolm X

Across the divide, across the Mason-Dixon and back back backward in time. Deeper into the South, deeper into the labyrinth,
following the line that connects, searching for the minotaur, the
monster to blame for the way things are and have been, looking
for someone to hate, wanting something ominous to happen.
Deeper I slide into the South whose past owns my nights, owns
the darkness of my imaginings, and lurks in the shadows of my
dreams, lurks in my memory like the hideous monster of a childhood nightmare. Deeper into the past that the South clings to
in a deathlike grip.

Confederate battle flags flutter along my route. They hang from
front porches. They dangle in pickup truck rear windows. They
are pasted on car bumpers, decorate caps and jackets and shop

windows. They color the covers of books. They are a constant reminder.

The South.

I drive the motorcycle with near abandon. By now I, who had never ridden before, am comfortable on the machine after already so many thousands of miles, and so many more to come, comfortable with the bike's speed and with its power, comfortable with its size and with its heft. I have learned by doing, learned to ride by climbing on and holding on, have seen the beauty in this beast and have learned to love the animal. Now I live constantly with it. I have become one with it and through it have become one with the road. I can feel every rut and every ridge. I anticipate every turn.

I lean far forward and hunker down on the bike. I see clearly, almost presciently. Long before I am upon it I know where the gravel lies and the patches of oil, the slick pavement, the wet spots. I know the bike's moods, it knows mine and I am safe. It's like riding a horse. When I breathe, the bike breathes. When I shift my weight, the bike compensates. When I look away from the road to focus on a distant blur, the bike drives itself. The bike reads my thoughts.

The bright sun glimmers off the asphalt. Mirages hover in liquid mist inches above the road. The day sparkles all around, a kaleidoscope. I am alive to the heat pouring down like rain on my back. My senses awaken to the smells of tobacco and growing corn. I speed through a hot tunnel of bright green on either side of me, suspended in a cocoon of rushing wind and vibration, the sound of the wind, the sounds of the engine. My heart pounds loudly inside my helmet.

I run through the gears. Up to fifth. Down to fourth. Around the tractor slowing in the road. Up again to fifth. Seventy-five, eighty-five, ninety miles an hour. When the road clears and straightens, I take the bike to a hundred and ten.

Corn fields surround me. Bean fields and tobacco. Clapboard houses line my route. Dirt farmers and their families look up to watch me speed by. Like flies languid in the dense autumn heat, they sit slow-moving on rickety front porches, the women in soiled gingham, the men in torn undershirts, their bellies swollen from too many beers and from diets designed with little more in mind than to quiet the long night's hunger. They are poor and they are very tired, even the young ones among them, the babies and the little children in shoes too big that have been handed down from some older relative or bought from a neighbor's yard sale. There is surrender in the soft smiles of them all, and something akin to resignation. Poor like soil that has played out, tired like overworked mules, fatigue in their faces, they gather in groups and sit on the steps. They watch the cars pass like a parade.

An old man in a rocker sits alone in the shade of a tree. Slowly he waves, but too late. I have passed him before I realize the gesture of his hand is a wave. Too late to throw up a hand in return, I tap two toots on the horn and send them back to him. I speed on as if in a hurry, as if something down this road is waiting for me.

But no one waits for me, only Bowling Green and lunch.

Why Bowling Green?

Why, then, the cop?

Why turn left when the road right seems just as fair? Why the motorcycle, this make and this color?

Why anything?

Five years ago, I canoed down the Mississippi. I saw an Indian canoe as the only suitable vessel for such a journey on such a mythic American river—something about getting closer to the water and to the spirit of the river, something about the canoe's connection to American history and to others who had gone before me. I see now that I did not choose the canoe, any more than I chose to walk across the Sahara, or to squeeze with eight others into the back of a car built for six and travel Africa, or to steam up the Congo River on an ancient barge held together by magic and spit. No, I did not choose these things. The canoe, the steamer, the camel, and now this motorcycle, I realize all of a sudden, they chose me. And none of it could have happened any other way.

I did not choose Bowling Green. Nor did I choose the South. Bowling Green, the South, the cop down the road: they—or the weaver—chose me.

My life, it often seems, is not my own, its loss the price paid, perhaps, for casting aside map and itinerary without which, as Robert Frost would have said, way leads on to way. The goal blurs and the journey itself becomes the destination. Nothing goes as planned for rarely is there any plan. And control of one's life seems to lie in the hands of some greater power.

That is why Bowling Green. That is why the South. That is why the cop, and why the turn left instead of right. It could have been no other way.

I ride as if I were, but I am not in a hurry, not going anywhere in particular, just going, traveling in the vague starting patterns a weaver makes, zigzagging back and forth, up and down, the way the wooden block slides back and forth across the weaver's loom. Not until the cloth is well along can patterns and textures in the weave be discerned, not until the tour is nearly done. The journey will define itself by the woven patterns revealed at a distance, by quite simply what is and what has been, by what the South has been and what the South is. Not by any design I have in mind. Only by what I discover. I surrender myself to the will of the weaver.

It is seventy-odd miles from Owensboro to Bowling Green, seventy miles from the Coon Hunters' Club. If time mattered, it would be little over an hour's journey. But time has warped. Time has vanished. Today seems like yesterday, seems like tomorrow.

Time as time has become meaningless, has become like the road, merely a means of getting from one place to another, from now to some moment hence. Time is the road I'm on. No more than that.

Distance too has lost its meaning. If I go ten miles or ten thousand, it's all the same to me.

The tunnel of green all around envelops me, transports me in time, backward and forward all at once, a time tunnel, the present blurring into the past into the future, the green fields eerily liquefying into visions of occasions yet to come, giving way then to remembrances of events that never happened to me—but that happened. What is real can hardly be distinguished from what is not. It is like a dream. It must be the heat. I must be hallucinating.

Specters of the past loom in the clouds. The South is as the South was—and always will be, though nothing is forever. The past and the present coexist here as nowhere on earth, side by side, as though the one cannot live without the other, the way evil sustains good, the same too as white and black in the South are inextricably linked. You can hardly think of the South without thinking of blacks, could not have one without the other. And how can you think of blacks and their predicament without considering their links to the South?

The distant past is as fresh in the South as yesterday. History is a living thing still played out, forever battled, the future at stake, the past winning at least as often as the present. The effects of history and the effects of the battle are evident in the many angry eyes, the suspicious glares, the friendly smiles, in a man's hands and in his thoughts.

It is a very hot day. The wind blows slowly. Dust spirals in the fields. Heat swirls all around. The wispy clouds that had been hanging on the horizon are now thunderheads roiling together and threatening an autumn electrical storm. They billow in the sky's high breeze. I run inexorably on, toward those clouds as if toward the future. They slide overhead and all around, suggesting shapes that my imagination can play with, but not playful ones, no swans, no elephants upside-down, no faces of dead presidents.

In the clouds before me I see hooded men dressed like angels in flowing white robes. They are burning the symbol of their Christianity, and at the same time incinerating Christianity itself.

And in the clouds behind me, as real as any hallucination, lurks the fat-bellied figure of Bull Connor, surrounded in the clouds by policemen and dogs.

How can it be real? How could it ever have been real?

May 1963. Birmingham, Alabama. A hot day in a very hot week. The streets are crowded with young blacks protesting against racism, against not being able to sit at a lunch counter or swim in a public pool, demonstrating with no weapon, defenseless hands, nonviolence.

And then comes Bull Connor. The man whose given name, Eugene, is so genteel, but whose nickname speaks of the fury and violence that pervades the South.

Bull Connor is a fleshy man with a soft puffy face, large ears, and a glass eye. His belly hangs over the top of his belt. He looks like a hick gas station attendant, a good old boy at the Coon Hunters' Club. But he is the Commissioner of Public Safety, in effect the sheriff of Birmingham. He controls the police. He controls the police dogs. The fire department belongs to him as well. It is on his orders that these weapons, the police, the dogs, and the hoses, are loosed on the black crowd.

Most of them are high school and college students. Most of them do not resist.

The dogs attack and bite them. The water from the hoses slams into them with force enough to take the bark off trees.

Day after day they are repulsed back to the black sections of town. They are beaten and bloodied. Others are arrested, more than two thousand in a five-day stretch. And for the time being Connor's edict holds: "We ain't going to segregate [he means integrate] no niggers and whites together in this town." He doesn't want blacks and whites eating at the same lunch counters, or using the same toilet, or doing anything else together either.

Whatever was this man named Bull thinking, that he and his dogs could hold back the swelling tide of the past surging into future's momentum suddenly upon him? Did he not care how history would remember him? Or did he think what he was doing would be too small for history to remember? Did he think his name would go down in the book of heroes? Or do men not think of such things? Did he think he was doing what was good, what was morally right? Or was he not thinking at all, just re-acting the way his daddy would have reacted, the way his daddy would have wanted Bull to react?

Bull Connor's face still hangs in the clouds.

It is a dream. It is a very hot day. I need a break, but I speed on as if in a hurry, as if time will save me. I am afraid to stop. I worry that fear and anger will overcome me. (I am afraid too of this almost unthinkable other thing taking shape in the clouds, an impossibility that shall for now remain nameless.)

And so I hurry, trying to outrun the fear and the anger. But I cannot escape them. Time puts no distance between me and my nightmares. They travel with me. The South is my nightmare.

Time, it seems, has healed no wounds. The old sores open. The past is indeed as fresh as yesterday, my own past awakening in me just by my being in the South.

The sun is high overhead. I have on a black leather jacket and it's hot. Even at eighty miles an hour, the wind rushing by me is not enough to cool me. I stop the bike when I come to Hartford, Kentucky, stop to stretch my legs, to cool off, to clear my head.

There is a sameness to American small towns. As you approach the town, the houses get closer and closer together. Sidewalks appear. Trees lining the road at the outskirts give way to utility poles. Buildings crop up. Cars are parked roadside. Suddenly you are in the center of town.

So too with Hartford. One minute you are on the outskirts, the next minute you're in it. Only the houses closer together to warn you.

I pull to the curb and stop at the corner. I shut off the engine, get off the bike, and have a look around.

The buildings are low, none over two stories high, old and made of brick. A few shops, a courthouse across the street, a tiny library halfway down the next block. Right here on the corner where I stand is a bank. I can see my reflection in its big glass windows. Standing here with my helmet on, my black jacket shining in the sun, gathering heat, I look like a road warrior hellbent on finding trouble. Beyond my reflection I can see the bankers and their customers regarding me with small town curiosity, the recognition and suspicion of strangers. When they see me watching them watching me, they look nervously away.

I peel off jacket and gloves and finally the helmet. I drop everything right on the ground. I stretch and flex. There is a phone booth on the other side of the street. I walk over toward it.

And of course here comes the cop, down the steps of the courthouse and right toward me.

He is the spitting image of Bull Connor to me. But then all cops are Bull Connor to me.

I prepare myself for trouble.

I have not been very lucky with the police. Every encounter with a cop on duty has been disaster, and I long ago lost my every-kid's desire to be one of them, long ago lost my respect for them as a profession. Not a single encounter has been friendly.

As a seventeen-year-old kid, just beginning my wandering ways, traveling the country by bus, I sprinted across a busy street in downtown Houston. A motorcycle cop spotted the crime, hurried up behind me, screeched to a sudden stop.

"Boy!" he shouted at me. (I was young, yes, but why do they always have to call you "boy"?)

"Boy," he said. "You better have some ID."

I handed over my driver's license.

"You ain't up north, boy," he said. "And down here we take jaywalking serious." He kept calling me "boy" and my heart was beginning to pound. I didn't know why.

"Now there's two ways for a boy like you to end up," he said. "In jail. Or in the morgue." He waited. "Now what's it going to be?"

"Pardon me?"

"Pardon me, *sir*," he corrected, but I didn't oblige. Looking back on it now, I suppose he wanted me to lower my eyes, bow my head, and apologize. I looked him in the eye instead and frowned seriously. I wondered what jail would be like. He stared back.

Eventually he let me go.

"You be careful, boy," he said finally. "And from now on cross the street like you're supposed to—at the light."

I had forgotten about the entire incident until now, repressed it, the psychologists would say.

Five years later, another situation that I did not so easily forget. The Los Angeles police were not so easygoing.

Once more I was traveling by bus, in the station and trying to buy a ticket to San Francisco. Twelve people stood in line ahead of me and my bus's departure had just been announced over the PA. In a panic I asked each person in front of me if I could skip ahead. But even with their permission the ticket agent refused to sell me a ticket.

"Why not?"

"Because you jumped in line," he said. But no, that couldn't have been it.

"I asked first. You saw me. And everybody agreed."

I turned to them all for confirmation. They still agreed.

"Doesn't matter," he said. "Now get back at the end of the line or I'll call security."

"Go ahead and call security, you jerk. I'm not moving until I get my ticket."

Security came, but what could they do? I still wouldn't budge. But then the police were called. One tough cop kept fiddling, as tough cops like to do, with the pistol in his holster. I thought it might be a good idea to get back in line, but not before I told them all, cops included, what jerks they were.

The line moved quickly—of course. Without the panic and without the fuss I would have had my ticket by now, been on the bus and gone. And that made the entire incident all the more frustrating.

The cops stayed right beside me. They gloated now about how easy it could have all been if I had just stayed in line in the first place.

"That didn't take long," one cop said. "Now did it?"

But I was still angry.

"You see?" he said. "We're not such jerks, are we? We're just doing our jobs."

I saw red.

"Calling it your job doesn't make it right," I said. "But no, you're not a jerk. You're very little more than a pea-brained penis-head."

Now he was the one who saw red. Before I could finish insulting his mother, he grabbed me by the wrist and yanked my arm hard behind my back. He twisted my wrist until the skin burned. I struggled. Together the two cops slammed me to the floor and while one of them held my head against the filthy tile, the other cop handcuffed me. Then they dragged me off and threw me into a little holding room with a couple of drunken vagrants trying to sleep off their DT's. The room reeked of vomit and urine, the odor of stale alcohol and sweat. The two cops pushed me in and bounced me off the walls a couple of times. They punched me and one of them kicked me hard in the stomach. He had been trying to kick me lower, but I sidestepped and he missed.

They didn't book me. They merely harassed me, held me there just long enough that I missed my bus.

I brooded about this incident for a long time then, but put it behind me. Never funny to begin with, it is now even less amusing, almost absurd, slightly sad, and, when I think of the returning black soldier who had his eyes gouged out at the bus station in 1945, infuriating.

Like my father's old stories, over time my own remembrances take on new shapes, gain in significance, alter my outlook. What's most important, they connect me to my father in ways I had never considered. They connect me to so many others.

As I was driving in New Jersey the police pulled me over one evening, searched me, searched my car. My offense? I had changed lanes without signaling.

"With all the maniacs out here driving a hundred miles an hour, since when," I wanted to know, "do you pull people over and search their cars for changing lanes without signaling?"

In Delaware, another cop, another search, another lie.

"Come on," I said. "Why'd you really pull me over?"

I was smiling. I wanted a good laugh and would have gone along with this joke if only they had guts enough to tell the truth. But what could they say?

"You were speeding. We clocked you doing seventy-five."

I had just gone through a toll booth. It couldn't have been more than five seconds from a dead stop.

"Does this look like a race car to you?" I said. "It doesn't to me."

They looked through the car and told me to open the trunk.

"Have you guys got probable cause?" I asked.

They looked up then, paid me more serious attention.

"Are you a lawyer?"

Now it was my turn to lie.

"You got it," I said. "I sure am."

They left me alone.

The police and I just don't get along.

I was arrested once simply for walking down the street in a high-income—white—neighborhood.

"Somebody called in and said there was a black man walking in the neighborhood."

"Oh, yeah?" I said in a panic. "Where? I didn't see him."

The cop didn't find me amusing. When I refused to show him my ID, he hauled me off to the police station.

And then this last unfortunate encounter that came just before I left St. Louis on this motorcycle.

I had ridden the bike down to the Central West End to meet a friend for lunch. As usual, I was late.

The West End is described as a fashionable part of the city, crowded with chic little shops and cafés. In spring and summer when the weather is sunny and warm, people sit outside at these cafés and enjoy the open air and watch the goings-on. At one of them my friend sat and watched the entire happening.

I had parked my bike down the street. I was late and was walking quickly. As I crossed the street in front of the café, a tan car turned sharply across my path and into the alley. Two men jumped out, one black, the other one white. They were not in uniform. They never flashed a badge. But I knew right away they were cops. Their haircuts. The car. The way they swaggered when they walked toward me. They made sure I saw the guns hanging from their belts. The one cop kept a hand on his pistol.

The black cop hurried to me and yanked away the helmet I carried.

"We need to have a word with you," he said and shoved me toward the car. "Let's see some ID."

"What for?"

"You match the description of a man shoplifting up the street."

"Was he on a motorcycle? Was he carrying a helmet?"

"He was carrying something. Could have been a briefcase, could have been a helmet. Let me see some ID."

I refused. He threw me against the car and searched me anyway. He yanked my jacket off my back and went through it. He found nothing. He took the wallet from my pants pocket and went through that too.

"I think we're going to run you in," he said. "How would you like that?"

I had to think about it. I didn't want it, but I wasn't about to give in to them and cooperate. Finally I raised a finger to the woman waiting for me, just to make sure she knew it was me, and to tell her I'd be a moment or two. If they dragged me off to jail, I didn't want her to think I had stood her up.

"Is she waiting for you?" the black cop asked, as if that made a difference, as if a shoplifter wouldn't have a friend waiting, wouldn't want to break for lunch.

I didn't answer.

The white cop got a brainstorm. He decided to call in the information from my driver's license. In a second he came back.

"I think we can let you go," he said.

"Why? Did some bozo cop catch the real thief?"

"No," he said. "It turns out that you don't match the description after all. The guy we're looking for is five foot three."

"Five foot three," I shouted. "Does he have a beard at least?"

"Well, no. But he is black," he said, as if that justified everything. "Sorry, but hey, you understand how it is."

"Well you can just kiss my ass," I said. "Because no, I don't know how it is."

"Hey, hey, hey," the black cop said, trying to calm me down. "You don't have to make a scene."

"You pull up, snatch away my helmet, rip the jacket off my back, search me like I'm some sort of a criminal and *I'm* the one making a scene? You must be out of your mind." I was shouting, going crazy.

"Don't make this any worse than it already is," he said.

"It can't get any worse than it already is," I said.

I put my finger in the black cop's face. "You especially," I said through gritted teeth. "You ought to be ashamed of yourself."

Being black is still the crime. And every cop, black or white, is Bull Connor to me. Every cop is a southerner at heart.

And now here in Hartford was another one. A southern one.

He had a slight paunch that hung over his belt, but otherwise was lean. He wore a clean white shirt, sweat stains at the armpits, collar buttoned to the last button but one. Clipped to his belt was his pistol. I waited for him to touch it, was sure he would before long.

Hartford is the county seat. The courthouse sits up on a grassy hill. At the base of the hill is a retaining wall. On the very corner is the phone booth. That's where I was when the cop, a deputy sheriff, came to me.

I was thumbing through the little phone book hanging from a small chain. You hardly ever find directories hanging in phone booths anymore. People rip pages out of them. People steal them.

I was trying to find a phone number for the Coon Hunters' Club. It wasn't listed. When I dialed directory assistance, they didn't have a number for them either. So I stepped out of the booth and leaned against the wall. The cop was waiting for me.

"How y'all doing?" he said.

"Okay." Suspicious. Cagey. "How about you?"

"About as well as can be expected," he said. And then he touched the gun. He tugged at the waist of his pants and adjusted the way the gun hung on his belt.

His accent was soft, hardly southern at all, almost midwestern but slower and with a slight twang.

"Sure is hot," he said. He pointed with his chin across the street. "Is that your bike over by the bank?"

"Yeah."

"Sure is a pretty thing," he said. "How's she run?"

"Smooth," I said.

"And fast, I bet."

"Fast enough," I said. "Speed limits, you know."

"Yeah, right." I don't think he believed me.

"You're loaded down," he said, never taking his eyes off the bike. "Going far?"

"Just to Bowling Green right now. After that I'm just going."

"Living every man's dream," he said. "Ooo-wee! That's just about heaven."

He started to walk away, around the corner and to his car parked there, but he came back.

"Hey, you ain't lost, are you?" he asked. "You looking for something you can't find in that phone book?"

"Well, yeah. I'm trying to find a number for the Coon Hunters' Club I passed a while back."

"You passed it on this road? How far back?"

"Not too long ago," I said. "Back between here and Owensboro."

He scratched his head and shook it. "Naw, sir," he said. "I don't remember ever seeing no Coon Hunters' Club on this road."

"But I just saw it."

"Naw. Not in this county. If it was here I'd know about it. I know where just about everything is in these parts. That must have been back in Daviess County. And you won't find that number in this phone book. This here is Ohio County."

He gave one more long glance toward the bike, shook his head and smiled.

"You be careful on that thing," he said. "I'm not going to tell you to have fun. That's not something I even have to worry about, is it?"

He walked away, still adjusting the gun on his belt and pulling at his collar. I heard him muttering to himself. "Man oh man," he was saying. I couldn't tell if he was talking about the heat or talking about the bike.

I took a long look at the bike myself. It certainly was a beautiful machine, big and blue and sleek and all loaded down, two black saddle bags, one on each side, a canvas duffel strapped to the luggage rack on the rear, and a fishing rod attached. I admired my choice. The first bike I ever owned. The first I ever rode. BMW. K75s. A sport bike that looked like a racer but built for long-distance touring. It had six miles on the odometer when I picked it up, twenty-two at the end of the first afternoon I owned it. The dealer and I went to Forest Park on it and he taught me how to ride it. Twenty minutes it took and he told me I was on my own. By the end of the next week, I had put six hundred miles on it. The bike was ready for its first routine service, and I was ready to hit the road. I wondered how the odometer would read by the time I got home again.

I crossed back over and suited up, slowly for all the world to see and envy, jacket, gauntlets, helmet. I looked like a road warrior, I *felt* like a road warrior. As slowly as possible I climbed on. A light squeeze on the clutch handle and the kickstand retracted by itself. I stuck the key in the ignition and started the engine. An instant of slight pressure on the little green button was all it took. She fired right up. I said to myself: Ah! Those Germans! as I always did when I had climbed on and was about to take off. When I applied the brakes, the red light on the instrument panel went off, telling me the rear brake light was working. Ah! Those Germans.

I checked for traffic. I put the bike in gear. In half a moment I was gone. I forgot all about Bull Connor and the hateful past, forgot I was in the South. And for the moment I was back to my old self, a tall man with a beard, now with a hot-looking motorcycle. I was king of the world again. Being black hardly mattered.

IV

The best-laid schemes o' mice an' men
Gang aft agley.

—Robert Burns

The year I took to the road was meant to be the year I bought a house and settled down somewhat, the year I could finally, honestly and without hesitating or fudging answer the question: Where is your home, where do you live? I had my eye on one of those rehab deals in some desperately rundown inner-city neighborhood—itself an adventure—where you can buy a big house, old and tired, for about twelve dollars and a promise to revitalize it, which I was eager to do: eager to make something with my own hands, my own sweat and a few tools, something beautiful out of nothing special, out of something ugly. Never mind that I'm no carpenter and know nothing about electricity or plumbing or construction. I can handle a saw. I can drive a nail. And I can learn.

But I hadn't any money—not enough income anyway to buy

and redo a house, but yes, money enough for a more modest adventure, money enough to buy a motorcycle, money enough to hit the road.

Once I took to the road, I imagined it might become the year I would learn to hit a curveball, long after any threat of a baseball career was over. That threat ended in 1969 when I was thirteen. I couldn't hit a curveball then either, nor even a well-thrown fastball. So I wanted to spend the summer going from batting cage to batting cage, in every small town I came to, punching in quarter after quarter, hour after hour, swinging at every pitch the mechanical arm threw at me. I would start off in the little league cage and progress until I was up to major league speed. I would wait for the machine to click into gear and for the yellow light to come on, and then stare down a ninety-mile-an-hour fastball, one after another after another. Timing, a good eye, and quick wrists. That's all it takes. I didn't want to try out for the majors. I just wanted to be able to hit the damned thing.

This is what American men and young boys aspire to, the happiness of hitting a baseball, the same as they dream of one day hitting the road.

But way has a habit of leading on to way. The goals do blur. You learn to take the bends in the road as they occur, the hills as they arise, continuing on until a dead end bars the way. You turn. You take what the road offers. You follow where it leads.

I could no more have bought a house and settled down than I could have avoided the South. The road I was on headed south. Even when it had gone north it was carrying me south.

I sped along Highway 231 toward Bowling Green. All seemed suddenly right with the world. It was autumn in the South, which is quite unlike that same season anywhere else. The sun shone so hot the day would have seemed full-blown summer to a New Englander. There was not a trace of coolness in the air. The leaves had not yet given thought to changing color. But once you got used to it and accepted it for what it was, once you put out of your mind notions of autumn's chill, the heat was magnificent.

The sun traced its path in the southern sky and radiated full on my face. Inside the helmet was like an oven. I opened the visor to let in air. The heat had been debilitating. Now the wind rushed inside the helmet and was invigorating. It rushed into my eyes and made them water. A bug smashed against my cheek.

I unzipped my jacket. The wind slammed against my chest. At eighty miles an hour, I began finally to cool down.

Tobacco fields patched the land. Houses here and there were scattered, simple and made of wood, most of them painted white. There were few cars on the road.

Then all of a sudden, as if out of nowhere, traffic began to get heavier. Trees cropped up where farmers' fields had been. The yards got smaller. The houses started coming closer together. Bowling Green lay just over the next hill, and I slowed down.

At the edge of town Highway 231 turns east. It merges with Highway 68 coming in from the right, from the west and south, and together the two roads, now one, come to an abrupt end about two hundred yards farther on. The road dead-ends into a hospital. What appears to be the main branch carries off to the right, but forks as well off to the left and up the hill. The road left and the road right both seem about the same, just as fair. I can't say why—the wind, the smell, the way the bike leans—but I'm in the left lane. When the light turns green, I turn left.

The left fork takes me along a few twists and turns and carries me into the center of town. Perhaps the road right would have done the same; I'll never know. I probably won't be going back that way. But this is where I want to be. This is where, I suppose, I need to be.

In the center of the square there is a little park that lies dark green, cool and moist in the shade of trees and shrubs. There are freshly painted benches, none of them occupied, and the park looks like the perfect spot for an afternoon nap. My shoulders are tired, my lower back very stiff. But I'm also hungry.

I park the bike in the shade and strip off the hot riding gear. I hook the helmet on one of the bike's foot pegs. I tuck the jacket under one of the straps that holds the duffel on. Refusing to worry about any of it for more than a second, I leave it all on the bike. I stretch. I loosen up a little. Then I stroll around the square. I want to find food.

On all sides the square is surrounded by shops and stores and what used to be a movie theater. Repair work is being done to the façade of one of the shops. Ladders lean against the side of the building. The men who climb up and down hang on with arms hooked through the rungs. With one hand they hold buckets and brushes and tools. The free hand chisels away old paint, applies new colors, mortars bricks in place. And as I have been watching these workers, they have been watching me. One of them calls down. "Hey! Nice bike."

I wave up, a feigned casual air, but I'm thrilled, as proud as an envied child with a new toy.

Around the corner and down the incline from the bank, there is, at the far end of a parking lot, a place to eat. All I really want is a sandwich. A greasy burger will do, some chips and a cold drink to take back to the square. According to the sign hanging over the door, this place, Mariah's, calls itself a delicatessen, but it's a bit fancier than a sandwich shop. I can tell as soon as I enter. They're going to make me sit, put a napkin in my lap, and wait until someone comes to serve me. Lunch could take an hour or more. With luck, since I've missed the noon rush, it won't take too long. I'm aching for my nap.

The tables are butcher blocks lacquered shiny. Wooden chairs, a few booths, lots of light flooding in through the windows. It's the kind of place office workers, clerks and secretaries, treat themselves to only once in a while. Salesmen treat each other to lunch here and compare notes, an excuse to have a few drinks in the middle of the day.

Off to the left is a bar with those high tables where you have to stand up to eat and drink. That section is empty and would suit me fine, but a skinny young man in a white shirt and black trousers that are too long comes to me the moment I step through the door.

"May I help you, sir?"

"Yeah." I answer looking around, not looking at him, not overly polite. "Can I get some lunch?"

"Right this way, please."

He yanks a menu from the stand and leads me into the back room. It's empty, away from the few other customers. And he sticks me in a little booth in the corner.

"How's this?"

"Fine," I tell him, but I don't really know. How can I be sure?

I'm dressed pretty shabbily, a sweaty T-shirt and a pair of old dingy trousers. You can't tell that I've just gotten off a motorcycle, that I'm touring the country and that I have an excuse for looking grubby. To him I probably just look scummy and poor. He may even be wondering if I have enough money for lunch.

A funny thing about restaurants, you can never really know why they seat you in a particular spot. A section for those who smoke and one for those who don't. Tables for two, tables for four or more. Certain places for young men alone, perhaps. Spacing the customers when possible to offer a bit of privacy, to give all the waitresses an equal shot at tips. Or. . . .

Does he tuck me away in this corner to keep me out of sight? If yes, is he hiding me because I'm grubby, or because I'm black?

The South wins again.

I *am* black. I know that. I can't stop *being* black. But I don't have to be reminded at every turn, do I? I certainly don't need to remind myself, to limit myself in that way. And it *is* limiting, confining. Once you start thinking in terms of race, everything that happens, every person you meet, every circumstance, everything on earth always gets defined in terms of race, ours and theirs, us and them. And everyone else becomes *THOSE OTHER PEOPLE*.

It's so tiring, the constant racism, the constant wondering and worrying, the constant vigilance. Is it this, is it that? It steals your energy, clogs your pores, makes your hair fall out. It makes your food taste funny.

Did someone spit in my drink?

A cute little waitress comes over, young and very happy, as if there might be nothing at all on her mind more important than her boyfriend. There's a college nearby. She's probably a student. She smiles sweetly. She pours iced tea into my glass.

"Do you know what you're going to have?"

A burger, fries, and a small Caesar salad.

"Is there someplace I can wash my hands?" I would like to sound as gruff as possible, displeased as I was about being stuck in the corner, but facing her smile and her politeness, it isn't easy.

"Yes, sir." She points. "Right through there and make a left."

When I come back I slouch across the booth. I lean back against the wall, arms folded across my chest, and put my feet up. I close my eyes, shut out thoughts and light. Darkness softly enfolds me.

From somewhere I hear singing. Negro spirituals far in the distance. Someone singing the blues. "King" Oliver on Bourbon Street.

A little black kid tapping my shoulder, asking if I need a shine, wearing the cap on his head backwards. In the barbershop behind him, black men beckoning but I can't tell if they're calling the boy or if they're calling me. Big smiles. Happiness pouring out. Until the explosion. A bright light. The boy vanishes. The barbershop disappears in the flash.

The sun has shifted. The bright sunlight streams through the window and stings my eyes. Rays of light cross the room, dust suspended and swirling in narrow shafts. I blink a couple of times to clear my vision.

I must have dozed.

Outside in the street, two motorcycles are roaring past. The bikes are old, the kind that make much noise and sound like cannon fire.

One man rides solo, the other has a woman strapped to his back. Both men have long hair, their big potbellies bouncing on their thighs. The woman looks haggard and hard. She wears no helmet.

I take a deep breath and smell food.

The waitress has set my plate before me. She stands above me, smiling like an angel of mercy, holding the pitcher of tea, poised to pour more as soon as I nod yes.

I smile kindly and thank her. Even if I wanted to be gruff, with her there it would be hard even to pretend. She disarms me with her own kindness.

"Having a hard day?"

"About like all days," I reply. "Thinking too much, I guess."

"We all get those days now and again," she says, sounding like an old veteran, preparing for a career of missed opportunities, still waiting tables when she is old and divorced with kids to put through school. I'm waiting for her to call me sugar, the way old waitresses often do.

"And there's nothing you can do about them," she says, "but smile a little. I find it always helps if you smile a little. Sometimes it even helps you beat the heat."

She smiles.

"If you want more tea or if you need anything else, just holler."

I settle back and relax. The burger's not bad.

It comes to me now that the waitress reminds me of someone, a young ballerina I once met in Washington, D.C. I had gone with a friend to fetch her from the airport.

"Did you have a good flight?" I asked her.

"Yes, sir."

She was about nineteen, about the same age as this waitress, very pretty, and like the waitress, much too polite.

"You're from the South, aren't you?" Even without the accent it was evident.

"Yes, sir," she said. "From Mississippi."

I wanted to ask her if in Mississippi they always called black men "sir," but I preferred to imagine that she had been raised to be polite to all her elders, to call all men "sir," and to say "yes, ma'am" to all the women. It was nice. But she made me feel old.

"You don't have to say 'yes, sir' to me," I told her. "I'm not that old. Okay?"

"Yes, sir," she said.

The South.

When I had finished eating, the waitress came and cleared the dishes away.

"Dessert?"

There was nothing on the menu I wanted.

"No. I'm quite satisfied," I said. "Unless . . ."

"Yes, sir?"

A gush of air escaped my nose, a little laugh.

"You don't have a coconut pie stashed in the back somewhere, do you?"

"No, sir. We sure don't. Sorry."

She left the bill. I checked her addition to make sure there wasn't a mistake. Sure enough, there was.

I debated, but not long, whether to point it out. The mistake was in my favor.

When she came back to collect, I pointed out the error.

"It seems," I said, "you forgot to add on my salad."

"Sssh," she whispered. "I didn't forget. But you looked hungry and real beat. I thought I'd treat you."

She smiled. I'm sure I was frowning.

There is something about unmitigated generosity that brings out the paranoic in me. It is not much different from unprovoked hostility. At some point you sit up, you look around, and you wonder, Why me?

Was it her, was it me? Was it the full moon? Or something in the air?

When I finished my lunch, I went back to the square and lay on the grass. The ground in the shade was cool and damp. I put my jacket down, lay on it, used my helmet as an uncomfortable pillow. I lay there looking up, watching the sun shift in the sky, watching the branches part in the slightest breeze and come together again. The bright light sneaked at odd intervals between the gaps in the leaves. Shadows crossed my face. I covered my eyes with my left arm. It wasn't long before I had fallen asleep.

I don't know how long I lay sleeping in that square, but I awoke stiff and not much refreshed. In fact I was just as tired as when I had started the nap, maybe more.

On the bench near me a man was sitting, watching me. He startled me. I sat up quickly and stretched. He watched me awaken.

"I never like sleeping on the ground," he said. "I never get comfortable."

"I don't like it much either," I said. "Bugs crawl on you and you start to itch."

"Yeah, that's it all right. You wouldn't think something so tiny as an ant could irritate you so. Then you get a blade of grass in your ear and you think it's a big bug going for your brain or something. The slightest things start to drive you crazy."

I laughed.

"Exactly," I said. "I know exactly what you mean. I'm a city fellow; I have to be really tired before I can do it, before I can sleep on the ground."

We laughed together, old friends already, sharing something as simple as itching and scratching.

"Then you must have been mighty tired," he said. "The way you were snoring."

I giggled, put my finger to my chest and put on that *Who, me?* expression. He nodded.

"I guess I was."

He was funny the way he just sat there.

I stood up and stretched some more.

"And I'm still tired."

"Is that your bike? She's a beauty."

He scooted over on the bench, the first movement he had made. There was plenty of room. He didn't have to move. But he slid over by way of invitation for me to sit beside him. We shook hands. He held mine a long long time, almost as if he were reading me through my skin and bones and the texture of my palm. And as he read mine, I read his.

His fingers were long and bony, the skin scaly. The palm of his hand was calloused and rough. His grip was strong. He was a farmer, I guessed, or maybe a carpenter. The sun had darkened his face. His eyes were pale.

He grinned. He looked hard into my eyes for longer than was acceptable. I stared back, locked onto his gaze and refused to blink. He squeezed my hand harder. I squeezed his. His stare became uncomfortable. Then it became unbearable. I flinched first. I looked away.

"Where are you from? You're not from around here."

"No, I'm not."

"What the hell are you doing down here?" he said. "You on vacation? Because if you are, this is one hell of a place to spend it."

"I'm just passing through," I said.

He said his name was Franklyn. He had lived in or near Bowling Green all his life. And yes, he had been a farmer, and he had been a well digger, and he had worked in construction.

"Whatever it takes," he said. "That's what I'll do."

I stroked my beard in thought. My hand smelled of Franklyn's hand, a strong odor that was the smell of the grass I had just lain in, the smell of the soil, the smell too of sweat. A man's history, the battles he has fought, won and lost, can be read in the lines of his face, in his smile and in his eyes, but in his hands as well.

I looked at my own hand.

"And you, I figure, work in an office," he said. "But you don't like it. You'd rather be out—I won't say fishing, because you're a city boy—but you'd rather be outside. Freedom, motorcycles, and all that. You got you a bit of education and you're wondering why you haven't made a million dollars."

I just shrugged. We both laughed.

"Everybody wants to make a million dollars."

The breeze picked up warm and gentle. It caressed my face. I closed my eyes to feel it and the sun came through the trees.

"Nice, isn't it?" he said. "Almost a little too nice."

I looked at him. He had closed his eyes too, doing what I had done.

"So how have you been getting along?" I asked.

"Well, to tell you the truth," he said, "I've been wondering why I haven't made a million dollars too."

He laughed out loud. His head tilted back and his laughter pealed across the square.

"But how are you going to make a million dollars," he said, "just sitting all day on a park bench?"

A leaf had fallen onto his shoulder. He flicked it off.

"When I figure that out," he said, "man! I'll really have me something. But in the meantime I'll just sit here and enjoy the sun and conversation with a stranger. That's almost like having a million dollars, don't you think?"

"Better," I said.

"Well," he said. "That depends on the stranger and on the conversation."

We sat a few minutes looking out across the square. It was a little busier now. Teenagers had come down to hang out.

"Look at those kids," Franklyn said. "Black kids, white kids, just as natural together. You'd think they didn't know nothing about what used to go on. Maybe they shouldn't."

"Has it stopped?"

"Hell no, it ain't stopped. It might not never stop. But it's a damn sight different in a whole lot of ways than it used to be. Funny thing is, I can't always tell if that's good or bad. One thing's for sure, it ain't never going back to the way things was. Too many people like you won't let that happen."

He looked askance at me.

"Right?"

I took a deep breath.

"I'll tell you another thing," he said quickly. "They ain't never going to let you forget you're black, that's for sure too. White people, black people too. They're going to force you to be black and to think black and to act black. And those kids would do better the sooner they realized it. One of these days they'll split up and go their separate ways. The white boys will forget they ever had friends who were black, the black boys will live like they don't know anybody white. That's one thing that ain't changed."

I saw then that he was much older than he first appeared. I had guessed him to be forty-five or fifty. He had a youthfulness about him. But in the way he now squinted, the sudden melancholy, the deep furrows when he wrinkled his brow, and the harshness of his memory, I put him now at about sixty. He had seen and been through plenty.

His voice was suddenly very heavy. He stared out straight ahead, gazed far past the scene playing out in front of us, and he talked cheerlessly as if to himself.

"They have no idea," he said. "No idea what we went through to get here, no idea just how far they've got to go. They think everything's cozy. They think all they have to be is good as the next man, as smart, or as rich. They don't know it yet but they'll find out that that black kid over there could be the most likable kid in class—hell, in all of Bowling Green—everything a mother could want in a husband for her daughter, but if her daughter happens to be white, even if they've been friends forever, the minute they want to go to bed together or have children together or get married together, ain't nothing else going to matter but the color of his skin. And it'll make him think there's something wrong with being black. He'll forget just how good it is to be black, and it'll make him crazy. But that's just the way the world is, sorry to say."

The joy had been sucked out of the air. He tried to get it back by slapping me on the knee. Now when he spoke, he looked at me from time to time, but his smile was still weak.

"Take, for example, you," he said. "Now, let's just say you're an artist and you painted a picture. If you're a black artist, that's what they're going to call you. A black artist. And they'll expect certain things from you and they'll limit you, try to make you fit in. And white people won't collect you or they won't take you serious. Not just a painter or a politician, but a black this or a black that. And the same goes for women. That's so you'll always know this ain't where you're supposed to be. Just like white basketball players. They say, 'Aw, he's pretty good for a white ballplayer.' And they'll compare you to other black artists and try to make you feel you're not really good enough to be compared to the main bunch of artists, or ballplayers, or whatever the thing is. Of course you and I know they're just scared. Ain't that what it is? As soon as they let black people in fair and square, black people just seem to take over. A lot of times it seems like black people are just better at a whole lot of things. Like baseball and basketball and a whole lot of other things. Smarter too. Because black people see the world different. Maybe that's why black people don't get a fair shake. And maybe that's why America's in decline. Things have changed, all right, but I don't think things have changed enough."

Franklyn kept talking. I heard his voice but my own thoughts carried me a little farther on. I was thinking of black writers and black literature, and what makes them black. Is it only the color of the writer's skin, or is it his state of mind, what a writer brings to his work, his subject, his outlook? A black writer's point of view can be very different, but it doesn't have to be. And if it isn't, is it still black literature?

The reader too brings with him certain expectations.

What makes the characters in a novel white or black? If the

author doesn't tell me, do I automatically imagine that they're white—characters in a novel, voices on the radio? Is this what the dominant culture has done? And if the author is black, do I assume his characters are also black? What has the culture done to my expectations and to my assumptions?

Think back to the people I saw up around the Coon Hunters' Club, the children who ran down to the road, the old man who waved, the women in gingham, the fat-bellied men in torn undershirts. Were they black or were they white? If I don't describe them in terms of color, what color does the imagination supply? The color of the reader, or the color of the culture? Close your eyes. This man I'm talking to now, Franklyn, is he black or is he white? Can you tell from his being, what's important to him and the way he talks, or do you have to look to know? Or does it not matter?

Of course it matters. He's black and how he sees the world is different precisely because he *is* black.

The waitress was white. The men on the ladder, they were white too. The cop in Hartford of course was white. And every one of those country folk lining my route to Bowling Green was white. And it matters. In some way it matters a lot.

Then Franklyn stopped my reflections and shocked me.

"Maybe it doesn't matter at all," he said, as if he were reading my thoughts. "Maybe it's like Jesus. We all know Jesus was a Jew, going to the temple, singing in the choir maybe, with a rich and soft tenor voice. What do you call those Jewish men who sing in the Sunday choir?"

"Cantors, I think," I said. "And you mean Saturday. The Jewish sabbath runs from sundown Friday to sundown Saturday."

"Whatever," he said. He looked at me with impatience. "Anyway, we all know Jesus looked more like that terrorist fellow— what's his name? That man in the PLO."

"Yasser Arafat."

"Right. Well, Jesus probably looked more like him than like the handsome wavy-haired blond with blue eyes that we always see in pictures and statues. But in some black churches, Jesus looks like an African. And in South America I bet Jesus looks like an Inca Indian."

I scooted to the edge of the bench and turned to look at him full-face. He was smiling, happy that he had got my attention, that he was the genius.

"Maybe a character in a book doesn't have to be one thing or another. Maybe he can be everything depending on who's doing the reading. Just like Jesus. And it doesn't even have to make sense. Maybe that's why I stopped going to the movies. They steal away your imagination. And they cost too much."

My frown melted into a broad grin to mimic Franklyn's. He was looking straight ahead, but he felt my smile and he beamed and he looked at me.

"What's the matter?" he said. "You can't imagine that deep thoughts would pass through this old head of mine? What else you think a man does when he sits all day on a park bench?"

We made together at that moment a joyful sound, our laughter running together and ringing out across the park in melodious harmony, his the bass, mine the baritone. The kids across the way turned to look at us. It was impossible to tell if they were laughing with us or at us or not paying us any attention at all, but anyway they were laughing.

"I'm a park bench philosopher," Franklyn said, still laughing. "But to tell you the truth, I just thought all that stuff up."

"But anyway, you might be right."

"Maybe so," he said. "And maybe people read other people like they read the characters in a book. Their history and your history will meet. And when they see you—you, I'm talking about now—maybe one man will see something completely different from what another man will see. The way you carry yourself. The way your eyes light up when you smile. The warmth in your hand. It's not easy to miss your intelligence. And something else too, but I don't know what it is. They won't see in you what they see in me, that's for sure. You're the new generation. You ain't never had to bow. Men can see that in your eyes."

His eyes sparkled with a new idea. He raised his hand and pointed a finger—aha!—to the sky.

"Maybe you can be like Johnny Appleseed," he said. "Maybe you can teach them."

But I didn't know then what he was talking about and we fell silent.

"I sure do love that bike," Franklyn was saying now. As he had invited me to sit, now subtly he was inviting me to leave, to get back on the road and on my way.

"I'd love to be off going everywhere," he said. "But I surely do not envy you. I think you must be kind of nutty, riding around the South on that thing. People down here are still a little bit crazy. Everybody's got a gun. And you're more than a little bit exposed, you know. But I guess you know what you're doing."

"Perhaps I don't," I said. "But the Lord watches over fools and babies."

"I sure hope so," he said.

We shook hands once more and I got up to leave.

"I do wish you luck, brother," he said. "And I wish you peace, with yourself and with other men. I hope you find whatever it is you're looking for. But damn! Couldn't you have looked for it in a pleasanter place?"

And I uttered these words for the first time, just to provoke: "Maybe the South isn't as bad as we think."

"Oh, it is," he said. "Maybe worse."

"Well, look," I said. "I met you, didn't I? And you're not so bad."

"Yeah, I'm not so bad. When you look at it that way, maybe the South's not so bad either. It's as bad as *I* think, that's for sure. But maybe you'll find something different. Maybe it'll treat you different. Maybe it's all in how you've been used to seeing things. You're bringing with you a different history; maybe folks really will see it in your eyes."

He frowned, squinting again and looking into my eyes as if to see what difference there might be.

He came with me as I suited up and climbed on the bike.

"You know," he said, "in a more perfect world we would all be blind. Then a man's color wouldn't matter and there would be no assumptions to make."

Then he realized. He shook his head.

"Naw," he said. "We'd just find some other way to hate each other. To hate ourselves, too. That's all it really is anyhow."

V

Pride of race will come to the Negro when a dark skin is no longer associated with poverty, misery, terror and insult.

—Carl Sandburg

What do people see when they see black?

Long before the road turned south, I was riding up the coast of Maine toward the Canadian border. Autumn hits the northeast early, and I wanted to get in a little fishing before cooler weather set in. I wanted to have a peaceful, perfect time watching the whales in Nova Scotia. I wanted to cruise along the sea and eat fresh lobsters. There is nothing sweeter-tasting or more tender than lobster pulled from the sea and plunged directly into a vat of boiling water. An ear of corn or two, maybe a salad and a beer, but nothing fancy to compete with the delicate flavor and texture of the lobster. Every time I passed a sign that said FRESH LOBSTER I wanted to stop.

I spent a night in Bath, Maine, at a little inn. A couple from California were the only other guests. They had retired and were traveling really for the first time in their lives. They had driven cross-country. They had laid a map on the coffee table and were plotting out their route, picking spots for trout fishing. I told them my favorite spots in Vermont, New Hampshire, and Maine.

"Do you fish for trout?"

"I don't go anywhere without my rod," I said.

Then I told them some of the great places I had fished for rainbows and browns and brookies—Montana, Vermont, Scotland, South Africa. I suppose I was bragging a bit. The man was astounded. I showed him my fly rod, a very nice one—a very expensive one. He was more than a little bit jealous.

After breakfast the next morning, as we were saying our good-byes, as the husband was packing the car in the driveway and I was loading the bike, he and his wife complimented me on my good fortune and on my deportment.

"It's too bad all black people can't be as articulate and non-threatening as you," he said. He meant it as praise. I was insulted.

"What makes you think they're not?"

"All we ever see on TV are radical blacks, criminals, and preachers. Maybe you ought to go into politics."

And then the real insult.

"Tell me," the man said. "How in the world does a black man come to take up such an elitist and expensive hobby as fly fishing for trout?"

"Fish are color-blind," I said. "They can't tell."

He didn't get it.

"You know what I mean," he said. "You've been all around the world. You stay in the kinds of places that I've always wanted to stay in, you do the things I've been saving up for twenty years to do."

As if his desires and mine should be so different, as if all black people are poor, on welfare and food stamps.

"I've had to wait all this time and I'm only just now able to do it. Are you rich?"

"No," I said. "I just act like it."

"Then what's the secret?"

"Attitude," I said. "Attitude is everything. You never get to do anything if you work all the time. You get to do even less if you listen to what other people say you can and cannot do."

What does this man see when he sees me? A glitch, something gone wrong, an aberration. An intelligent, nonthreatening black man that he wishes all black men could be. He just doesn't understand, does he?

Still I sometimes wish I could be what other people see as an ordinary black man, poor and blighted and easy to ignore, with the cares and concerns and interests of common black men. Then they would see nothing uncommon in the things I do, the places I've been. And oh how I wish that all black men could be as fortunate as I have been. For privilege is punishment. If all black men and women who wanted to do these same things were able and allowed to, then what I do and have grown used to would not seem so rare, would not be evidence of privilege, and I could be without the burdens of best behavior, duty and obligation. I could be left alone. I could rid myself of other people's expectations. There is advantage in privilege, certainly, disadvantage as well, punishment and responsibility. Always responsibility.

One thing is certain. One way or another we pay for all we have and all we are.

If I am well mannered, even-tempered, and good natured, it is to my detriment. Perhaps I am a coward after all, afraid to reveal the anger and the rage that boil within.

Or have I, in some way, been a traitor all these years?

I'm thinking of the grandfather in chapter one of Ralph Ellison's *Invisible Man*. As he lies dying he tells his son, "After I'm gone I want you to keep up the good fight. I never told you, but our life is a war and I have been a traitor all my born days, a spy in the enemy's country ever since I give up my gun back in the Reconstruction."

But does he mean a traitor to the white men he deceived, or traitor to his own people who followed his example and subjugated themselves, perhaps even bought into the lies of inferiority and promises of heaven, promises that their patience one day would be rewarded?

And which have I been? Which of these lies did I sell my soul for: the biggest lie of all, perhaps, the one that claims that all men are created equal and that in this land of opportunity the cream rises and all who apply will be considered on their merits, on the content of their character and not on the color of their skin?

(Somehow still I do believe it.)

"Live with your head in the lion's mouth," the old grandfather says. "I want you to overcome 'em with yeses, undermine 'em with grins, agree 'em to death and destruction, let them swoller you till they vomit or bust wide open."

But I feel sometimes that I was the one who did the swallowing, greedily, selfishly gobbling up the lies, at best clinging to hope, grasping at straws, and at worst doing whatever it takes to survive. Without the hope of tomorrow, there is no hope. And like the most desperate Jew in a Nazi death camp, I sold my soul perhaps for a chance at survival, for a chance at tomorrow, even to the point of being won over to the other side. I feel as if I have been colonized.

The road turned south once and for all, though I didn't realize it at the time, as I passed through the part of Connecticut that is ritzy suburb to metropolitan New York City. I stopped to visit my brother who lives there, in Stamford. He had been invited to a cocktail party the evening I arrived. He wanted to drag me along. I was grubby and very tired. I didn't want to go.

"Come on," he said. "We won't stay long, I promise. There should be lots to eat and drink."

I was very hungry.

"You'll like this," he told me. "They're your kind of people." By which he meant refined and well mannered, the kind who hold their pinkies out when sipping tea or champagne. He was making fun of me. I was not in the mood for jokes.

I had spent a year in Africa amid poverty and suffering. I had been casually insulted by a well-intentioned gentleman in Maine. I had been harassed and practically strip-searched by U.S. Customs on my return from Canada. A woman in Saratoga Springs wouldn't even walk on the same sidewalk with me.

"I don't think I'm in the mood," I said. "I think I'm tired of those kinds of people. I've had enough of polite society." But Tommy didn't believe me. So we went.

There are two me's—at least—and Tommy was right: one of me is very comfortable with refinement and with elegance. I have indeed been colonized.

I have striven to be included in the culture that prevails, but have come to feel lately that I do not fit it. I wonder if I ever did fit.

Instead I feel powerless and I feel useless. That is what it is to have been colonized: wanting in, but forever on the outside.

The party was held in the home of Sam and Carla Mancini. My face and my brother's were the only black faces there. But Sam and Carla probably see themselves as very liberal. They think they live in an integrated society. They think the whole country is an integrated society.

I wondered how in the world I had learned comfort in the company of these others.

The party was one of those dreadful affairs where you spend most of your time hovering over a table of hors d'oeuvre because there's not much else to do. It was as boring as death. My life flashed in front of my eyes. Footprints in the sand, right to the edge of the shore. I could not see where I was headed, but I was reminded how I had come to be there. I had been on the road to that table all my life.

Long ago when I was in seventh grade I found myself sitting in a classroom side by side with the *crème de la crème*, as they called themselves, of my hometown. I had taken the entrance examination for a private school founded in St. Louis by a group of stern British monks who had come from England at the request of wealthy St. Louisans wanting a Catholic school that was a cut above for their college-bound boys. Somehow I won a spot in their midst, learning French and Latin, studying Greek and calculus and Shakespeare.

For some reason I never questioned if I belonged with them, these sons of doctors and industrialists and beer magnates.

Their families were among the wealthiest and the oldest, the most influential in St. Louis, I suppose, the most respected and prestigious, certainly among the Catholics. There were other nonsectarian prep schools in the area, and private schools for boys and girls of other faiths, but I doubt any of them at that time carried the weight and snob value of the school for boys lorded over by the severe and aristocratically arrogant monks from North Yorkshire.

The boys who attended were the brightest the area had to offer, groomed for this, most of them, their futures loosely outlined by the sometimes rigid, sometimes flexible and fragile boundaries of money, education, expectation, and exposure. Could any of them have imagined a future life as a long-distance truck driver or thirty years' drudgery on an assembly line in some factory? Rather, the gods had reserved for those boys chairmanships of the board, prestigious positions as giants of architecture, high-powered attorneys, skilled surgeons, pillars of society. Like fathers, like sons. Positioned since before birth. They by prosperity, I by proximity.

My first year with them I was one of only 5 blacks in that school of 214, one of only 2 in my class, but I was too busy to let the numbers worry me, working hard to keep up. And if I did sometimes feel different, the feelings were more about being poorer rather than about being blacker. No one called me nigger. I never once heard the word even in anger, not when I fought Jim Niemann for a particular seat on the bus to school one morning, nor even when David Tucker hurled me to the gymnasium floor on a Saturday afternoon and sat on my chest until I cried uncle and surrendered only to get up and taunt him again and again— for what I cannot now remember. Each time I came at him he would throw me to the floor until finally I realized I would not win this battle. I burst into tears like some sissy, vaingloriously giving the fight one last attempt by swinging a folding chair in his direction. Then I quit, Tucker holding out his hand to shake mine.

I was one of them, I guessed, learning their values, swimming daily in the foamy white surf of wealth, absorbing, learning new ways to balance with the old, until I remained *who* I was but no longer what I was, in a way half one thing and half another. And then the new ways consumed more than their rightful half, metastasizing within until only outwardly did I resemble the black shell that housed me.

And I never questioned my belonging; they never let me. Almost as if by some design or conspiracy, they made me feel, parents and sons and the rest of their families, that I really was one of them.

Every Friday after school, it now seems, I was invited to dinner in the Baldwins' home. Each Friday I would be there hanging out with Tom, and each Friday at dinner time I was told to phone home and ask if I could stay for supper. We would sit sometimes in the kitchen to eat but most often in the dining room, cloth napkins in our laps, water goblets sparkling, silverware shining, and someone would serve me until I had taken my fill. Later someone would drive me home.

In summer the afternoons were spent hitchhiking with John Niemann and swimming in Bill Sciortino's pool. My weekend nights were spent playing poker, stretching the late nights into early morning in the homes of the Berglunds, the Hefferns, the Brinleys.

The Niemanns never had a Christmas party that I wasn't expected to attend, the Aviolis never failed to invite me to their New Year's celebrations. The Barrys still consider me their seventh son.

I cannot remember now why or what we talked about, but when our revolving poker game took us to the Tobias house, Sherwin senior would often invite me into his study and we would chat. Dr. Sciortino would often do the same. And Dr. Avioli seemed to have expectations as high for me as for his own children, his wife once saying to me: "We're expecting great things from you one day."

(She never said what or why.)

Once again, as in my childhood neighborhood—but different—being black hardly seemed to matter.

My sensitivities were the same as everyone else's around me, my desires, my aspirations, my outlook. My ambitions were the same as theirs and the life I thought would be mine was no different than the lives they dreamed of: doctor maybe, or corporate executive; a magnificent house in the suburbs, a passel of children, a happy family, comfort and the fast track to a million dollars. The well-worn American dream.

Oh yes! As black as I am, I come to realize how white men have made me. As much as by any black man, I have been shaped by white men, and they continue to make me. Ought I now hate them for what they have done?

Two winters ago one of them, Dr. Sciortino, died. I was more than saddened, so numbed that at the funeral I could hardly speak. I could not remember the name of Bill's wife, forgot even that he was married. I was flooded instead with memories as alive and as warm as my tears that very cold morning.

I spent the morning in a haze of memory. The gray-haired, bespectacled doctor was once again sitting in his big easy chair, smoking cigars that cost an ungodly sum and came wrapped not in plastic but in sealed metal tubes. I had never imagined there could be such a thing. His eyeglasses were dense and I never clearly saw his eyes, but I'll never forget his smile and how he would sit in the dimly lit room surrounded in a fragrant cloud of smoke. His hands were strong with the skill and knowledge of his profession. When I injured myself one evening on the basketball court and we had gathered, as was our custom, in his kitchen to drink soda, Dr. Sciortino called me into his study and put his hands on my right thigh. He felt the warmth of my leg with his thumbs and pressed the sore spot where I had been kicked. He knew in an instant what had happened, what was wrong, and told me what I should do. I was profoundly impressed, as impressed as I had been the first time I walked through his pantry and found not a few six-packs of soda or even a case and a few cans of juice, but cases and cases of summertime refreshment stacked high as the ceiling, and not just one brand or two, but several. It was Aladdin's treasure, pure enchantment for a kid limited at home to one glass of orange juice in the morning, and if we were lucky enough to have it, one soda in the afternoon. "It's bad for your kidneys," my father would tell us. "If you're thirsty, drink water."

Not so with the Sciortinos, nor with the others who invited me into their homes to eat their food, swim in their pools, and be part of their lives. They shared with me their wealth, their ways, and their expectations.

Somehow Dr. Sciortino's death marked profoundly the end of one period in my life. And the start of another.

It was then I went to Africa.

There is another me waiting to be unraveled, another me I have only begun to discover. The other me was shaped in part by white men too, long before I was born, and is as black and as outraged as can be. The other me showed up at the Mancinis' cocktail party in Connecticut.

I was back from Africa, still thinking about the Invisible Man's grandfather. And I started to think about my own grandfather, my great-grandfather, my great-great-great-grandfather. If they could see me now, they who had been slaves, and sons of slaves, what would they think? Would they be proud or disheartened, marvel at how far I had come, or saddened because I had got no further? Would they see a spy in the enemy's country? Or would they see a traitor who has done whatever he can to survive?

I had tried but found I could no longer "overcome 'em with yeses, undermine 'em with grins, agree 'em to death and destruction." They had swallowed me and now at the party in Connecticut, I was going to leave the revelers—a few of them, anyway—vomiting just a bit and busting wide open. I was heeding the grandfather's other admonitions.

I tried to avoid confrontation. I tried not to be conspicuous, to be in the room without being in the room. I tried to vanish into the woodwork, to blend in with the surroundings. I tried, as I always tried, to disappear without leaving, to keep my feelings to myself and my big mouth shut. But once it was discovered that I had been to Africa, that I had spent a year traveling there, I became the sudden center of attention. I was drawn in.

"I bet you were glad to get home."

"I was," I said.

I was standing by the table of hors d'oeuvre. I had just shoved into my mouth a tortilla chip with crab dip on it and I was eying some sort of bean concoction. I wanted more to eat. I reached for a couple of little sandwiches.

"I bet you saw some things in Africa that made you think, didn't you, things that made you really appreciate what we've got here."

"No argument there," I said.

"And I bet you think this country is just about the best place on earth."

I poured myself another glass of wine. Before I took a sip, I finished chewing the piece of lemon chicken I had bitten into. I took a moment to think.

The party was somber as a funeral. Laughter came in titters, disagreements in hushed tones. The loudest sound was the clinking of a fork on china.

Outside on the back patio a young man was talking about the U.S. troop buildup in Saudi Arabia and the imminent war against Iraq. He was not part of the conversation inside, but I could hear him.

"I hope we do go to war," he was saying. "I just want to see what happens."

"You can't be serious."

The group around this man was aghast. The genteel reaction was predictable. War is a terrible last resort, the failure of diplomacy, and let us pray for peace.

"Sure," he said. "Let us all pray for peace and let us hope that utopia one day arrives and that the world will all make sense. Until it does, you should know that in the real world wars are not always fought for just causes against enemies you have a serious need to see destroyed. If they were, the United States and the Soviet Union would have started shooting long ago. War is about winning, so you pick your spots. It's about dominance; it's about flexing muscle. It's about making the country feel good when there's really nothing else to feel good about, something we can all rally around and support like good little citizens, something to make us forget for a while the rest of what's going on and what's going wrong. And sometimes, when you're a warrior tribe like we are, it's just wanting to know how strong your army is. That is what this war is all about. This one has nothing to do with our strategic interests or naked aggression or any other nonsense the president wants you to believe. Otherwise we could just send in a squadron of bombers and blow the hell out of Baghdad. This is a test; this is only a test. We haven't had a real war since Vietnam, and we lost that one. You can't count those big bully fights we keep picking against the likes of Grenada and Panama. This time it could be for real. The Iraqi army is battle-tested from eight long years of desert warfare against Iran. This is merely a test to see if the U.S. Army is any good. And I'm sorry for the lives that will get lost, but death is inevitable and just like those guys in the Pentagon, I'm dying to find out how good we are—if we are."

I can only imagine how my face must have soured, how it must have silently roared. I bit my lip. My hand started to shake. I shoved the hand into my pocket. I tried to stop myself but couldn't.

Get hold of yourself, I thought. *You've only had one glass of wine; you can't possibly be drunk.*

I was prodded.

"Well?" someone said, I don't know who.

In almost slow-motion I looked around the room and took in the comfort of upper-middle-class living. It was, in a word, taste-ful. Everything so tasteful and so neat. The paintings hung with care. The porcelain figurines and objets d'art decorating the shelves and tabletops. The furniture so carefully arranged. Even the colors had been chosen according to some scheme. Not a thing was out of place.

This is the life I had been prepared for, a life of ease and comfort, gentility and good taste.

But suddenly that decorous life no longer appealed to me. It seemed somehow so inadequate, as if something terribly impor-tant was missing. It did not reflect the world I had recently come to know. It lacked truth.

The house had all the worldly signs of refinement, all the comforts one could reasonably want. But it lacked realness and grit. It was sterile.

A house full of affluent, intelligent people and they didn't have a clue about the real world. It was like a cartoon, not real at all. The conversations were carried on in hushed murmurs, static noise.

And on the patio a man was advocating war for the sole purpose of testing an army. Killing people as if it were some sort of game.

No wonder the world is in the shape it's in.

My head was spinning. My vision blurred. I felt sick to my stomach. I tried to resist but found at last that I could not control myself. After Africa, who can? Suddenly I was back at the checkpoints with soldiers' rifles stuck in my ribs, with beggars and starving children swarming at my side, with illness and utter powerlessness at my throat.

In the course of a lifetime there are experiences so powerful that they become part of us. A place we've been, a thing we've seen, something heard or read or done. These events are more than mere memory. They shape us. They define us. They alter the way we think and feel, and the way we see the world. Ernest Hemingway said it of Paris, that if you have the good fortune of living there in your youth, *"then wherever you go for the rest of your life, it will always stay with you, for Paris is a moveable feast."*

Africa had become my moveable feast.

Africa was with me still. The sufferings of other black men and women would remain with me always.

And then there was my childhood. I could not forget where I had been, how far I had come and the unfairness of fortune. The landscape of my memory was littered with friends who had not escaped. I could not forget them. All of a sudden I was bothered by what it means to be black in this country and to be a man and to be a black man.

I took a deep breath. I looked at my inquisitor, and he looked at me with a smirk that said he knew he had me: that America was paradise, and that I should appreciate living here.

"You just don't understand, do you?" I said. "You haven't got a clue."

I can hardly describe what happened next. From my lips, through no control or desire of my own, all the anger of the ages funneled into me and then spewed out again. I lost half my mind. In the torrent of my venom I reminded him that I was black.

"What do you mean?" he said. "What has that got to do with anything?"

"It means that I understand everything about you," I said. "I know where you're coming from and what you're thinking. I can get inside your head because in so many ways I am like you. I have your same twisted dreams and aspirations. I know what you want and I know what you feel because this culture has taught me to think like you. But you don't know a thing about me. You don't know who I am. You don't have an inkling what it feels like to be black. And what's more, you don't even try. You don't even care."

He was stunned. He didn't know what to say. He stared for a second, then stammered, and then he was quiet.

"I care," he said. "What makes you think I don't care?"

"Because if you and all the people who claimed to care really cared," I said, "things wouldn't be as bad as they still are. Africa is not the only place with inhuman poverty and injustice."

He wanted to talk to me about New York City.

"The greatest city in the world," he called it. "It's got everything, rich and poor, black and white, side by side. People of all races live together and they get along fine. It's truly a melting pot."

"What New York City are you talking about?" I shouted. "There's a hundred thousand homeless people living on the streets there. And blacks and whites and Koreans and Jews killing each other every day. Don't you read the papers? You can't be this naive."

"I spend a lot of time in New York," he said. "I never have a problem."

"You think that because you can't see the problems the problems don't exist," I said. "I don't know what part of New York you've been hanging around, but come with me tomorrow. I'll show you a New York you've never seen before. I'll show you places where you won't even want to get out of your car. Even in daytime. I'll show you places where the poverty and suffering will make you sick."

He stammered, didn't know what to say.

"I'm almost thirty-five years old," I said. "I have almost surpassed my life expectancy. According to the statistics, because I am black and because I am a man and because I live in a city,

I've got a better chance of being dead or at best on drugs or in jail than I have of seeing my next birthday."

Then the host joined in. He offered that things might not be as bad as they seemed. He said, "Certainly black people are a lot better off than they were in the past." Bill Cosby, he pointed out, made forty million dollars last year.

I looked at him like he was crazy. Then I lost the other half of my mind.

"Because one black man made a lot of money," I said, "you think things have gotten so much better? What's wrong with you people? Are you so blind that you can't see anything?" Now they were all listening to me.

Climb inside my head, I told them. Climb in and see what it's like to be black. See what it's like to always wonder if what happens to you is happening because of your color. See what it's like to constantly be under suspicion, to always be seen as criminal or deficient. Can you possibly know what that feels like? And if a man as fortunate as I can feel this way, can you imagine how the less fortunate must feel?

The system is stacked, I told them.

"I'll tell you one thing," I said. "If I were poor and destitute I'd go where the money is, I'd stick up *your* neighborhood. I'd break into *your* house. But the way justice works in this country, it doesn't pay to break into your house. Listen, if a black man kills another black man, he gets a light sentence; if he kills a white man, he gets life in prison at least, the death penalty probably. The same is true for burglars. The system is stacked. If I were a criminal, I wouldn't steal from some miserable wretch as poor as I am; what am I going to get, a TV, a stereo? I'd steal from somebody who's got something I can really use. I'd steal from somebody who benefited most from the injustice. And you can bet we'd find a solution pretty quick if all the poor people stopped robbing and stealing from each other and started coming up here to your neighborhood. If they started marching into ritzy white neighborhoods and torching rich people's houses, you can bet that would shake up some things."

It went on like this for forty minutes. And it got worse.

"The best thing we can do is to burn it all down and start all over," I shouted. "Just line up all the people who aren't trying to make it better, line up all the people teaching hate, and shoot them. In fact, we ought to just line up everybody over the age of thirty and start shooting. Or over the age of twenty. Or even fifteen. Just line them up against the wall and get rid of them all."

"What good would that do?"

"It would be a start. There wouldn't be any people left to teach their kids to hate. I would say kill everybody over the age of five, but somebody has to be around to raise the kids."

"But you're over twenty," he said. "You're over thirty."

"Start with me," I said. "I have gained from the way things are. I'm part of the problem. Shoot me first, set fire to my house. I'll make that sacrifice. What sacrifice will you make?"

The hostess was sobbing now.

"There's no point going on," she said weakly, as much to herself as to her husband. "Can't you see you just can't get through to some people?"

A young woman had pulled my brother into the kitchen. I heard her say, "Why isn't your brother more like you?"

"More like me?" Tommy said. "I'm the hot-headed one. He's the one who's always so polite and quiet."

"He's so hostile and malicious!"

"I am malicious because I am miserable. Am I not shunned and hated by all mankind? You, my creator, would tear me to pieces and triumph; remember that, and tell me why should I pity man more than he pities me? . . . Shall I respect man when he condemns me? Let him live with me in the interchange of kindness, and instead of injury I would bestow every benefit upon him with tears of gratitude at his acceptance. . . . If I cannot inspire love, I will cause fear, and chiefly towards you my arch-enemy, because my creator, do I swear inextinguishable hatred. Have a care; I will work at your destruction, nor finish until I desolate your heart, so that you shall curse the hour of your birth."

These words of Frankenstein's creation leapt burning to my ears.

"I guess he's just seen too much," my brother was saying.

Once in the car my brother howled out in glee.

"Big Ed!" he shouted. He seemed happy. "Should I call you Mr. X, or will Malcolm be all right? You were a raving madman!"

He started to laugh.

"Did you see their faces?" he said. "They thought you had brought the revolution. They thought it was right outside their front door. They thought you were serious."

"What makes you think I wasn't?"

"Right, Malcolm," he said, and we laughed.

"You're just a sheep in wolf's clothing," he said. "I know it and you know it too." He laughed until he nearly convulsed.

"But they sure didn't know it," he said. "Wait till I call your mother and father. Wait till I tell them how their baby boy was carrying on, shaking up the suburbs and scaring the white folks."

He was genuinely thrilled. And then he got quiet and a little bit pensive. He slowed the car and looked at me.

"Welcome back," he said.

We passed under a street lamp and the light caught dimly in his eyes. The laughter had gone. A wrinkle furrowed his brow. It lasted only a second, and then it was dark again.

~

I rode on quietly. The South was on my mind. The South was within me. And the prospect of going there left me brooding, for if things were as they were in the North, how bad then would they be in the South?

Africa had become a moveable feast for me because I had been there. The South was a moveable feast long before I even thought of going there—it had begun to affect everything I saw, every person I met, everything I thought and felt, long before I mounted the bike and headed out on the road.

It would not be an easy holiday tour, this much I knew—a journey not only across the South but back in time as well and into the future, and, most importantly, into the mind of a black man.

I wished the Mancinis and their guests could travel with me.

ॐ

The road south carried me through New York City to Coney Island, out into the harbor beneath Miss Liberty's blind eye, out to Ellis Island.

I hadn't been to Coney Island in fifteen years. I had never been to Ellis Island.

How different Coney Island seemed to me now. The gauzy curtain of time throws a soft haze over old memories, and everything is colored by newly darkened bifocals.

I walked along the beach and remembered my first roller coaster, how I had adored it and how after each ride I had stood in the long line waiting for the thrill to repeat. But with each ride the thrill lessened, wide eyes narrowed, innocence receded as innocence does, like an aging man's hairline. It was never the same.

Nor was I, as I walked in the shadow of the Cyclone, the name for that old roller coaster, and could not conjure up that long-ago rush of excitement. Too many years had gone by, too many other emotions barred the way, too many ghosts had come between.

The ghosts that haunt the cold stone halls of Ellis Island are not black ghosts. They whisper only part of the story. Photos on the walls, old tables and chairs left neatly in place, the past echoes quietly as if the fury of the world passed through these rooms and left nothing but serenity.

Ellis Island is a national monument, but where is the black person's Ellis Island, where the monument, however rusted over in the shame of chains and slavery, to immigrants from Africa? No reminders that blacks are, have been, and will always be part of the history.

Perhaps because the reminders would be too filled with shame and pain. For all.

And so, no reminders here in the North, the liberal and urban North, no reminders of the riots in 1864 New York or in 1917 Chicago in which blacks were picked out for slaughter, the thirty-nine dead blacks, the thousands left homeless after race riots that same year, 1917, in East St. Louis.

Life in the South was a horror that many blacks fled, the flight from Egypt. But what of this place they fled to, this promised land? Better? Or did they find that the South truly begins at the Canadian border?

When I am in church—on the road or in my hometown—why is my pew always the last to fill? I know how Catholics like to sit alone with their God, how they will always take an unoccupied pew. I prefer an unoccupied pew myself, and that's usually where I find myself. Unless mass is absolutely packed, Christmas or Easter, or unless I'm in a black church, I am always the only one in my row, always the last one anybody wants to sit next to. I am forever sniffing my armpits in church to see what's the matter.

No wonder my hair is falling out.

No matter what I do, good, bad, or indifferent, always it seems I am reminded just how black I am.

No wonder that the links in this chain are wrapped tight around my neck and yanking me south.

I do not believe in predestination, nor really that the gods in whose hands our lives lie have some carefully designed strategy. But from all quarters the South had been singing to me the song of the Sirens. If there are these gods, perhaps they from time to time shift the winds to see what we will do next with the new circumstance of our lives. If there is a destiny, perhaps it is a constantly shifting one, and it is up to us not merely to live it but to discover it based on all we have seen and heard and felt.

Our human hearts are like bits of sponge soaking up memory and experience, swollen with a little bit of this, a little bit of that, and a small taste of some other thing: a small child afraid in the darkness, a little boy crying in the back of a classroom. We either surrender to our anxieties, to our shame, or we fight them and redefine ourselves. Otherwise we are not masters of our fate, not much better than the choiceless animals, mere hostages to circumstance, more amoebae than men.

We may be the sum total of all we have seen and heard and felt, but we are not hostages to that past, not unless we choose to be. We are connected to our past selves the same as we are connected to our ancient ancestors and to history, by a time line that has run since always, a road winding through mountains and ending just in front of us. The road ahead must be blazed, through the trees and over the mountains, by each of us. It is a road that has touched time and all that time has ever tasted.

With one eye on the past we look ahead, emptying ourselves to leave the layer of rocks upon which we stand and reach above, shinnying up to the next level, one foot remaining on the level below to steady us until we can hoist ourselves higher. We climb. Perhaps from there, from the next level, we can find a better view.

And so with these thoughts and memories I came to the shores of Lake Cumberland in Kentucky to pitch my little one-man tent. The sun was going down. The fire at the horizon slowly died out. The sky had taken on the quiet colors of late evening, steel gray in the east, palest blue overhead, misty rose in the place where the sun had last smiled. Most of the boaters had surrendered to the coming darkness, had driven their boats to the landing and were winching them onto trailers. A few grasped at the last straws of daylight and stayed out on the water just a little while longer. Some sped across the lake, back and forth, dragging skiers behind, trying to roar the evening awake. The loud motors of their boats spoiled the stillness. The water swelled into mini-tides and sloshed heavily against the shore. Others fished. It was the best time for that. The evening had taken away the heat. Insects settled on the water. Hungry fish were splashing after them. A fisher could hardly miss at a time like this. Only the darkness falling swiftly, and the motorboaters, could send them to shore.

When all had left the water and the area, I lit a little fire. Up on the hill was a small stall, toilets and showers. I went up to find water.

The boaters had all gone home. I was the only one left, the lone camper. I was alone on the earth.

The water in the lake settled down and smoothed over as if a chill wind had turned the surface to ice. Trees became silhouettes in the fading light, then shadows barely reflecting at all off the water. A star appeared. Then another. The sky lost the last color it would see till morning. The evening tired. So did I.

Crickets awakened one by one and sang their night songs. Birds called their mates to nest. Frogs on the banks croaked a startling sound, bass to the symphony. And at the very instant that all was darkness, the symphony crescendoed to silence.

Then it started again and I fell from my trance. I was in the South.

The smoke from the fire drifted to me. The scents of growing tobacco that had filled my head all day now filled my memory. I sniffed my hand. It still smelled of Franklyn's, still smelled of southern soil. Although I had never smelled it before, it was a familiar smell, like a taste in my memory, like home. The night smelled the way the South ought to smell. Green and dark and smoky.

It was bizarre. I felt suddenly and strangely at ease.

I stumbled down the hill with the water and found my way. I opened a sack of rice.

Rice, I think, is a miracle.

VI

In thinking of America,
I sometimes find myself admiring her bright blue sky
—her grand old woods—her fertile fields—
her beautiful rivers—
her mighty lakes and star-crowned mountains.
But my rapture is soon checked when I remember
that all is cursed with the infernal spirit
of slave-holding and wrong;
When I remember
that with the waters of her noblest rivers
the tears of my brethren are borne to the ocean,
disregarded and forgotten;
That her most fertile fields drink daily
of the warm blood of my outraged sisters,
I am filled with unutterable loathing.

—Frederick Douglass

The sun has not yet risen and dew coats the grass with glitter. Liquid diamonds hanging from branches and from leaves drip to the earth as a breeze from the south and from the west whispers warm through the trees. A mockingbird calls the morning to waken. Light appears at the edge of the sky, and acrid fragrances sail aloft. The sulfur smell of gunpowder and rotten eggs rises strangely from the earth, drifting, stinging the senses awake. The scent of pine and damp soil perfumes the morning. Soft moisture bathes the air, a fine mist hangs, light fog floats in stripes across the lake where a lone hawk glides above the water. A fish splashes. The hawk dives and disappears into the fog. Somewhere a propeller plane mutters unseen across the sky, too far away to shatter the stillness. It is a morning so cool and so beautiful, so full of promise, as all mornings are, so delicate and so fine that serenity enters into me as gently as water into sand.

I take a deep breath and hold it. Slowly I let it out and take another. The moist air smells sweet and I can taste it as it warms around me. I can taste it on my tongue.

I fill my lungs. I breathe slowly, easily. For this moment at least, I am at ease.

Now I know why the journey: because I have felt the weight of civilization and have sought relief. I have sought renewal.

You cannot know true satisfaction unless you once have known want, nor hunger until you have tasted plenty, nor serenity until torment has torn at your soul. Until this moment I never knew how tormented I was.

I never knew—or perhaps I did—that my father's anger has always been my anger, that all black men's suffering and shame has been my own. What my father and my grandfathers knew, I know. What happened to my brothers happened as well to me, and will descend again to my children yet unborn. We as a people carry these burdens in our genes, pass them from one generation to the next. They are part of who we are.

Beyond the superficial, beyond station and skin and circumstance, there are things shared that make us who we are, something that separates us, distinguishes us—whoever WE are—from the mass of others. Call it collective history. For Blackamericans it is, of course, the experience of slavery which marks and demarks us, the shame of it, the pain of it, the bewilderment of it, and the guilt too, perhaps, for having let slavery happen.

I wonder if Jamaican blacks feel as homeless as Blackamericans do. Or Brazilian blacks. I wonder too if they have so little pride that they will look to find their roots generations behind them in a land they never knew and in a people they are not now.

Blackamericans are not unique in their migration to this hemisphere; slavery is a tie that binds all North and South American black men. But others gained their freedom earlier. They outnumbered white men, revolted, and took possession of whole countries. Others made peace with those around them until the various cultures fused. Other black men are Brazilian, Bahamian, Jamaican, Cuban, Haitian. But we in the north, we are neither one thing nor another, a hyphenated people, reminding ourselves of the blatantly obvious, the richest of the lot and the poorest. We know not who we are, nor where we belong.

In Africa black men will tell you this: "From this great distance you seem to have everything. Here in our little villages, very often we have nothing but this, and this is more than wealth: we know who we are. We can look back one hundred years, two hundred years, we can look back forever and we know who our fathers were, where they were born, how they died and where they are buried. But you, American man, you can only look back a few lifetimes and then you are lost. You have everything but this: you do not know who you are."

Orphaned at an early age and suffering the indignity of a hostile foster home, a Dickensian orphanage, we carry a double burden: this loss of identity and the shame of slavery.

I think I know why white men hate us so—that we were slaves and they were not. Perhaps too that we were slaves and are no longer, for who among men does not long for servants to assure him of his greatness?

But apart from slavery . . . (And didn't whites come to America as slaves too? Seventy-five percent of the white immigrants who came to the colonies south of New England between 1620 and 1780 came as indentured servants and bondmen.)

But apart from slavery, are we, black and white, so woefully dissimilar? What the African says about black Americans, couldn't it just as easily apply to white Americans too? Do they know who they are?

We are mongrels in this country; we are mongrels all.

So what apart from slavery and suffering and skin makes a black American black? Or are slavery and skin reason enough to bond us all in suffering? Or is it, as Franklyn said in Bowling Green, largely other men who make us?

Black immigrants from Haiti. They will for a time remain Haitian-Americans, maintaining two cultures. But the culture that surrounds them eventually will alter them. They will have drunk the water and breathed the air. They will have learned to walk the walk, to talk the talk. They will have absorbed. They will one day, I think, their sons and grandsons, their great-grandsons continuing to live in New York, no longer be who the parents were. They will no longer be Haitian. They will be American. And what's more, they will be this new thing. They will be niggers as well. Not because of the color of their skin, but because of the way white men treat them. White men will see color and react to it. And these once-Haitians will have absorbed in two generations the pain of three hundred years. And their way of seeing the world will change.

Slavery's impact touches more than black, but white as well, the shame of it, the lasting pain of it, the bewilderment of it, and the guilt too for having let slavery happen. It has left all of us less than whole.

As I was about to head south, sometime during the long autumn eve leading to war in the Arabian Desert, General H. Norman Schwarzkopf, commander of allied forces arrayed against Iraq, appeared on television to prepare his country for war, get us ready to hate, give us permission to kill and cheer slaughter. Referring to the Iraqis, soldiers and civilians alike, Schwarzkopf said that they are not part of the same human race that we are.

When the war was over, and this man was transformed into an American hero, there were parades and celebrations, jubilation in the streets for our victory over the enemy, for our mastery and superiority over them. No one recalled Schwarzkopf's vocabulary of hatred. No one asked where sentiments like his come from or where they lead.

Not part of the same human race.

Words meant to envelop a country and unify it in the warm glow of patriotism and pride.

Not part of the same human race.

They are just the words of one man, but they have a way of entering the collective psyche, the collective awareness, just as they have been taken from there to get cycled around once again. They become the consent we seek to look at other peoples and to hate them, to see in them profound differences from ourselves, to give them nicknames they never deserved and to make jokes about them, to mark them, to force them into concentration camps and to exterminate them, to enslave them, to annihilate them as a people, to steal their land and corral them onto scrubby reservations that would hardly support a pack of coyotes, to burn their villages, to shut our eyes and close our minds and stand idly by while others do the dirty work. *They*—these others—called out the dogs and set them loose. *They*—these others—blasted the children with firehoses. *They* did the humiliating, the mutilating, the shooting, the maiming, the killing. *We* are the innocent. *We* had nothing to do with it at all.

We protest these crimes. We cannot see how we perpetuate them. But the sins of the fathers have a way of staining the souls of the sons, a way of settling into the collective memory of a nation. And they will not go away. They have stolen our innocence. They have damaged us. They linger, much as slavery lingers, and they affect how we see and how we are seen by others. Most importantly, our sins determine how we see ourselves.

We are an old nation now, an old world. The bill has come due. We are now paying the price for the sins and indiscretions of our youth, for the bad choices we made in a long line of history. It can be no other way. The bill always comes due.

Not part of the same human race.

Yes, I know why the journey. Simply this: I seek salvation.

I seek a confrontation with the South and with the past, face to face—a baptism of the spirit, a reconciliation, and, in the end, a salvation. I seek a new way of seeing.

I gaze into the water at the edge of the lake. In the bottom of the pool a dark face stares back at me, a face I hardly recognize anymore, the face of a stranger. It is a tired face, a face that does not smile. In this face there is no serenity. The eyes squint. They have become piercing and hard, not as wide around as I remember them. They have about them the look of fatigue. There are puffy circles beneath and the eyelids too are softly swollen. Perhaps that is from sleeping on the ground, or perhaps they have been crying. Perhaps they are about to.

There are more lines in the brow than before. The lips are clamped shut. The beard is grayer than it ought to be, longer, wilder looking. There is something almost menacing in this face, but still it is a pleasant face, not, I would imagine, a face to fear. If I saw me coming toward myself, I would not run and hide.

Nor would I panic if my daughter brought home this face to meet me.

So what is it about this face, these hands, these arms, that makes white men fear me, that makes me so repugnant to them? Not long enough ago they would have refused me a seat beside them at a lunch counter. They would have gouged out my eyes for using the same toilet. They would not have wanted to fight beside me, die beside me, live beside me. What is it that makes them even now refuse me a place at table, begrudge me a decent job, a happy existence, a home in the neighborhood, membership at the country club?

Perhaps this, now I begin to see it, is how it is to be black in America, what it really means to be black, to live always with these questions branded, like a slave owner's markings, on your being, on the back of your mind, on your memory. To look in the mirror and see a face that is hated and feared by men and women who have never laid eyes upon it.

But no. Not this face. Not this gentle, peaceful face. It can't be me. It can only be the idea of me they hate, for they do not know me really. I hardly know myself.

The wind catches the water, and the water laps gently against the edge of the lake, its sound soothing and inviting, luring me close. The face blurs in the ripples and vanishes.

I scoop my hand into the cold water and rinse my face. I wash the sleep out of my eyes. Another scoop and I taste the water. I rinse my face again. I touch my hand cold to the back of my neck and then, still not quenched, I rise. And the water beckons.

Like baptism.

Swiftly then. Like a child. Before fear prevents me.

A lightning-quick and crazy dip naked into the lake, frigid, heart-stopping madness. Startled awake and then suddenly numb, I am intensely alive one minute, dead the next. Resurrection in reverse. Goose bumps riddle my flesh, clothe my nakedness. Arms flapping, hands clutching, fingers squeezing, I rub sensation back into my body. Hands grope frantically for skin, for legs, arms and shoulders. I am alive again and as happy as Lazarus. Giggling, screaming, freezing, arms wrapped tightly around my ribs, I hop barefoot over stones and sticks, dashing wildly uphill to the stalls and a shower, praying with the fervor of a religious fanatic that I will find hot water.

Oh, the joys of solitude!

When I am alone I am not black. I am not tall. I am not deformed. I am not ugly. When I am alone I am nothing more than a voice whispering, a mind wandering, a spirit soaring. There is just a hint of brown at the inner corners of my sight. If I move my eyes down I can see the brown skin of my nose. I can see the black shadow of my mustache. But unless I lift my arms or move my head and look down at myself, I am colorless, shapeless, two eyes looking out, and yet utterly whole and perfect. An abstraction. A thought. An idea. When I am alone, without other men's opinions of me, without their eyes attempting to define me, without the ways they treat me, their reactions to me, their fear and their loathing and their disgust, even their kindness, without other men I am simply me.

I wish I could stay in these woods forever, escape this civilization we hold so dear. For if men and women are civilized, I think I should prefer the trees and the remote company of animals.

The dreamer in me searches from time to time for escape from civilization, and I seek renewal in a new skill, a new place, a stranger's face. It is, perhaps, why I drive fast, why I seek the thrill of danger—a reminder of my mortality and a momentary escape from it as well. To float in the clouds, to plunge into an icy lake, to race down a ribbon of road. Time suspends, elongates, has no meaning. The clock dies and for the briefest moment that seems to last and last, I am alone with only my thoughts, with only myself. It is why I have come south. To find myself.

Will I surrender to hatred? Or will I find peace? The roots of our discord lie buried in the soil of the South, this place that makes us who we are. If the seeds of brotherhood could be planted there, would they not grow alongside the weeds of hatred and choke them out?

The thrill of not knowing. This is my addiction. The wondering what lies beyond the trees, around the bend, over the next hill. The hoping one day to stumble into a miracle.

Over the mountains of the moon you ride, and into the valley of shadows. Along the way you acquire some things, you lose some things. Someone you once held dear has died. Someone you used to be is no more.

Don't look back, the man said. Something might be gaining on you.

But look back we must.

I have not previously explored the South. I do not know it, yet it is not a land altogether unknown to me. How could it be? I feel the place in my bones.

Here is where my people lived and died. Here is where the new breed was born, where denial and fear slowed the rhythms, where suffering slowed the singing, where the wails became blues, where what joy there was became soul, became jazz, where hope was the religion, where warmth, passion and bitterness were the heritage.

The color red flashes, streaks across the corner of my vision, vanishes, and flashes again. A cardinal darts from branch to branch. When it alights, it sings three long slurred whistles, four crisp chirps.

And suddenly that which yesterday was unthinkable takes shape in the trees. I conceive the inconceivable and this time give voice to it. Could I like this place?

But how could I? How could a black man ever like it here in the South, here where it has never been good to be black, never even been all right to be black? How could a black man ever feel comfortable here?

I had this fleeting notion that even if they don't like blacks in the South, at least they know us, recognize us. They grew up with us. It must be very hard indeed, I thought, for a white person to live in the South without at the very least knowing someone black. Not so in the North. You can pass your entire life in a cloistered suburb and never see, except on television, a black face, never encounter a black person, talk to him, get to know him, shake his hand.

But no, I have hated the South and feared it since long before I can remember, since before I was born. I have inherited the dread as all blacks have, have heard too long the stories linking me to the horrors of the past. I have hated the South for the poison it spread, for the venom that has left black people less than whole. I realize now that I must reconcile myself with that hatred. I must make peace with this place.

The bike is packed and I have once more found the road. From the top of a rise I look out across a great vale of green glimmering through the mist. Perhaps on some stagecoach a freed slave rode through this valley on the way west to Tennessee. Light-skinned enough that he would have been allowed to ride the coach. Light-skinned enough that his grandson would have discovered arrogance, tested himself, and been forced to flee north.

The sun begins to rise, stark white in the colorless eastern sky. Above the sky is blue.

Bravado aside, rage and anger on hold, I wonder what will happen once I find the soul of the South and touch it.

My hand reaches slowly to touch my forehead, then slowly down to touch my sternum, left shoulder, right shoulder, hands together, and a little prayer.

Oh God, help me on this road. Protect me. Keep me from harm and keep me from anger. Help me to find the peace I seek.

VII

But my pen stubs its toe on this nigger reality
which is like cataracts and old men.

—Mbembe Milton Smith

The road under my wheels shines as after a heavy rain, the smell of wet pavement rising with the morning mist and crowding the space inside my helmet. The sun has climbed into the southern Kentucky sky but not very high, the air is warming but not yet warm, the road to Somerset has not yet dried. Above the eastern horizon a line of thick clouds waits to snare the rising sun and hide its shining, to cast the earth in shadow, to play tricks on the eye with shade and with shafts of light. Shapes form, faces and figures, a guessing game for children, a premonition for me. In the clouds looms something ominous and almost familiar, but something I can only vaguely make out, ever changing in the light wind, the clouds drifting in and out of one another. A new shape appears. A face, perhaps. Someone I know. Someone I have yet to meet.

Or perhaps only a storm advancing. Rain and winter on the way.

The air blows softly, crisp and fresh on my face and on my hands. Quickly, though, the bike gets up to speed and the wind whips past me at eighty miles an hour. Now suddenly the air is freezing, and so am I. Cold rushes by me, cold surrounds me, cold enters into me. Cold that has been transferred from the air to the metal of the bike's gas tank now releases itself into me. My thighs grip firmly around the tank and the cold of the metal creeps into me there, settles around my legs and spreads down to my toes, up into my back and ripples all the way through my body. I find myself shivering. My teeth chatter. Soon the morning will shake away its chill, and the moisture that has settled during the night will shrink away like a distant memory, but for now the air remains very cool. I ride gloveless and the wind numbs my fingers.

As I come to the top of a high hill the bike slows and stops itself in a patch of bright sunlight that soon fades away. A shadow washes over me. Clouds have come to block the sun and there is no warmth. I am shivering from the cold, yes, but shivering as well from a feeling of dread that suddenly has fallen down upon me. Call me a coward, but fear once more has its hands around my throat. I am at last, completely and utterly, in the South, in a southern state of mind, and fear of this evil place grips me still. I know what the South was once; I do not know what the South has become.

Nor can I tell which comes first, this fear or the anger that goes along with it, but there they are, side by side, and they never quite go away. Nor perhaps can they ever, for once you have experienced racism from the receiving end and have been made aware, once you have felt its sting, thought about the pain of it, the stupidity and the senselessness, brooded about it and obsessed about it, once you have known the shame and the degradation of racism, this fear and this anger both come alive, and they cannot be gotten rid of. Not easily. Nor ever completely.

Yes, I know what has been and I am angry.

I do not know what will come and I am afraid.

I stop to rest, to take a deep breath and to look down across the valley that spreads out before me. The hill I am on falls away abruptly and then flattens out before beginning the gentle undulations that recede like an endless sea rolling to the horizon and beyond. Like the sea these hills seem eternal and unmoving, yet they are alive with ceaseless motion and music. Their shapes and their colors change with the shifting sun, with the coming and the going of light and shadow. The wind blows and the tall grass dances. The pines and the oak trees sway. And if you stand perfectly still holding your breath until silence surrounds you, you can hear the quiet whooshing of their leaves brushing together. The sound sails on the breeze and over the hills, caressing my ears and soothing my thoughts.

My gaze drifts lazily up one faraway hill and down the next until sight can see no more, but can only imagine what might lie over the last hill I can see, and the next one after that, and still the next.

The sunlight comes and goes. Clouds move with the wind, and shadows slide slowly across the landscape like a caravan of spirits creeping through the valley, following along after the creek that winds through a crease in the terrain. My mind follows after them, over these hills, along this valley, back in time. Suddenly I find myself nostalgic for a time I never knew, a time long ago when life was simpler and a man could change his life, change his luck, change even the way the world presented itself to his eye and to his mind; all these things simply by heading for the darkness of the unknown and setting out to see what lay on the other side of the hills.

As my mind begins to wander, my eye is snared by the brusque movement of horses that a moment ago were grazing placidly. Now they are galloping joyfully to music only they can hear, stopping suddenly and rearing, snorting, grazing again, oblivious to me, to my fears and to my angers, oblivious to the world. All in the valley below seems as peaceful and as perfect as God intended it to be and seems untouched, except for the fences, by the hand of man. I cannot help but wonder, the same as George Custer couldn't help but wonder in the predawn as his gaze drifted lazily across a western plain: How must it all have been before we came and impured not just the land, but the spirit of the land, when all was future and all was perfect with nothing but possibility?

The sun was just coming up and mist still hovered over the land. An encampment of Native Americans in the valley below was waking to the new day. Smoke was rising from their lodge fires. The dogs were barking the morning into day. Even Custer had to behold and wonder. The Seventh Cavalry was preparing to attack, ready and more than willing to slaughter the old men, the women, the children, even the dogs. And Custer paused. *"What was the(ir) world like,"* he asked himself, *"before we became part of it?"*

What indeed?

When Custer looked out across the plain all he could see was raw wilderness. The future and all its ripe promise. A Native American regarding the same view at the same time would not have seen the same thing. He would have been looking not so much and certainly not only at the future, but at the past as well. His history was there, the story of his people hidden in the tall grass and buried in the hills. The things that explained who he was lay in that prairie, in those forests, lay in the fields and in the mountains, in the streams and in all those things that were being stolen away from him. And as he looked out across his own valleys and plains, must he not have wondered what had happened? Must he not have said to himself in his native tongue, *"Something has gone horribly wrong. This is not the way the world is supposed to be."*

It is impossible to imagine what he felt, but not so hard at all to imagine that he felt it, for I find myself thinking the same thing: that something has gone horribly wrong, that the world is not supposed to be like this. No one, not man, not woman, not the tiniest child, ought to be afraid in his own home. And yet here I am, home at last and very much afraid.

Yes, this is my land. Here in this southern soil, my people were known. Long before I was a glimmer in my father's eye or a worry in my mother's womb, my roots were planted, fertilized by the living, perhaps the suffering, and the dying of my ancestors. Here in these hills my ancestors walked and toiled. They breathed this air, and tilled these fields. They lived and died to become these hills, these trees, this land. They became these things so that I might be. And their voices whisper in my ears.

I owe them this journey, if only to smell this soil and breathe this air and see these trees, if only to remember them and what they endured for my sake. This land is home to me, bought and paid for with the sweat, anguish, and joy of those who went before me and willed it to me. This air is familiar to me. This land is familiar to me. I could recognize the smells of this land, the sounds and the tastes of this place, with my eyes closed, for in my dreams I have visited this place a thousand times. This place haunts my nights and owns my reverie, created my childhood and the stories my father has told. I have not been here before, except in lightest passing, but indeed I *have* been here before. I may not stand where my ancestors stood, nor tread the same patches of earth that they once trod, but they were here, somewhere here. I can feel their presence.

And somewhere here there is proof that they truly existed. Wouldn't it be wonderful, a miracle almost, if as I traveled this land I stumbled across concrete evidence of some long-ago ancestor of mine, some great-great-grandfather who perhaps had been—no, surely had been—a slave?

A thousand waves of fear and excitement surge over me.

This land is mine. I have come to reclaim it. My roots are here. This land is me. Fear or no fear, I cannot distance myself from these hills, from this soil, these smells, this past. Nor should I want to. I am these hills.

The wind grew stronger and howled for a moment and then settled down. The clouds swirled, formed new shapes. Quite suddenly the weather turned serene, and a warm peaceful wind drifted over the land. The sun found a large gap in the clouds and peeped through. The day began to warm. The warmth wrapped round me. A sense of quiet elation settled upon me and enveloped me like a cloak draped over my shoulders. A hand soothed my back and my arms. Sounds like voices whispered soft syllables in my ear. The words I could not make out, but the earth was talking to me—the earth or the past or some great ghosts hovering over the landscape and wandering in this valley.

And their voices murmured, urging me on. It was of course only the wind whispering over the grass.

I was in the South. I was home at last.

I took a deep breath. And then I took another, and then another and another, each one like the Magi, bearing a different gift. The South was happy to have me home and showered me with the gentle scent of pine from the trees on the faraway hills, with the strong equine smells of sweat and manure, with the rich smells of earth and grass, and enveloping it all, holding it all together in the precious package it was, the soft sweet smell of moist tobacco.

The clouds formed a new face then, without hair or nose or chin, but only mouth and eyes. The mouth smiled briefly, then stretched long and emotionless before shifting once more and falling passively into the billows below. The eyes, though, were unmoving. They did not blink or flinch. For the longest time they hovered there like the eyes of angels, just waiting and watching, always watching, until finally I looked away. A hawk had soared on rising thermals and crossed the path of my staring. I followed its gliding, its swooping and its sudden dive until it had flown out of sight. When I looked back to the clouds, the sun had risen fully above them, warm and bright, erasing all from the sky but the blue and the haze. The eyes had disappeared.

I was ready to travel. But which way now—which way to go?

When a writer first puts pen to paper, he has before him the paralyzing problem of infinite possibilities. But once the first word is written, the writer loses his will and it is the story which dictates. The writer becomes merely the medium through whom the poetry passes. The muse sits on his shoulder and directs him with whispers.

Likewise the wanderer. The spirit that persuades him sits on his shoulder and directs him too with whispers, with soft nudges, warm winds and rumors. The traveler merely goes where he is told.

The road before me was all mine, I thought, and I could follow any route I chose. But really I had no choice. There was only one path, only one right road. Everything that had already happened, everything yet to happen, were pebbles laid down to guide the way into the labyrinth and then out again. This journey had been preordained.

I hadn't pulled the bike very far off the road when I stopped to take my rest. I nudged the bike back on the road again. Coming over the hill and aiming straight for me with all the rumble of an earthquake was a gigantic rebel flag painted on the front of a huge semitrailer barreling so fast along the curves in the road that the truck seemed out of control. My mind said to get out of the way, but my body sat paralyzed on the bike for what seemed an eternity.

My gaze locked on the flag, the square red field crisscrossed with a great blue X bordered in white. Inside the X, thirteen white stars. The battle flag of the Confederacy. But much more than that to me. Symbol of racism, symbol of hate, a symbol that caused to rise in me all the rage I had ever felt and that splintered the fragile peace I had made with the South.

I hated this driver.

Perhaps this is what it is to be black in America, maybe to be black in any world of white men. To be black is to always be reminded that you are a stranger in your native land. To be black is to be surrounded by those who would remind you. To be black is having to be ever vigilant, never completely at ease.

I got off the bike and put one foot on the road. I wanted to startle the driver, not so much that he would swerve across the center line and possibly plow into anyone who might be coming round the bend, but I wanted to give him a scare. I wanted him to sit up and take notice of the crazy man in the middle of the road. I dared him to hit me.

The truck screamed. Its horn blared. The lumbering monster lurched and clattered as it passed. The driver made an angry face. I thought I heard him yell obscenities.

I put my helmet back on, my gloves and my jacket. I got back on the bike, started it up and gave chase. I wanted to catch the driver and challenge him. I wanted to know—and of course I knew—why he had that flag painted on the front of his truck. I wanted to fight him, hurt him, kick his truck and puncture his tires. I wanted to make him pay.

But it had taken me too long to get the bike in gear and going. By the time I was in pursuit, he was long gone. The road was too windy and unfamiliar for me to do much over eighty, and that truck must have been doing eighty-five. But for twelve hot minutes I sped after him. Then I slowed down and laughed at myself.

What would I do if I caught up with him? Scream at him? Bite his ankle while he beat me over the head with a tire iron?

This being the South he probably carried a pistol in the cab of his truck.

Hmmm. Perhaps I had taken so long with the helmet and the gloves for a reason.

Yeah, call me a coward.

I gave up the chase at the top of a rise that looked down on a small town in Kentucky called London. A tangle of roads came together in the junction below. Maybe the driver of that truck was down there somewhere waiting for me in the confusion of roads and traffic and fast-food burger joints. Maybe he was waiting for me a little farther on. I slowed.

The road I was on widened into a four-lane expressway, crossed Interstate 75, and then slipped back into a two-lane road winding into the mountains one hour to the east. The Daniel Boone Expressway crossed nearby going into the mountains as well, but it was superhighway all the way to somewhere and probably a toll road to boot, the route for travelers in a hurry. I definitely was not in a hurry. I didn't even know the name of the somewhere I was going. Like that song Sylvester the Cat is always singing in the cartoons: You never know where you're going till you get there.

No, this was not a journey about going anywhere in particular, nor about keeping time. It was perhaps more about losing time, about blurring it, contracting it and elongating it, erasing it. What a miracle if we could somehow erase time, retrace our steps to where we went wrong, start all over again.

If we could do that, I would come back one of these days to the rise in this road. No, farther back to when the truck with the rebel flag painted on it came racing over the hill and spoiled my morning. I would go back to the dawn, back to the lake, and start this day once more. I would not look up when I heard the truck coming this time. I would not allow him to harm the peace. I would get back on my bike after he had passed and I would come to this very spot. I would sift through the tangle until I found the road, the one that goes south before it goes east, the one that runs down through Corbin and Barbourville, Pineville and Harlan, up into the mountains and then down the other side. After that, who knows?

After that, who cares?

VIII

Fancy thinking the beast was something you could hunt and kill! . . . You knew, didn't you? I'm part of you? . . . I'm the reason why it's no go. Why things are what they are.

—William Golding

❧

There is hardly any wind. Clouds have gathered around the tops of mountains and settled in great gray clusters that do not move. Somewhere, not too far away, it is probably raining. But here the sun shines bright. The air is mild. I ride slowly and with the visor up so the smells can enter my helmet and surround me. But even with my sunglasses on and the air so calm, still the wind stings my eyes and brings them to tears.

Through my tears the world is softened as if seen through gauze. Reflections are ringed in halos, colors muted, edges fuzzy. Everything is bathed in mist as if it is the world and not I that has been crying.

It feels as if it will rain today. Moisture crowds the air. A certain stillness hangs over the landscape. An almost gloom permeates the tranquillity. There is a sadness in the air and not only because of what has been, though that is surely heartbreak, but a sadness too about what might have been. Melancholy wraps around all manner of memories, even fond ones, but always the saddest is this kind of reminiscing, this thinking backward and forward at the same time. We had such potential, but we failed each other. We failed ourselves. It is the smell of failure that hovers in the air.

If I had my choice I would travel this land without memory.

If I had any choice at all I would not look back; I would not look forward. I would live the journey of my life only in the moment, in this here and in this now, unencumbered by the past. I would respond to the world and to its people by what they do and think and say, and not by preformed feelings.

If I had my choice I would see this world through the eyes of a stranger. A stranger's eyes are so much clearer.

If I had my choice I would pick my route solely by the scents on breezes and I would ride carefree along these old roads forever. It is freedom I seek. Plain, simple and glorious. Freedom *from*, certainly, from time and from place, but as well freedom *to*, freedom to go, to do, freedom to be.

But there is no such thing as real freedom, especially no freedom for a black man, chained as we are, in other people's eyes and in our own, to the past. In the blackness of my mind everything has significance. Every incident is viewed as if through a prism, the light refracted, the hidden meanings dissected. Every man's motive becomes suspect. Every word must be weighed. I must be forever on my guard.

Perhaps in the years since hope, nothing has really changed. Perhaps nothing ever will. Perhaps race will always determine the roads we travel.

I pretend I have strength, I pretend I have choice, but long ago the choices were made for me. The road has been decided. I am an addict and I cannot choose.

My bike feels heavy, sluggish and unresponsive. It fights my control, no longer reads my thoughts. I am no longer completely at ease. It is as if I carry an inexperienced passenger who does not lean when I lean, who is nervous and tries to guide the bike.

I wanted nothing more than to take to the road and see new

places, to scratch this itch of mine and see what lies beyond the next bend. This was the old addiction, not so much to travel as simply to move, in the hope that in smelling its earth and breathing its air, tasting its flavor and meeting its people, I might find the soul of this land and touch it—never once imagining that I might find and touch my own black soul.

Instead I found myself at the mercy of a destiny I had not chosen.

I found myself in the clutches of a new addiction that I could not control. It was like heroin.

A cloud of euphoria surrounds you. You lie in quiet comfort. You lose the urge to breathe. You forget about thinking. You just want to feel the ball of warmth as it fills your center and begins to expand. It is so good and so soothing. There can be nothing better.

A bright light silently explodes inside your head. It softens into a glow, pink and golden. After a while it shrinks to a pinpoint of yellow with a red-hot center. Then all goes suddenly dark and finally you surrender to the familiar peace that conceals itself in the shadows. The darkness is safe, a haven. The darkness is your friend. The darkness is good.

Addiction is effortless and excellent—heroin is the best thing there is—as long as you don't try to fight it, to kick what has become habit. Once you have tasted the drug and slipped into its cocoon, everything becomes temptation. Everything reminds you.

Long I fought against the ease of addiction, fought against memory and against the will of the bike. I took the bike, or it took me, over the mountains and deeper into the South, back out again to places like Baltimore and Washington, thinking that if I removed myself from the source of racist thinking, I would escape the temptation and addiction of my own racist thinking.

But everywhere it was the same. I could not outrun the temptation. I ran smack into reminders at every turn. Everywhere was the past and painful memory, everywhere a reason for self-pity and self-loathing and anger, the bitter ease of being victim. This is the addiction.

Just east of the junction in London, Kentucky, on the right-hand side of the road, there was a restaurant attached to a small hotel. A charmless place made of brick and wood, it looked like it might collapse any minute. Nothing about it seemed inviting, nothing to recommend it apart from the fact that it was the only place around. I went in. I found myself listening to some inner voice that was guiding my every move. I thought it was the voice of addiction.

The walls were dark wood to suggest the interior of a log cabin. The place was dimly lit inside. I walked through the front door and stood before a glass display case crowded with candy bars and chewing gum, cheap cigars and a few souvenirs. Two ladies were yakking loudly. One stood behind the display case and leaned on the cash register. The other stood on my side of the display case and leaned on the counter, one hand resting on the glass, the other hand perched on her hip. She was almost blocking the doorway, with her back to me.

She was a hefty woman with the bad posture of one who works on her feet all day and never gets a moment's rest. She wore a dingy white uniform and her shoes were badly run-down. The right shoe was so twisted that the heel was gone. She shifted her weight constantly from one foot to the other, rolling her shoes onto their sides. A pencil was stuck in her beehive hairdo.

Neither woman greeted me. Neither noticed me standing there, unless they were making a point of ignoring me.

They were engrossed in conversation about a woman they knew who lived, they said, at the beck and call of a miserable, conceited bastard named Cliff.

"He's such a pretty boy," the one with the tired feet said. "He really thinks he's God's gift."

"Well, he is single. He's young. He's not bad to look at. And after all he is a man."

"Yeah," the one said. She shifted her weight to the left foot. "But if he called me late in the night do you think I'd get up, get dressed, and run over to his house the way Alice does?"

They both paused for a moment. Suddenly they burst into laughter.

"In half a heartbeat," the one behind the counter told her.

Their gossip had about it an air of harmlessness, but its edges were sharp and malicious. They didn't like the woman who ran after Cliff. They disliked her for chasing him, they disliked her more for catching him. They were jealous.

"The way she comes in here acting like she's all happy and everything, like she's got something the rest of us ain't got. It makes me sick. And him that she's got, he ain't so much. He makes me sick too."

It was casual gossip, not much different than gossip generally is among intimates.

"I've seen you sometimes flirting with him mighty hard," the one was saying to the other.

"Well, like you said, he is a man. And if Alice can latch on to him, I'm sure enough good as her, and maybe he's looking for a little variety. She makes me sick too, the way she thinks she's so smart all the time."

Their tongues were barbed and sharp. They spoke candidly to each other, as if I couldn't hear what they were saying. As if they didn't care if I could hear. They spoke as if I were an invisible man, or not there at all.

In days of slavery, so I've read and so I've been told, white men and women very often would speak frankly and openly in front of blacks, servants and slaves. The whites would reveal intimacies that would kill them of shame if anyone white ever heard these things said in confidence. But they were so unconcerned about a black man's eyes and ears and a black man's opinion, it was as if blacks in the same room did not exist, were not there, or could not communicate secrets. It was as if they were family pets, incapable of understanding.

The waitress pulled the pencil from her hair and scratched her scalp with it. Finally now she looked over in my direction. Before she said another word to her friend, she pointed with her chin the way into the dining room.

"Find yourself a seat," she said. "Somebody will be right with you."

She did not call me "sir."

And nobody came to see about me. The two women went on talking about Cliff and about men in general. I was completely ignored.

I sat in a booth near a window. It seemed the only well-lit place in the room. Behind me was a shelf of old books leaning against one another, stacked in disarray, most of them covered with dust. While I waited for any attention at all, I pulled down one of the books and leafed through it. It was a history book, the *American Heritage History of the Law in America,* and from page 72 this notice leaped up and stung my eyes:

CAUTION!!

COLORED PEOPLE OF BOSTON, ONE AND ALL

YOU ARE HEREBY RESPECTFULLY CAUTIONED AND ADVISED,

TO AVOID CONVERSING WITH THE WATCHMEN AND POLICE OFFICERS

OF BOSTON

FOR SINCE THE RECENT ORDER

OF THE MAYOR AND ALDERMEN, THEY

ARE EMPOWERED TO ACT AS

KIDNAPPERS AND

SLAVE CATCHERS

AND they have already been actually employed in KIDNAPPING AND KEEPING SLAVES. Therefore, if you value your LIBERTY, and the WELFARE of the fugitives among you, SHUN them in every possible manner, as so many HOUNDS on the track of the most unfortunate of your race. KEEP A SHARP LOOK OUT FOR KIDNAPPERS and have TOP EYE open.

April 24, 1854

It wasn't much of a reminder, but there it was. I could not outrun nor blot out the memory of how it used to be. I was in the South, all right, the South full of reminders, the South which is a symbol of how it used to be, *why* it used to be, and why it still is today.

I did not stay to have breakfast.

The South.

I hate this place. How in the world could a black not hate it here, a feeling, thinking, remembering black man? After all that has been, it would take a miracle—evidence of absolute blindness or of greatest hope—not to surrender to bitterness and hate.

I hopped on the bike and rode like a demon, rode for hours and hours and hours, rode as if my life and my sanity depended on getting as far from where I was as fast as I could. I stopped for gas, got back on the bike, and rode some more. I talked to no one, except to thank the man for the gas. I knew there was no one I could trust, and no one who would trust me. In every smile I saw an evil motive, in every glance a leer. The South loved me no more than I loved it. I hated this place, all right, hated it for what it was doing to my mind. I was becoming paranoid and obsessed.

The South was winning.

No mere place could conjure up the images that are awakened here. No mere place stirs the emotions the way the South does. Just as that rebel flag is a symbol, the South too is a symbol. More than place, much more than physical boundary or political distinction, the South is a way of thinking, a way of feeling, a crucible of ill will.

It is not the soil of your native land that gives you strength, and it is not air that sustains you. It is not the trees that make you proud, nor the whispering wind that makes you afraid. It is the spirit of the land that defines your emotions. It is the people who live there who give a place its character, like-minded people sharing history, sharing ideas and tendencies, sharing narrow-mindednesses. The South is a state of mind.

In the winter of 1860–61, eleven states seceded from the Union. Texas was one of them; Kentucky was not. And yet Kentucky is the South to me. Texas feels something else entirely, Southwest perhaps, half-Mexican, almost another country, southern only in the sense that they grow cotton there, had an allegiance to the Confederacy, and that it has its share of racist rednecks—Texans, not southerners. Texas lacks, at least in my opinion, the feel of the Deep South. Across the rest of the South there is a common outlook.

The Confederate alliance arose from a perceived need for like-minded people to join together while separating from those damned Yankees—*those others* who shared neither ideology nor culture, but only so insignificant a thing as history. The South chose to ignore shared origins, shared blood and a shared past. The South chose to forge a new and separate tradition, which now holds me hostage and makes me hate this place. In all this time it seems nothing, absolutely nothing, has changed.

It had not been my intention to cover every square inch of every state, but merely to enter this state of mind. Now I had done it. And now I regretted it. I did not like this feeling of always being on my guard, always reading between the lines.

I longed to break free, longed simply to ride over the mountains of eastern Kentucky and get lost in the rising mist.

In the blindness of my newly discovered racialism I had lost sight of my original purposes, to head for the open road and just go, to find the perfect cheeseburger, the perfect milkshake, the perfect coconut cream pie.

I wished for an easier time of it, a simpler voyage, and could have found one if I had just turned west and headed for California.

I rode like an escaped prisoner. Just trying to get away. Yet, oddly, I continued to ride south, toward the prison, not from it, faster and faster until everything in my sight became a blur.

Suddenly somewhere there was a sign.

JESUS HABLA ESCUCHA Y CONTESTA EN ESPANOL
LLAME 754-2032

It flashed momentarily at the corner of my sight. It came into focus and was gone, passed before the words could register in my brain. But the sign snared my attention. I slowed and made a U-turn in the middle of traffic. I went back.

On the left-hand side of the road, what used to be a bank had been turned into a church. I pulled into the lot.

The drive-up window was still there where some teenaged teller used to sit all day. Now the window was covered over by a thick shade. I couldn't see inside.

The carport for the drive-up window was also still standing. I stopped beneath it and rested in the shade. A billboard told me I was in Corbin, Kentucky.

It could have been the main street of almost any small town in America. Fast-food joints lined the road. Car dealers crowded next to gas stations. These are the threads now that link all American regions and cities and small towns. Denver looks like Dallas looks like Detroit, Pittsfield looks like Springfield, Connersville looks like Fresno.

But I was in Corbin, Kentucky, in the South, and what struck me as strange was not the assurance that Jesus answers prayers. After all on the corner where stands the Daviess County Coon Hunters' Club, there was a similar promise, that God is the answer.

That corner was linked to this dusty parking lot of sand and gravel by a thread of religious fervor as surely as by the road. But what struck me as odd was that the sign was written in Spanish. I had not expected to find a Latino community in the South.

JESUS HABLA ESCUCHA Y CONTESTA EN ESPANOL.
LLAME 754-2032

Everyone knows the Bible gets banged like a drum in the South, beaten more loudly here than anyplace else in the world. Everyone knows that Jesus's name is invoked at every opportunity here, that everything is done under the veneer of Christianity. Everyone knows too that this is a land where Christian ideals have never been given even half a chance, let alone truly applied.

I was not surprised to see a sign urging religion. But in this neck of the woods, I was not expecting a sign telling me that Jesus speaks, listens, and answers in Spanish. Or in any other language, for that matter. Why would anyone not white, not Anglo-Saxon, want to live in the South?

I kicked the dust from my boots and rode on, deeper and deeper into the South, on and on.

I was bound all right, bound to this place, to this road, bound to this new way of thinking and seeing. This country had seen color for such a long time. I was beginning to see it too, color and nothing else.

The virus was in my blood now, the fever was upon me, thick and heavy. I had to break free. There had to be a way.

IX

Don't look back; something might be gaining on you.

—Satchel Paige

🐌

But how can a man not look back? Are we not tied, all of us, to the past?

I was brooding and I was serious, but the big man beside me was laughing. He was howling. In fact he looked like he was baying at the moon up in the sky, the pale moon left over from the night before. He leaned back. His mouth fell open. His face aimed straight up. Then he put his hands on his big jiggling belly to keep himself from shaking apart and he bellowed with laughter.

"What you're saying makes sense," he said. "But all that stuff you're talking about, none of that stuff ain't never happened to you."

I was talking to a white man named Andrew, a gas station attendant in Raleigh, North Carolina, telling him all about my wanderings. He had come down, he said, to watch people getting on and off the morning train—the same as he did every day. The train, on its way from Florida to New York, had just pulled out of the depot. Together we watched it shrink away like a distant memory, around the bend and out of sight. Andrew had said how much he wished he could have been on it.

"Me too," I said. "Me too."

Now he was laughing—at me. Earlier when he had first found me, I had been sitting on an old wooden dray, digesting an early lunch I had just eaten at the café around the corner—greasy burger, french fries, a stiff piece of coconut pie. I was resting beside the railroad tracks, staring into deep space and dreaming, watching passengers board the train, when Andrew came up beside me and smashed my brooding with questions about my bike. Now that I had told him about my journey he was mocking me.

"What are you getting so bent out of shape about?" he said. "All that was a long time ago. Ain't none of it happened to you."

But it did. All of it.

In a most insidious way, didn't Nazi Germany happen to every Jew who has since been born? Isn't it still happening, aren't the effects still being felt—and in a way, by all of us?

The things that have happened—the shadows cast, the footprints that are left in the dust—they alter the landscape of our experience not just for the moment but permanently. From the death camps to slavery to the simplest injustice, can you not see, then, how the world has been formed and how everything reminds us of what we were and what we are and what we will never be? One thing stems from another and leads to still another. All things come together in the moment we call now. And unless we can look beyond the here and now and see what effect our actions will have on the events that follow and on those who will come after us, we will selfishly and foolishly continue to leave chaos for others to decipher and unravel and endure.

These things did not happen to me directly, I said, but they happened. And they are still happening. And as they affect the world, they affect me, the way I see and am seen, the way I act and who I am, the way I think and feel, the things I choose to eat.

Once your consciousness is tapped in a certain way, you see things differently. Everything reminds you, everything becomes significant.

Absolutely everything.

There is a hotel in Asheville, I told him, called the Grove Park Inn. F. Scott Fitzgerald used to stay there when he came to the North Carolina mountains to escape the summer swelter of New York City. All I wanted to do was spend a couple of comfortable nights there, walk in the shadow of Fitzgerald's literary greatness and hope his ghost might still linger on, might breathe on me and infuse me with his spirit and his art.

Is this not why we visit the boyhood homes of our idols, to see how they lived? Yes, but also in the hope that by touching the walls and floors and furniture they had once touched, sitting in the same chairs, seeing the same view from porch or window, breathing the same air, we might somehow touch their shadows and absorb their greatness.

Thomas Wolfe, who wrote *You Can't Go Home Again,* grew up in Asheville. I thought that if I could breathe the air that he inspired, and that inspired him, perhaps that same air could inspire me.

But all I could think of as I walked the grounds of the Grove Park, all I wondered about as I wandered through the rooms of Wolfe's white clapboard house, all that bothered me, was my admiration for men who must on some level have been racists.

Was F. Scott concerned about the things that concern me? Was Wolfe, was Hemingway? Did they ever try to put themselves in my shoes and wonder how it might have been to be black and excluded? Did they even care, or did they and everyone around them merely thank their lucky stars that they had avoided the misery of being black, and then go about business as usual?

Why didn't they fix the world? Why didn't they try?

How can I admire such men and want to be like them? How could I be comfortable in a hotel that I would have been barred from only thirty years ago—within my lifetime!

There used to be a Howard Johnson's on Kingshighway near Natural Bridge in St. Louis, in my old childhood neighborhood. I went to buy an ice cream cone there once when I was little. They refused to serve me. I didn't know why. I had money. I wasn't acting silly. But they told me I couldn't come in.

I was just a kid. What did I know about racism and segregation? How was I to know that being black was bad, that being black made me hateful? My parents and friends loved me. How could someone who didn't even know me despise me?

My parents had always refused to go there. As a child I never knew why. As an adult I can see more clearly. Now that I know, I utterly refuse to spend money in any Howard Johnson's restaurant or hotel.

"But you're punishing them for things that happened in the past," Andrew said.

How else to let them know that they cannot get away with being willfully evil and then later, after the damage has already been done, simply apologize it away by saying they didn't know any better? How can that be any different from Nazis in the death camps who excused their guilt by saying they were only following orders?

I have Jewish friends who will not visit Germany because they remember what the Nazis did to them there, who will not listen to the music of Wagner because Wagner was a virulent anti-Semite and because the Nazis used his music almost as theme songs of hate.

My friend CooChung Chao's mother had a fit because CooChung once bought a Japanese car. She remembers what horrors the Japanese committed in China, and she cannot forgive them.

"We all breathe the air of our times," Andrew said.

That's too easy, I told him. That just gives us an excuse for everything we do. Howard Johnson's should have known better. We all should have known better.

I cannot sleep in a Howard Johnson's hotel, cannot eat in a Howard Johnson's restaurant.

I cannot even look fondly upon that late summer day in 1964 when the St. Louis Cardinals baseball team won the last game of the season against the New York Mets. The victory gave the Cardinals the league championship and sent them into the World Series. I was there that afternoon. And when pandemonium broke out and the fans stormed onto the field after the game to celebrate, my brother and I were right there with them, running and screaming along with everybody else. We thought all the world was fun and laughter.

But I cannot now remember that day with a child's unmitigated joy, cannot remember old Sportsman's Park without knowing that St. Louis had the last big league ballpark with segregated seating. I cannot even think of major league baseball without thinking of injustice, without thinking of the great black ball-players in the old Negro Leagues who because of their color were never given a chance. I can think of very little from this country's past that does not cause my heart to break.

These things may not have happened to me directly, I told Andrew, but because they happened at all, they happened to me.

"Sounds like you're pretty outraged," he said.

"Outraged?" I said, thinking of the Mancinis at the party in Connecticut. "That's putting it mildly. I'm so far beyond rage I scare myself."

I don't see the world in simple ways anymore, I told him. I see everything in terms of history and race and am reminded at every turn, more than anything else, that not now or ever has it been all right to be black. And the question I need answered, the only thing that is going to keep me from losing my mind, is: Will it ever be in the future—can it ever be—all right to be black?

"Of course it's all right to be black," Andrew said, but he said it in an offhanded, casual way. "You ride a beautiful motorcycle. You sound educated. You look like you're doing all right, successful and all that. You're big, you're strong. I bet nobody gives you a lot of trouble."

You don't understand, I told him. I am an isolated case. Of course there are going to be individual success stories. And you're right, I don't have a problem with being black. I like being black. I feel there is nothing I can't do, nothing that's too good for me, and nobody better than me. There are better brains and better athletes, but nobody better. And absolutely nobody I'd rather be. The problem is that I am a freak. I am not the norm. Being black for a lot of people is not the picnic it is for me. I am very comfortable being black, yes, so comfortable in fact that I never gave it a second thought until now, hardly even knew I was black until I started feeling these things I now feel. Now being black is all I think about.

I am worried, I told him, for my unborn children.

A cop pulled me over for speeding in Henderson, I told Andrew. It was about an hour from Raleigh. He was a white cop who didn't give me any trouble, but he didn't make it easier either. He was gruff and serious, didn't make small talk, didn't smile. He just unpleasantly wrote out a ticket and gave it to me. I couldn't help think that if I had been white he would have been a little more congenial.

"But maybe he would not have," Andrew said. "Maybe he was just mean, or having a rotten day."

Maybe. But because racism exists, I have to wonder.

"I don't want to think like this," I said. "I never used to, but now I can't help it. I'm trapped."

So I went to the batting cage just outside Henderson and vented my frustration. I must have taken a hundred badly timed swings at pitches a little leaguer could have pulverized. I missed most of them.

Andrew had stopped laughing now and was listening intently as I ranted. Although he seemed very concerned, he did look a little confused.

"I'm not an educated man," he said. "I just work in a gas station, for God's sake. I don't think about these things. All I do is put a little gas in cars for people who don't want to do it for themselves. The big event of my work day is when I come down here and watch the trains pull in and out of the station."

"And dream," I said, finishing his thought the way I was sure he was going to, the way I wanted him to. "And dream of getting out of here."

He looked sharply at me.

"I never said that." He almost barked at me.

"What did you say, then?" I asked. "When the train pulled out you told me you wished you could be on it."

"Yep, I did tell you that," he said. "But you didn't hear it the way I meant it. I don't hate the South the way you do. I don't even know the South that you know. And you sure don't know the South the way I do."

"All I know about the South is its history," I said. "Its hatred and its injustice. And every day on this road I see how the South is doing all it can to hold on to its racist past. Rebel flags and little reminders all over the place. And I know too that if I'm going to get to the soul of the South, first I have to encounter the dark heart of this racist past. And that's what I'm doing."

Andrew was shaking his head.

"But why?" he said. "You're missing so much more."

"It wasn't my choice," I said. "Believe me. All I wanted to do was go across that bridge."

There is a bridge in Virginia that's seventeen miles long. It's actually part bridge and part tunnel. It skims so low over the choppy water at the mouth of Chesapeake Bay that I started to feel seasick as I crossed it. Then it dips under the surface of the sea—twice—so that naval warships based at Newport News and cargo vessels can slide in and out of the bay. It is a marvel.

Some years ago I lived in Dover, Delaware. Highway 13 passes through the center of town. Just about at the end of that highway, which goes through Maryland, then Virginia, is the bridge. Many times I promised myself that I would take the two-and-a-half-hour drive and cross that bridge, and then come back. But the bridge was too close, always there. And because I could do it anytime I wanted, I never felt compelled to do it. So I never did.

But now, being in the South, and riding around Virginia, as I had been before I came to North Carolina, I really had the urge to see what man can do when he puts his mind to it. I knew at some point that I would make my way to the coast and ride down the appendix that juts out from the bottom of Maryland, cross over the bay into Norfolk, and then ride back up toward Richmond before making my way to Raleigh and here to Andrew.

So I crossed from Kentucky into western Virginia and camped in the mountains. I ate country ham and red-eye gravy at a dingy diner in Marion. The coconut pie was not good. Then I woke early and rode in the silence of the morning mist.

You know how it is when you drive in the mist to the crest of a high hill or a mountain. When you get to the top suddenly it's very clear and you can see across the whole of creation, down into the valleys where the heavy mist lies, and up to the peaks that are not as high as you are but that rise above the clouds. The clouds and the mist swirl around the tips of the mountains and lie in stripes on the hillsides. The forests drip fleece. The fog feels like rain.

The sun awakens, rises, dries the air and warms the earth. As far as you can see there is green and green and still more green in various shades, striped with gray for a short while longer. And the road winds into the mountains like a wriggling worm that has no end. And sometimes it crosses your mind how ugly highways can be and yet on mornings like this, how simply beautiful.

Such beauty as this that runs along the Blue Ridge Mountains and up through the Shenandoah River Valley steals the breath away and stings the eyes. Such beauty as this brings the eyes to tears.

You would think nothing in this world, past or future, could spoil such absolute splendor.

But in this country Lee's Army of Northern Virginia fought campaign after campaign—to threaten Washington, to invade the North, to defend Southern soil. Up and down this valley and across the whole state, from the Rapidan to the Rappahannock, from Petersburg to Fredericksburg to Richmond and Antietam. The sacred soil of Virginia has been watered with blood and made fertile with corpses.

I rode the valley, I told Andrew, and followed the route of Lee's army into that small town in Pennsylvania. I toured the battlefield there—twice. For kicks I stopped at the souvenir stand and bought a Confederate soldier's gray cap.

I tramped through battlefield after battlefield, the ones they call the Wilderness and Spotsylvania, Antietam in Maryland, Manassas and New Market. My shoes were soaked with blood.

I could not tell how the other tourists thought of the war, the two noble causes, or of slavery itself. All I could think of was the slavery.

Heading ever closer to the coast and to the highway that would lead me to the bridge, I met a man who would become my friend. He lives on the edge of Baltimore. His name is Frank.

There is no nicer man. When my bike was stuck in the mud, he dirtied himself far more than I did to help push it out. I stayed in his home, became friends with his wife and three children, and when I left, the invitation was open to return. "Soon," he said. "Come back soon."

But one evening in his study I found my new friend wondering about me what too many strangers have wondered.

He was quite delicate about it, and we talked around it for a long time, but eventually he asked how I found time and money and where I got the interest to travel to faraway places—as if my world rightfully should be so small.

When we talked about the past, and he mentioned that his grandfathers had both been engineers, I saw at once the difference between his expectations for himself and his expectations for me.

All a black person can say when talking about deep ancestry is that his forefathers brought forth on this continent were not conceived in liberty, but were slaves instead, and sons of slaves.

My own great-great-great-grandfather was a slave, and family rumor puts him nearby, in Virginia. I hate him, hate him for not having the courage to die rather than endure the humiliation of slavery. Did he not think what his indignity would lead us to? Did he not care about those who would follow? Could he not imagine what effect his captivity would have on the psyches of the heirs of slavery—slave and slave owner? It would have been better to die.

Everywhere I looked there were monuments to the war to maintain slavery and to the slavers themselves, in the battlefield shrines and the society itself, but nowhere any sign of shame or remorse, instead only reminders that the war is not yet over.

At Appomattox Court House, the site where Lee surrendered his army and the war in the east ended, there is a plaque.

HERE ON SUNDAY APRIL 9,1865,

AFTER FOUR YEARS OF HEROIC STRUGGLE IN DEFENSE OF

PRINCIPLES BELIEVED FUNDAMENTAL TO THE EXISTENCE OF OUR

GOVERNMENT, LEE SURRENDERED 9000 MEN, THE REMNANT OF AN

ARMY STILL UNCONQUERED IN SPIRIT

"And that spirit is racist," I was telling Andrew in Raleigh. "The war is not over. Nor the spirit that led to it."

"Of course it is," Andrew said.

I disagreed.

Our government, the plaque says. *Whose* government, I wanted to know.

Over the capitol buildings of nearly half the states in the South flies a flag, I explained, that proclaims loud and clear how utterly unconcerned the South is about its black citizens—the same now as it was forty, sixty, one hundred, two hundred years ago.

"How do you expect a black person to feel," I said, "in a society that so blatantly reminds him how emotionally tied his government still is to a system that fought to keep his ancestors in slavery?"

Almost every state flag in the South takes its design from the flags of the Confederacy.

(Remember that there were four Confederate flags, all of them retaining the red-white-and-blue of the old federal flag, displaying their roots: the Stars and Bars, a blue canton with seven stars in a circle, three broad horizontal stripes red on white on red; the Battle Flag, a red field crossed by a blue and white X holding the thirteen stars of the original colonies; the Stainless Banner, a stark white field with the battle flag in the upper left-hand corner. The last Confederate flag was like the Stainless Banner but with a broad vertical red band.)

The state flag of Florida is a white field crossed by a broad red X; the state seal lies in the center. The state flag of Mississippi has the battle flag in the canton corner with three broad stripes of blue, white, and red. The state flag of North Carolina has a blue canton corner beside one red and one white stripe. The state flag of Georgia has a blue band holding the state seal alongside the Confederate battle flag. The state flag of Texas, a lone star in a blue field beside one red and one white stripe. The state flag of Alabama is a big red X on a white field. And right beneath this flag as it flies over the state capitol waves a taunting Confederate battle flag, right where George Wallace put it, symbol of hate, symbol of segregation, symbol of pride—for southern whites only.

Symbols are indivisible, Benvisti said. If it's mine, it can't be yours.

And this is exactly what the South seems to be saying: "We don't care if our symbols are hateful to you and upset you or remind you of our inhuman treatment toward you. We don't care because these are the sources of our pride and we do not concern ourselves with your pride. These are our symbols and not yours. And you do not share in what is ours."

It's as if in all this time we have learned nothing about sensitivity to others.

Those flags hark back to a struggle to hang on to an institution that denied humanity to a people. They glorify a tradition that excludes blacks. And if you want to start a fight, there is no quicker way than to suggest that the rebel flag ought never fly, or that the state flags of the South ought all to be changed.

"Well, you're right about that," Andrew said. "I sure don't want to see nothing changed. It's our history."

"And how do you think Jews in Germany would feel if the Nazi flag were still the official flag in that country?"

He rubbed his chin. I could hear the scratching sound his hand made as it ran over his razor stubble.

"Not very good, I guess."

"They would feel somebody was trying to tell them something," I said. "Symbols aren't everything but they go a long way toward maintaining or changing attitudes."

Everywhere, hardly anything to even suggest that blacks are part of this country and played a role in this history and its shaping.

In an old cemetery in Boston, Crispus Attucks lies in a grave. But if you didn't know who Attucks was, you would never suspect that a black man had fought in the American Revolution. Black men fought on both sides in the revolution. The English promised freedom to those black slaves who fought for the crown. And when that war was over, the English would not abandon them to a fate worse than slavery, but took them home to England. But are there monuments there to the blacks who fought and died for the empire?

It's as if black men and women have been erased from history.

Right here in Raleigh, I told Andrew—as if he didn't already know—the capitol is surrounded by statues and monuments.

A woman sits with a book, a boy with a sword kneels at her side. This is the monument to the women of the Confederacy.

Henry Lawson Wyatt stands nobly on a plinth. He was the first Confederate soldier to fall in the Civil War, at Bethel Church—June 10, 1861.

There are statues of George Washington, a man named Vance, another named Aycock, and a statue of Charles McIver. There is a monument to Samuel A'Court Ashe: patriot, soldier, legislator, Christian, citizen.

There is the great monument to Our Confederate Dead, and one to Worth Bagley, the first to fall in the Spanish-American War.

James Polk, Andrew Jackson, Andrew Johnson, three presidents with ties to North Carolina.

But the only hint that blacks ever did anything worth mentioning is a statue to the soldiers who fought in Vietnam. Two white soldiers carrying a dead black one.

But monuments everywhere to the warriors who fought to keep slavery.

In Richmond all along Monument Avenue, a beautiful tree-lined street, there are huge statues of Stonewall Jackson, of Jefferson Davis, of Robert E. Lee, of Jeb Stuart.

"It's so one-sided, so prevalent," I said, "after a while you get the feeling somebody is trying to tell you something."

Just across the river from Washington I had gone to Anacostia where abolitionist Frederick Douglass had lived. His home is a national monument, and that says something, but the day I was there, all the visitors were black.

Benvisti backwards: *Symbols are indivisible; if it's yours, it can't be mine.*

Andrew looked at me sadly and said, "Kudzu."

I thought he had sneezed.

"Kudzu," he said again, and I looked at him like he was crazy. "Kudzu?"

"Yeah," he said. "You've seen that plant that grows wild all over the place. I think it only grows in the South, but it comes from Japan, I believe. And it just takes over everything, covers everything. You see it growing in the valleys, at the side of the road, up the trunks of trees, across telephone wires. It consumes everything. It's kind of like racism. It's kind of like being obsessed."

I nodded.

"I guess it's true," he said. "If you want to get to the soul of the South, you do have to touch the dark heart of our racist past. Just like you said. But still, something about that ain't right."

Andrew was looking at me with his eyes round like saucers, but he kept shaking his head. He wasn't shaking it as if to say "no," he wasn't disagreeing with me, and he wasn't saying he didn't understand. He was saying: "Um-mm. That ain't entirely right."

Every time he shook his head he said, "Um-mm." He was telling me that the way I was seeing things was simply wrong.

"Don't you know?" he said. "Don't you know you ain't never going to be able to enjoy this magnificent machine and this trip if you don't stop acting like a fool? Just get on with it. 'Cause if you don't, you ain't never going to see the South. You're going see this thing you think is the South. And I guess in a crazy way, you'll be just like the racists you're screaming about. You won't be seeing what's really there, you'll only see what you want to see.

"The South is not that bad. We're just a race of people trying to hold on to our pride, that's all. If we had never fought the Civil War, who knows where we might be. I think the end of slavery would have come. I think it would have been more peaceful. But we had everything rammed down our throats. We had to push back. We had to find a way to form our own society along lines that weren't too unfamiliar to us. We already had a system of separation. We just exaggerated it. We had a wounded pride, and we were looking for a simple way to take away the sting. Nobody was thinking about the future. Nobody ever does."

He spoke softly and very slowly. Before he had said that he never thought about such things. Now he was telling me that all southerners think about such things.

"How could we not?" he said. "Even when we're not thinking about it, we're thinking about it. Just like you are. It's going to tear us all apart."

He gazed longingly up the tracks. He still wanted to be on that train. I could tell.

"Don't you wish you could fly away from here?" I said.

"Yeah, I do. But not to the North like you might be thinking. I never saw the North as some kind of haven where everything would be wonderful and different. I expect it's all pretty much the same. You look at the TV, and the things that are tearing us up down here are tearing you all to pieces up there. I never wanted to go north, I just wanted to go anywhere. It doesn't matter where.

"That train is going somewhere and I'm not," he said. "When the sun comes up in the morning, I'm going to be right here. I'm going to be the same old man in the same old place. And nothing is ever really going to change for me. I've spent my whole life around here. Just like everybody I know. I know the same people I've always known. I'm the same man I was twenty years ago."

He patted his belly.

"A little fatter," he said. He offered a smile that was not filled with mirth. "But the same man."

And the smile went away.

"I think the same as I always did," he said. "And I think the same as everybody around me. I don't want to go away and stay away. I just want to go and be somebody else for a while. When I come back, and sure enough I'd come back, maybe I'd see this place a little different. And everything else too. But I don't hate the South, and you shouldn't either. When you do, what you're saying is that you hate me. You hate my family and all my friends. And you don't even know us."

Now Andrew grew very quiet and very serious. He took off his cap and wiped his brow with his left forearm. He ran his hand over his balding head.

"You know," he said, "I once thought—and this was some years ago—that in twenty more years we would have this problem licked, somehow all sorted out and all together. Twenty more years. That's all it would take, I thought. Maybe it'll be twenty more years from now."

"Only if we're lucky," I said. "And only if we work really hard at it."

He was thinking. He had started to frown and now I could feel how my own face had wrenched tightly into almost a scowl.

"What can I do?" he said. "This is the way I am, this is the way we are. You can't expect us to change overnight and all of a sudden deny everything that we have ever been and be something completely new."

His question made me think of a man—Dan Jordan—I had met a short while back as I was riding up the Shenandoah Valley. I had stopped off in Charlottesville, Virginia, to send a postcard to a friend who had graduated from the university there.

It was a wet afternoon. I had been strolling along the downtown mall that runs the length of Main Street. I had eaten breakfast and browsed the book shops and as I was going back to the bike I met Eugene Williams. He was coming out of his office and was about to get into his car, which was parked next to my bike.

"Where are you from?" he wanted to know. I wanted to know how it was that everyone recognized me as a stranger.

He just shrugged, and we went back to his office to talk.

"What are you looking for?" he asked.

"Home," I said. I don't know why I said it. It just slipped out.

"Home?"

I nodded. "Some place where I can find peace and feel at ease," I said.

"Home is not some place you find," he told me. "Home is where you find yourself. No mythical promised land that you can dream about. You've got to sink your bucket where you are, dig a well, plant a little garden, and make the best of where you are. That's what we're trying to do around here. Trying to make things better right here, right now."

His organization, Dogwood Housing, is trying to help poor people buy their own homes. He sends out a newsletter encouraging people to face up to the problems of the community and take charge of their own lives and make things better. He points out problems. He offers solutions. He gives advice. He guides young people.

Eugene Williams is my hero.

"It's not all about the white man," he said. "We need to take care of ourselves a little bit better. You'd be surprised how many of us start to make it and then just abandon the rest of us. We are part of our own problem."

He invited me to his house for dinner that evening and his wife stuffed me until I couldn't walk. The next morning I went to see the man Andrew in Raleigh made me think of, Dan Jordan, who is the executive director of Monticello, Thomas Jefferson's old estate. Eugene had given me Dan Jordan's name and told me he would be an interesting man to talk to. I phoned him and we made an appointment. Then I went to interview him.

We talked formally a little while. He told me how they were actively engaged in trying to include blacks into the history of Monticello. After all, Jefferson had owned slaves his whole life. He freed only seven of them, all of them skilled workers and artisans Jefferson expected to prosper as free men. Jordan seemed to want that side of the story told. He wanted it known that Monticello would not have been the great place it was without the help of black men and women.

But the interview degenerated quickly into a friendly chat. I wasn't so interested in Jefferson and the past as I was in Jordan and the future. And I asked him point blank, "If a man grows up in a racist society and is a product of it, even with the best of intentions, do you think he can ever stop being a racist?"

He answered the question quickly and just as matter-of-factly as I had asked it.

"He will always be a racist," he said. "I don't see how you can take out what's been bred in you, not in the society we live in. All you can do is pretend. You may not be able to change those inherent attitudes, but if you try real hard, and pretend real hard, you can, I think, change your behavior. And that will help change the attitudes of the next generation."

He told me just a little about his daughter.

"She lives in New York," he said. "And I'm sure she's dated black men. I'm not real comfortable with that, but it's a new world and I've got to get used to it. You can't keep holding people back."

Dan Jordan is also my hero.

"Maybe I can't change," he said. "But I can keep from forcing my racist attitudes on my daughter and let her make up her own mind. If we all did just that, and stopped teaching hate, maybe the world would sort itself out. But it's a struggle. It won't happen overnight."

"You can't expect us to change overnight," Andrew, the gas station attendant in Raleigh, later said.

"Not overnight," I said. "I can want it, but you're right, I can't expect it. But what you can do is open your mind. Try to see in a different way. Try for just a little while to see the world the way I see it. Then maybe you and I can share some kind of understanding."

He was nodding. His frown softened, but only a little.

"I tell you what I'll do," he said. "I'll meet you halfway. You have to open your mind too. Try not to hate the South so much. We might surprise you. Some of us are, but most of us are not bad people. You might even find that you like it here. And wouldn't that be something?"

"It would," I said.

I reached out my hand and he took it. He held it and said, "One more thing."

"What's that?"

"Stop looking back so much," he said. "You've got to get on with it."

"What do you mean?" I asked.

He let go of my hand.

"Do you know why I really come down here every day? I come down here," he said, "to look at the pretty girls getting on and off the train. They remind me what it was like to be young and not have a care and have at my fingertips all the world's possibilities. When you get old, and I'm not very old, you begin to see how all your possibilities have disappeared and how much time you've wasted. All those things you thought were so important aren't really such a big deal after all. And you start to see how all those dreams you had are never going to come true."

He took my hand once more and squeezed it.

"Everything is not ugliness and suffering," he said. "You can find some goodness if you look for it, and you can find a bit of happiness and you can find success if you don't let yourself get sucked under. For the sake of that great-grandfather you were telling me about, the one who was a slave, and all your ancestors who were slaves, don't waste too much time. Just get on with it."

He slapped me on the back.

"Promise me," he said.

I promised him I would try.

"And don't hate your ancestors," he said. "I don't think that's a very healthy thing. People will do almost anything to survive. That's why we have been fighting so hard to hang on to a way of life."

Then he walked me to my bike. I got on it and rode away.

X

The head must bow and the back will have to bend,
wherever the darkey may go.

—"My Old Kentucky Home"

ë

This is what I know about my great-great-great-grandfather.

He was a slave. His name was Joseph. He made and mended
harnesses. Born in 1795, he was owned—inasmuch as one man
can own any other—by a man named John—John Harris of
Goochland, Virginia.

In 1832 Joseph was legally manumitted. The reasons are not
clear. Family rumor has it that Joe might have been—even must
have been—John's son. What other reason could there have been
for the emancipation, for Joe's light complexion, and for the fact
that Joe, a slave, had been taught to read and knew how to write?
His master John Harris could do neither.

I had seen the last will and testament that Joseph recorded in
Shelby County, Tennessee—written in Joe's own hand and signed

by him. It is a document that has floated around the family for years.

A copy of the emancipation deed I found in Richmond, Virginia, in the State Library and Archives. It was not signed by John Harris. He could only make his mark—a small but steady X.

Know all men by these presents that I John Harris serv. of the County of Goochland and State of Virginia, have manumitted, emancipated and set free, and by these presents do manumit, emancipate and set free, a negro man slave named Joseph and sometimes called Joseph Harris, who was born my property, and I do hereby declare the said Joseph Harris to be entirely liberated from slavery, and entitled to all the rights and privileges of a free person with which it is in my power to vest him. He the said Joseph Harris hereby emancipated is a man of yellow complexion about five feet seven inches high and was thirty seven years of age on the 12th day of July last.

In testimony whereof, I have hereunto set my hand and affixed my seal this 5th day of September Eighteen hundred and thirty two.

                                                    his
Signed, sealed and delivered   John **X** Harris
in the presence of   mark
NW Miller

In Goochland County Clerks Office 5th September 1832

This Deed of Emancipation was this day presented to me in the said Office and acknowledged by John Harris serv to be his act and deed, and admitted to records

                                          Teste, *NW Miller*

The language of the deed suggests that Joseph had already been granted his freedom. He might have bought it. He might have been given it. But he seems already to have had it. For some reason now he was being given it explicitly, perhaps because he had earned it, and like a son with his inheritance, wanted to leave with it.

Of course everything was subject to the discretion of the slave-holder. John's son or not, Joseph remained legally a slave. And even if Joseph had earned his freedom, or saved up money to buy his freedom, still he would have been hostage to the kindness of the man whose property he was. After all, the property of a man's property, his time and the fruits of his labor, is that man's possession as well.

But often slaves were allowed to earn and keep extra pay for doing extra jobs or for growing and selling crops on their own time. Many slaves were hired out—to work on other farms, in other homes, in factories. Many were given Saturday afternoons and Sundays off. What money they might have earned working these extra hours, many would have been allowed to keep. That money, earned and squirreled away behind a loose board or beneath a few rocks, could have bought freedom.

As a skilled laborer Joseph might very well have been hired out—and often. John might have kept part of the wages, the rest he should have given to Joe.

Perhaps John was an honorable man, setting a price and then living up to his word, letting Joseph buy his freedom with the money saved. Perhaps he then let Joseph stay on, working for the lower wages that a black harness maker would charge. Working for John and for others in the county, Joseph could save still more money before setting off down the road to find whatever adventures awaited.

And now with enough money saved, Joseph wanted to leave. He wanted to find his place and his fortune in the wide world. He wanted his freedom. And John, true to his word, let Joseph have it.

But in the deed there is no mention of the price of Joe's freedom. If this had been a cash transaction, the price should have been recorded.

But it doesn't matter. Whatever the case, whether he bought

his freedom or was given it as some sort of birthright, before leaving the land that had been his home Joseph needed an official document to prove he was no longer a slave.

Patrollers roamed the countryside and lurked in the cities looking for runaway slaves. They made sure you were who you said you were, where you were allowed to be, doing what you were supposed to be doing. They stopped blacks routinely. Any slave caught without a pass was likely to be arrested and whipped.

Free blacks if challenged had to prove their freedom, either that they had been emancipated or—since freedom could only be inherited maternally—that either mother or grandmother had been born free. They lived, after all, in a society that equated black skin with slavery.

Free blacks were not entirely free, were slaves without masters, limited by what they could and could not do, where they could and could not go. In many southern cities they had to register their names and occupations. Often they had to wear badges. Free blacks arrested in faraway places without proof of freedom were apt to be forced back into slavery. Sometimes, proof was not enough.

But the allure of the city was worth the risk, worth the insult and subordination. The allure of the city was obvious. There was opportunity there. There were jobs and money there. And there was freedom.

Not every runaway slave went north. Many escaped simply to anonymity in the closest southern city.

Cities like Richmond in Virginia and Charleston in South Carolina swarmed with black faces. The air was alive with black sounds—music, laughter, voices.

Away from the city, free blacks continuing to work on the farm were not much better than slaves. Some whites assumed that any black they saw was a slave, and dealt with him accordingly.

But in the city every black was not a slave and was not treated as one; nor was every black unskilled or unambitious. In the city there were blacks of every stripe.

In the city a black man could get lost in the crowd. In the city, free blacks and black slaves hustled along the sidewalks, bought and sold, shoved and shouted along with whites. The city was a more cheerful place. It was, perhaps, enough to know that slavery did not have to be a permanent condition. There was hope.

And there was life.

Fifty percent of Charleston's population was black, 40 percent of Richmond's, and the unskilled labor force in those two cities was 70 percent black—although in Charleston three out of four black men worked at skilled trades. The unskilled labor pool was 50 percent black in Mobile, 40 percent black in Nashville.

Blacks worked in tobacco factories, ironworks, construction crews, railroad companies. They were in the shops and on the streets. Blacks were plentiful. And they were conspicuous.

In the mornings the cities belonged to the blacks. Workers ran to the docks and hurried to the factories. Domestic workers went to the market. Drivers raced their wagons and carts noisily through the streets. Laborers repaired the roads, dug the ditches, manned the textile mills. The black presence was powerful and essential.

Free blacks were carpenters, millwrights, barbers, and tailors. Free blacks owned property, houses and farms and grocery shops. Free blacks owned slaves.

Free blacks made shoes, free blacks made perfume, free blacks made harnesses.

Goochland is only thirty miles from Richmond. Able to read and write, intelligent, Joseph surely would have accompanied John into town from time to time. He would have seen the possibilities afforded blacks in the urban environment. He would have wanted to test himself in those waters. If he had been living as a free man, he would need formal proof. An official deed of manumission was required.

And so one late-summer afternoon, John rode over to the Goochland County Courthouse and freed his son—if indeed he *was* John's son.

If he was John's son . . . The phrase causes me to stumble. Both pride and shame are bound up in it.

For days I pored over genealogy records in the State Library and Archives. I checked marriages, deaths, deeds, wills, I checked the census and the tax rolls, everything that was recorded by Goochland County for the state of Virginia. I followed a trail of property deeds and title transfers until finally I found John Harris's family and traced it as far back as the early eighteenth century, back to when this country was still England's and the land prices were still in pounds and shillings and pence. Probably John's family, possibly my family, had been here long before I found them.

His family, possibly my family, were speculators. They bought land and then sold it.

His family, possibly my family, were English or they were Scottish.

His family, possibly my family, were merchants. And they were successful. And I ought to be proud of them.

But my pride cannot outweigh my guilt.

John Harris's family, possibly my family, were also slave owners.

If Joseph Harris was indeed the son of John, then not just the blood of slaves but the blood of slavers ran in Joseph as now it runs in me.

If I am to be proud of what others have done before me, proud of these things I did not do, then I must feel guilt and shame as well for the horrors I did not do.

And which shame, that of slave or of slaveholder, should be the greater?

I was thinking for some reason of Joseph's mother. I know nothing about her. I wonder who she was and how she was, wonder as well how she endured being torn between joy and sorrow. She had conceived and for nine months would carry the joy that would be born a slave. The world her child would enter would not be the world she wanted for it. What a hopeful and strong woman she must have been.

No wonder John was attracted by her and drawn to her. No wonder he wanted her.

She likely had been a slave on the Harris farm. Although the southern edict has always been against black men loving white women, white men could do as they pleased. And one warm October night, John, wanting company, wanting a woman's warmth, walked in the darkness to where this nameless woman of my past sat, and he entered without knocking.

John Harris owned only three hundred twenty-five acres. His was no great plantation. He only held four or five slaves. He was probably a very humane man. His slaves might very well have liked him. He might have carried on regularly with the women on his farm before he married, and again after the death of his first wife and before his remarriage. So far there had been no accidents. But on this October night, the moon and the stars were aligned: the woman was fertile. John's lust was strong. And that night when he entered without knocking and took hold of his property, in a moment as fleeting, as stirring and mysterious as a heartbeat, the blood of slaves and the blood of slavers mingled. The act was both momentous and casual, so casual in fact that it was being repeated at the very same time on countless farms all over the South.

I wonder if John would have stayed the night. Or did he take his pleasure quickly? I try to imagine his face, his manner, his way of walking. But I can see nothing. It must have been a very dark night.

The following July, Joseph Harris was born.

This man's face I can see clearly. I see him in the eyes of my father. His smile lives in my father's smile, his laughter in my father's joyful noise. When I look at my father, in the same way that I see myself, I also see my great-grandfather Joseph. When I look for Joseph against the night sky, it is my own face I see. I hear his voice in the whispering of the wind, and it is my voice as well. I feel his hand press against my heart.

Joseph. I call him and he answers me.

So. It was not the voice of addiction that had urged me on. It was the soft voice of a man I had never met until now.

Until now I never knew him. Until now I never understood.

From the distance of centuries and the distance of different worlds, Joseph Harris at first seemed a coward to me. And my voice was accusing when I cried out to him.

Great-Grandfather, why did you suffer the hardship and humiliation of slavery? You could have fought against it. The arrogant blood that runs in me, that I took from my father and will give to my children, surely it came from you. Where was your courage and your pride when time came to rise up against injustice

*and pain? Why did you not think of me and the effect your actions
would have on my life? Why this cowardice? Where would we be
now if you had stood bravely and said no?*

When I think of my great-grandfather with his head lowered
and his eyes to the ground, I think of my father who in his day
was also forced to bow his head and avert his eyes. And I am
shamed. Having inherited arrogance, my father inherited cowardice as well. Having gone south to tempt fate and to test his
limits, he learned his limits and had to eat his pride. And oh!
how that must have hurt him.

If it hurts me now, how it must have hurt them then, proud
men reduced to groveling, backs bent, heads bowed and eyes
averted, voices humble and trembling with fear. When I think
of them I feel their pain. How easy it is to hate them for it.

I ask myself how they could have done it.

I ask myself if my great-grandfather was a coward and the
answer has always been yes. Of course he was a coward. But then
again, he had to be.

He had been a slave. As fortunate as he was, still he carried
the burdens of slavery, the insecurities of slavery. You don't go
overnight from slave to free man in your thinking.

As free as he was, as light-skinned as he was, he was still a
black man. He thought like a black man, was still plagued with
the worries and fears of a black man.

When he moved to Richmond, he would not have wanted to
draw attention to himself. Like other black men he would have
wanted a low profile, would have tried to be as anonymous as
possible. He disappeared from the tax rolls; the census takers
could not find him. When he sought housing it would have been
where the other blacks did, in back alleys, in stables and ware-
houses, in shacks on the edges of town. Where white residents
refused to dwell, blacks both free and slave came together and
formed communities. Comforts and services were few, but these
hubs were vibrant.

In the cities slaves had been hiring out on their own time since
at least as early as 1712. That year the South Carolina legislature
complained that the practice of slaves hiring themselves out
would grant them too much independence, and a chance to in-

dulge in drunken behavior, to entertain evil ideas and develop bad habits. Slaves negotiating for pay, for housing, and for food struck many white southerners as undermining the very foundation of slavery. But the practice continued, and the white working man had to compete with the hired slave the same as he had to compete with the slave working for no wages.

(Naturally, resentment and hostility grew between blacks and poor whites. And violence often broke out as factory owners used blacks as strikebreakers—but still nothing like the great race riots that erupted in Boston and Philadelphia and other northern cities.)

As the southern economy expanded and the purchase price of slaves increased, those who could not afford to own slaves had to hire them. Cities hired slaves to collect trash, build bridges, maintain roads. Slave owners could cut expenses by letting others provide food and housing and clothing for slaves, as well as payment for their work. The slave owners could take in fifty cents a day for a slave. And if the slave could bargain for more than that, or find a job that paid more, he could satisfy his owner and still have a little money for himself. With this little bit extra he could set up house on his own and live away from his master. He could even hope one day to buy his freedom.

Until then, living out—as it was called—was liberty enough for the slaves, even if their lodgings were nothing more than squalid huts and makeshift shacks, dingy and dreary.

But they were away from the masters' gaze.

Some slaves were fortunate enough to rent houses, and while many families had never before found themselves in such favorable circumstances, these lodgings were often not much better than the shacks and huts the poorest of them stayed in. They were rickety and cheap, but still they afforded a degree of privacy and independence. And if a husband and his wife were owned by different masters, living out in these shacks and rented houses enabled them and their families to stay together.

In many cities, blacks were not restricted to certain areas by their race. Blacks lived in all parts of most southern cities. Not until after the Civil War would the South learn the strict segregation it would become noted for. And it would look north to places like New York, Boston, Pittsburgh, and Chicago to learn it.

Until then, as strange as it sounds, blacks were an accepted and integral part of the community at large. Considering the social climate, free blacks, because of their skills and their enterprise, had earned a rather high degree of respect and approval in cities all across the South.

At the same time blacks had their own community as well. Free blacks and slave blacks visited freely. They got together for church activities, interacted at social affairs. They assembled in public houses for drinking and for lively conversation. There were dances and weddings, they celebrated new life, they buried the dead. They were a community that had in common work and race and circumstance. They had the same oppressors and the same fears. They lived in the same two societies—the one black, the other one white.

And the white society was dependent on the black one. The white society lorded over the black one. And the white society was afraid of the black one.

Blacks free and slave could have divided, but they didn't. There was more that bound them than separated them. They associated freely. And the white society feared this as well.

In 1822 Denmark Vesey gave them reason to fear.

Vesey was a blacksmith who had purchased his freedom in 1820. He lived in Charleston. It was his plan for blacks both free and slave to rebel, to assemble on the night of June 16, attack the guardhouse, and take the arsenal. Then they would murder the whites, pillage and set fire to Charleston. Afterward they would make their way to islands in the Caribbean.

The plot was discovered. Thirty-five blacks were executed. But the hysteria didn't die. Concerns grew about the association of free blacks and slave blacks. It was feared that free blacks would inflame the slaves and preach rebellion, that free blacks would deliver freedom papers from ex-slaves living in the North to slaves still in the South, that free blacks would hide fugitive slaves. For the sake of white safety and for the sake of slavery itself, laws were passed attempting to limit contact between free black and slave, to keep blacks out of the transportation trade, and to restrict alcohol from slave blacks. The laws were not strictly enforced.

Not until the 1830s.

On a Sunday night in 1831 Nat Turner stole up to his master's house and took the master's baby and killed it. There were forty men with him. They went to another house, killed a schoolteacher, went on and killed many more. During a month of rampage and rebellion and hiding out, Nat Turner and his followers killed fifty-five white people in southern Virginia, after which the South and black-white interaction changed forever.

William Lloyd Garrison's abolitionist newspaper, *The Liberator,* had appeared in Boston. Slaves found courage. The rest of the world pointed an angry finger at the institution of slavery. White southerners fell back and insulated themselves. Many had considered slavery an evil institution. They had hoped and assumed it would eventually disappear. Now suddenly they rallied to its defense and praised it as part of what made the South and its way of life different and good and pure.

Upon the shoulders of slavery now rested southern honor and trust and a way of life. Into slavery's palms men and women of the South placed their fortunes and their futures, their lives and eventually the lives of their sons.

Laws that had been on the books for a long time but never enforced were now seen in a different light. South Carolina began executing a law that prohibited the manumission of slaves. Any black person who could not prove he had been free before 1822 was forced back into slavery.

By the late 1830s state legislatures would allow manumission only by judicial decree. By the late 1850s most southern states wouldn't permit manumission at all.

In Richmond the ability of slaves to hire themselves out was eliminated. Blacks could not assemble without white authorities present. Free blacks and slaves both were restricted from entering certain parts of the city. Blacks could not smoke, stand on the sidewalk, or carry canes. Jails, hospitals, cemeteries were now segregated, public schools, restaurants, and hotels were declared off-limits to blacks. The railroads kept separate cars for black travelers. There was even a law in Virginia that all free black men had to leave the state within sixty days of their emancipation.

Segregation had arrived and being black suddenly became a bigger crime. And slavery suddenly became even more hopeless.

This was the backdrop against which Joseph Harris won his fragile freedom in September 1832. And still freedom was valuable enough to him that he left the Harris farm and made his way to the city.

Joseph Harris remained in the area for twelve more years. He showed up on census records from time to time, but the last record I saw of him in Virginia was in 1844, the year John Harris died.

Not including the three hundred twenty-five acres of land, John left an estate valued at $2,965.86. Among his property were beds and furniture, two cultivators and a black bull, thirty head of sheep and an ox cart, a deep red cow, nine hogs and nine slaves. It obviously had not been for humanitarian reasons that John had emancipated Joseph. John died a slave owner.

As best I can make out from the blurred handwriting:

Mahala and 4 children Tom, Louisa,

Rose, and Frances $1125.00

Toryan a Negro Man 400.00

John Ditto 500.00

Bob Ditto 400.00

Sulpha a Negro Woman 150.00

Nothing about them apart from this is noted, no mention of who the people were or what became of them, or of the too many others like them.

As for Joseph, he was not mentioned in the will, and maybe he did or maybe he did not attend his daddy's funeral, but he was there on October 31, 1844, when John's property was sold at auction. County probate records show that for thirty-seven cents Joseph bought horse collars and a harness.

And then what became of him?

Did he go to Richmond and try to lose himself in the city,

pass as a white man, take a job at the Tredegar Ironworks? The hours were long and the work was hard, but with bonuses and overtime Joseph could make much more as an ironworker than as a harness mender, maybe close to $100 a year. Maybe Joseph had a plan to make the most of his freedom. To travel the land and find a home. To take the name of his former owner, which was the only name he had, and get on with his life. Not to forget about the past—how could he ever do that?—but to leave it where it belonged, behind him.

When he had saved enough, when he had had enough of Virginia with its sour memories, perhaps he pushed further south toward Raleigh and the Carolina coast. Perhaps he tried his hand as a fisherman, or maybe he ran a ferryboat between the islands.

And each time the wind shifted, he carried on, down through Georgia and into Florida, across Alabama and Mississippi, and on until the great river blocked his path, and then north but not too far north, to Tennessee, where the rich soil was deep enough for a wandering man to plant his roots. There Joseph Harris found his home.

He took the money he had saved, applied his skills as a horseman, and started a stagecoach line. He bought land. He prospered. And in the same way that my father is happiest when his kids are home and around him, Joseph surrounded himself with his children and was happy.

Much of this is conjecture, of course, but by the time Joseph died in 1875, he had indeed started and operated a stagecoach line in western Tennessee. He had amassed a sizable wealth and 317 acres of land.

The land is still there. They call it Harris Hill. When Joseph died it was divided among his children according to terms set forth in a will of such sophistication that I wonder at it now, sounding like every white man who has ever asked me how it is that a black man travels the world and has as his hobbies skiing and scuba diving and fly fishing:

How in the world did a black man, a former slave, acquire wealth enough to leave behind at the time of his death five pages of final will and testament and 317 acres of land: 50 acres each to his daughter Martha and son Cornelius, 50 acres each to his daugh-

ters Mary and Lettie, 30 acres to his wife, Milly. The remaining 87 acres to be sold at public out-cry for one-third cash, the balance due in one and two years with interest and approved security. Where did a black man, former slave, gain such financial shrewdness?

Joseph ordered that the cash be doled out in equal shares among his children—except to his son James, to whom he willed ten dollars and nothing more.

Perhaps James was a bit of a goof-off. Perhaps he was a man, not unlike his father, with wanderlust in his soul. His father wanted James to settle down, be a farmer or a businessman, be respectable. James had different ideas. They fought.

Certain that James would only squander his share and amount to little, Joseph left him little.

James was the man who fathered Samuel, the man who fathered Melvin, the man who fathered another Samuel—my father. His blood is in my veins, and perhaps I am like him.

(My father also worried about me and my place in the world. For a long time he expected little from me, a writer, a dreamer, the one with different ideas. And we too have argued. But that is another story.)

James's brother Peter must have danced with uncommon visions as well. He left the hill and set off to find his own way in the world. Along the way he settled in the area known as the Delta in western Mississippi. He was a founding father of an all-black town called Mound Bayou.

It was a long way from the Harris plantation in Virginia to Harris Hill in Tennessee, and beyond; a long way from being a slave to being a landowner to founding a town. A long way to now. But here I stand, many generations and many fortunes hence. The torch has been passed. I carry Joseph's flame.

The mist recedes further from the mirror. The darkness brightens. I can see a bit clearer.

In all the kingdoms of the biological world, the instinct to survive surpasses every other. There is in mankind an intense instinct to survive. Joseph with his head bowed and his back bent was surviving. My father, when it was his turn, his eyes averted and his voice trembling, he was surviving. At the same time, it was more than survival of self. It had to be.

When Joseph stepped a free man out of the Goochland County Courthouse that September afternoon the day was very warm. It was a partly overcast sky, the clouds billowing up from dark bottoms to threaten rain. But the tops of the clouds boiled into the heavens and the sun struck them there and they gleamed almost golden. The light that late afternoon had such an amber quality that Joseph's skin darkened and seemed almost tan.

John went home without him. Joseph wanted to be alone. It was one of those moments best savored in quiet solitude.

Joseph did not shout his joy. He took his pleasure quietly, almost portentously, as he looked backward and forward at the same time. He stood on the hill of the courthouse and remembered. And then he looked forward and thought about his children and his grandchildren and his great-grandchildren, the same as he had thought about them every day of his captive life. He had been thinking about me.

I was the reason Joseph endured, the reason he could not stand up and say, "No, I refuse, I will do your bidding no more and you will just have to kill me." He would have died, and the future would have died with him.

"*The struggle of today is not altogether for today,*" as Abraham Lincoln said in 1862. "*It is for a vast future also.*"

I like to think that if I had been a slave, if slavery had rested on my shoulders and the shoulders of others like me, then slavery would have ended early. There can be no slavery without the complicity of the slave. I would rather have died. But then, I am not very forward-looking. I cannot see much farther than next week. I cannot see six generations from now, as Joseph and the others could, do not seem to care about the future as much as Joseph and the others did, would not sacrifice even half as much.

I turn to face the whispering wind, turn to thank my great-grandfather for what he endured for my sake. I turn to ask his forgiveness for not knowing sooner. And for not holding the torch higher or carrying it farther, for not having more to show for the pains he endured for my sake.

I'm sorry, Joseph.

There is no sound in the trees, no noise in the air, but I feel his gentle caress upon my face.

Joseph. I call out and wonder if he can hear the love in my voice.

I climb on the bike and ride west out of Richmond. Joseph rides with me. Along Monument Avenue the statues of Lee and Stuart and Jefferson Davis do not seem so chilling as before, not so frightening in their symbolism, for now I have a symbol of my own. I have a champion.

XI

*Do not wish to be anything but what you are—but be
that perfectly.*

—Francis de Sales

I settled into the saddle of my bike and rode, taking my time,
going slowly for a change. I did not guide the bike. I did not
know the way. Nor did I need to. I went where the wind blew
me.

From Monument Avenue it is a left turn onto Glenside Drive,
and then a right onto Patterson, which is Virginia Highway 6.
This is the road that runs from Richmond to Goochland.

At the crest of a hill not very high I stopped the bike and got
off. I wanted to lie for a moment in the grass. I wanted to feel
its coolness against my back before the sun dried the earth and
heated the air. I wanted to watch the cloud formations before
the sun cleared them away.

It was going to be a hot day. I took off my jacket and strapped
it to the back of the bike. Then I lay back and looked up. Some-

thing very magical and reassuring was suddenly in the air. I no longer felt alone.

Overhead the clouds struggled to conspire. A little more moisture in the air, a little less warmth, and they would have swelled together into large thunderheads. But the sun was too strong. The clouds surged upward instead of out, gathered the warm light into their white fleecy folds and then dissipated. Light now flooded the hills. The temperature rose.

In the sudden warmth a hatch of gnats and midges and small moths burst forth in great swarms. They hovered in ever moving clouds, frantic to fulfill their destiny, to survive this short while before death, to mate and lay eggs. For a year they had lain dormant waiting for this moment. Now it was upon them. The air was charged with new life.

Above, a sparrow fluttered by. In its beak it held dried grass and something that looked like a chewing gum wrapper. The sparrow darted into the trees. It had a nest to build.

In the distance, pine trees huddled against the now cloudless horizon. Houses dotted the hills, and kudzu covered the earth. The broad leafy plant filled the gullies along the side of the road. It clung to the bases of trees. It climbed telephone poles and stretched along the power lines that hung over the highway. It grew thick and lush and the air smelled of its growing.

It was like a dream, a very hot day, nothing but the flies moving, no sound but the chirping of distant birds.

From this hill, a hill that Great-Grandfather might have stopped to rest upon before heading to Richmond and then south toward his future—from this hill, all of a sudden the South didn't look so bad. I relaxed, crossed my legs at the ankle, folded my arms behind my head. I closed my eyes and drifted into a dream-like state. I didn't want to sleep. I just wanted to dream. Serenity was overtaking me. I wanted to slide into it gradually, wanted to feel it fully.

Now the almost unthinkable, having taken shape once before in the clouds, was forming in my mind and reaching my lips.

What if I ended up liking this place?

There was magic in the air, all right. Suddenly I was at ease, more than comfortable. Even after all that has been—and how could this be possible?—I no longer hated the South. I no longer feared it.

But then, why should I?

There have been more fearsome times than these. Others faced them. Others survived them. Others with more reason than I will ever have to fear and to flee braved it out and stayed when the prudent course would seem to have been to turn away from the South and make a start somewhere else.

The prudent course might well have been for Joseph, as light-skinned as he was, to try to pass, if he could, for white. But there is no sense denying who you are. There is, in fact, something evil about it.

Even in those hateful days, Joseph couldn't bring himself to do it. Long before black was beautiful there must have been something wonderful about it, about the color, about the skin, about the experience, some joy that was not worth losing or doing without, some hope, some sense of faithfulness, duty, and debt to the ones who had gone before, maybe even to the ones who would come after. Not everything after all can be measured in terms of comfort and self.

And there must have been something too about this place. After all that has been, how else to explain that there is even a single black person remaining in the South?

Why, for example, did Joseph not go north to make his fortune? Would it not have been easier there to find a better life for himself and for the ones who would come after? Why did he stay in the South?

What did he feel about this place that I don't feel, what did he know that I know not?

Of course it might have been not the South that held him, but the North that repelled him.

I was thinking of Roger Taney. Born in Maryland, educated in Pennsylvania, he became Chief Justice of the United States Supreme Court. In 1857 while deciding the Dred Scott case, Taney wrote that a black man had no rights a white man was bound to respect.

I was thinking of the great race riots in New York (1864) and Chicago (1917), in Boston and Philadelphia and Cleveland. I was thinking of the intense racial hatred that exploded in Boston when public schools were ordered desegregated in the 1970s. I was thinking of present-day Boston, and present-day Chicago, two of the most racially tense places in the world. I was thinking of a cocktail party in Connecticut.

And I was remembering that Malcolm X once noted that the South is anywhere south of the Canadian border.

The rest of the world points an angry finger at the South. The rest of the world sees the cinders only in the eyes of southerners. The rest of the world refuses to see the soot in its own eyes.

The South, in attitude and in effect, is probably not much worse than the North—only in degree and display. It's simply that the South has always been honest about its hatred and its prejudice. Northern intolerance has been subtle, therefore more pernicious and snaring.

Perhaps, as most of us do, Joseph simply preferred what was familiar, even if what was familiar was painful. Perhaps he pre- ferred the devil he knew to the devil he didn't, preferred hatred and despotism pure, and not, as Abraham Lincoln put it, mingled with the base alloy of hypocrisy.

As I find myself inexplicably now doing, perhaps Joseph found himself getting defensive about the South, the way many white southerners are, the way any man will defend his home, his family, and his ideas against outside criticism.

It was Joseph's home, after all. Like any Virginian he would have considered the South—and this state especially—as sacred soil.

When he departed, surely he left a bit of himself here. Just as surely he took a bit of Virginia with him and passed it along. My grandfather's middle name was Virginia.

What irrational love of sacred Virginia and of the South in general have I inherited, do I harbor and long to admit? In what weird ways is the South not just an ancestral home, but my home as well? How much of this place is within me?

In the workings of psychiatry, revealed secrets can suddenly unlock the gates to a flood of emotions and admissions. One little secret is all it sometimes takes.

I lie darkening in the sun. I close my eyes and shut off the outside world. I am alone, isolated, my thoughts humming inside my head like a mantra. I am completely relaxed. There is no sound now but the deep rhythmic breathing of meditation. My thoughts drift in front of me, unaided and unimpeded, floating in and out of focus like images in a dream. I acknowledge them, and they become real. Finally I admit to myself what I, a black man, would never admit to anyone else.

Of all the men who emerged heroic from battlefields in the Civil War to capture my imagination, only one wore a Yankee uniform. All the rest were Confederates. They were the same men glorified in the statues along Monument Avenue. They were Jeb Stuart and Stonewall Jackson and Robert E. Lee.

Forget for a moment the cause for which they fought. They were romantic figures to me. They were outmanned and outgunned and still they managed to avoid defeat during four long years of war. At times they seemed on the edge of victory. They were bold and flamboyant, they were brave and they were lucky. They were passionate about a cause, albeit an unworthy cause, and they had a valor about them that the inept Northern soldiers seemed to lack.

If you can separate the nobility of effort from the nobleness of the desired result, then these men and their Confederates deserve enormous praise for their bravery and for their devotion to duty.

Think of Pickett's charge during the battle at Gettysburg. It was obvious folly from the start.

Quietly General George Pickett urged his men: "Up, men, and to your posts. Don't forget today that you are from old Virginia."

Thirteen thousand brave men marched across an open field toward the waiting Union lines. It was failure for sure. But they marched on.

"Do not hurry, men," a Union general ordered his troops. "Let them come up close before you fire. And then aim slow."

It was impossible to miss. When the Union soldiers finally fired upon the advancing line of Confederates, entire regiments disappeared. By the end of battle, half of the thirteen thousand had fallen or were captured.

Think of Robert E. Lee. He was offered command of the entire Union Army. But his sense of honor and duty, his loyalty to his native country—Virginia—bound him to a lost cause.

We root for the underdog. We praise loyalty. We applaud patriotism. (In those days you were a Virginian, you were a Georgian. Your state was your country.) We honor devotion to duty. Why, then, can we not hold these men in esteem? They were fighting for what they thought was right—personal liberty, self-determination, right to property. But for the slavery issue and a way of thinking which is abhorrent to us today, their principles and ours are not that far apart. Why, then, are we not able to separate what they did from the way they were, their viler side from their nobler natures?

If that separation cannot be made, then we need to exclude from our list of heroes anyone who was born in a time and place whose sensibilities were different from our own, anyone whose ways of thinking were less perfect than our own.

Thomas Jefferson owned slaves.

George Washington owned slaves.

If their philosophies were so wonderful, why didn't they extend into the arena of human justice and equality?

How many great Americans hated Jews?

President after president has dodged the path to heroism, has preferred instead the politically expedient status quo.

Even the U.S. Constitution, so nearly humanly perfect, compromised in the end by declaring that blacks were not citizens, they were nothing more than property, and for the purposes of census-taking they were to be counted as only three-fifths of a whole person—a whole white person.

Does this thinking which is faulty to us now—I hope—tarnish their achievements?

Does their skill at one thing make it irrelevant that their feet were made of clay? Can clay feet keep our heads from rising into the clouds?

Babe Ruth played professional baseball at a time when blacks were not allowed to play in the same leagues with whites.

Babe himself admitted how great the players were in the old Negro Leagues. He could have protested against the color line, could have complained that in order for him to be great he would have to play against the very best, no matter what color. He chose instead to keep his mouth shut. And just by playing he gave legitimacy to the segregation. But it was the world he knew.

It's not a very good excuse, but it's an excuse.

We are formed by the world around us. It forms us, and we form it. We push the edges a little at a time. It is never fast enough for some, too fast for others, but in time we change and we grow, and the world changes with us.

We all have our sins. Not many of us are truly heroic. We all have our viler sides.

And so we grant to our heroes dispensations, the same as we grant to ourselves. Not a single one of us is completely and perfectly heroic.

If we are to have heroes at all we must separate the nobility that is in them from that which makes them just like us. We must pluck the flowers from the weeds and treasure the flowers.

A black man can admire Robert E. Lee for his valor and honor, for his bravery. A black man can love the South for its beauty and charm, and value it for its place—not a good place, but a place—in our history.

I awoke with a start. I awoke with a headache. And I awoke hungry.

It was time to continue on to Goochland and find a place to eat.

When I set out from Richmond I had had another purpose in mind. In the Library and Archives I had seen only photocopies of the documents pertaining to Joseph. In the Goochland County Courthouse I expected I would find the originals. I had wanted to see them, put my hands on them, feel their tangible evidence of Joseph and John Harris. I thought I would feel some great link to them, proof that I was really here.

I was thinking of Joseph as I put my helmet on and climbed back on the bike, as I turned the ignition key and pushed the starter button, as I put the bike in gear and got back on the road. I was thinking of Joseph and of the things he must have seen along his way that might have urged him on, that might have seduced him to stay, the people he met who would have shown him kindness, the towns where every door was closed to him. He would not have wanted the dust of those towns to remain on his boots. He would have knocked it from his shoes and moved on.

I was thinking of Joseph and I remembered Andrew in Raleigh. I remembered what he said about looking at pretty women.

"I don't want to have them," he said. "I just like to know they are in the world. There is so much ugliness around us. I just like to know that there still is some beauty in the world."

And maybe Joseph too. Maybe he was looking for a little goodness and a little beauty.

Having been a slave, he had seen enough ugliness to last a lifetime or two or several. Having endured, he had to have been a hopeful man. Having learned to read, he would probably have studied the Bible. He would have known that when God threatened to destroy Sodom and Gomorrah, Abraham drew near and asked, "Will you condemn the righteous with the wicked? Suppose there are fifty righteous in the city? Will you not spare the place for the sake of the fifty?"

And if for fifty, how about for forty or for thirty or for twenty? And God said, "I will not destroy it for the sake of even ten."

After all the evil he must have seen, perhaps Joseph was looking for ten just men. If he was to keep his hatred at bay and his hope alive, perhaps the search was necessary. Just to know that with all the ugliness around, there is still some beauty in the world.

Despite all that has been and surely all that will come in the future, I cannot allow myself to hate this place. For the sake of ten just men, I cannot allow myself to hate the South.

We all have a very long way to go. Hating makes the going slower.

Just before entering Goochland the road descends sharply and goes around a curve. Right at the top of that hill lives a family named Harris. They call the place Cedar Knoll. A sign hanging from a wooden post tells me so. I see the sign scarcely a moment before it is too late. I hit the brakes, turning into the gravel roadway at the same time, and skid to a stop. The bike almost falls over.

The house is quaint, hidden from the road by the cedar trees. I cannot really tell cedar trees from most other trees, but why would the Harris family call this place Cedar Knoll if these were chestnut trees?

It is a peaceful setting. There are no neighbors nearby. The air is still but fragrant with the smell of cedar. I would love to sit out on the veranda with these Harrises, sip iced tea and watch the birds soaring across the valley. I tell myself to go up and ring the doorbell. When I stick out my hand to shake I should say, "Hello, cousin." Some white man would either laugh himself silly or die of a heart attack.

I get off the bike, but only for a second. There's nothing to prove by shocking him. Or by getting myself shot. I already know he's my cousin. And anyway I'm very hungry.

Goochland is a very small town. It's only a few blocks long. There are no shops to speak of. There is a small library, a post office, and a gas station. And there is the Goochland Restaurant.

The restaurant sits away from the road, at the back of a gravelly parking lot. There are a few old cars in the lot, a pickup truck, a big trash container.

Inside, the restaurant is as elegant as it is outside. It is just one big room—and not very big, at that. A chalkboard menu promises home cooking, manicotti, apple cobbler, pork chops. Along the walls there are a few booths with fake wooden tables and orange plastic benches, in the center of the room a few tables with orange plastic seats. The floors are linoleum, and very dirty.

In a big wall case there are sodas for sale. A freezer holds ice cream. There is a rack offering potato chips and candy.

There is a low counter with a cash register on it. And in the rear of the restaurant there is a window behind which is the kitchen. Through this window the waitress shouts orders at the cook.

Apart from her shouting, the place is pretty quiet. In one of the booths there are a few ancient ladies sitting, smoking, gabbing. I can hear them clearly.

"And so some guy comes in here and says the Dumpster was on fire. Virginia went over there with him and he told her he seen the Dumpster was on fire. Now who do you suppose would set a Dumpster on fire?"

"And why?" another lady adds.

There is the murmur of general agreement.

A big yellow ribbon and an American flag hang from the center beams that support the ceiling. Thank God it isn't a rebel flag.

There is only one waitress and she comes to me. She is very skinny, has no hips at all, her blue jeans just barely hanging on to her waist. She forces herself to smile at me, but she sounds almost rude. She doesn't seem to want me here.

But then again, she doesn't seem to want anybody here. She doesn't want to be here herself.

"What's it going to be?"

I can't tell how old she is, forty-five or fifty. Her hair is black and she wears it cut very short like a young boy would. She has deep sacks under her eyes. Her sad face is bone thin and tired. I heard her say she's been working here for twelve years now, and I don't think she's the owner. I don't think she likes it here. But she looks like she has nowhere else to go.

I order pork chops and know right away the trouble I'm in.

She barks to the kitchen. "Hurry up and get some pork chops thawed out."

When they come, the chops are tough as shoe leather. This is not the southern-style home cooking I came looking for.

An old man in green pants, a blue jacket, and a cap slowly shuffles by. He carries a white plastic pail. He had been in the parking lot when I pulled up. Now he has stopped whatever he was doing to come sit beside me and talk to me while I eat.

"Where's that state you're from? Is that Missouri?"

He had seen my license plate.

"I was in Missouri once," he said. "In Mexico, Missouri. But that was back before you was born, way back in '43."

His hair was white and he had no teeth. He came to tell me that and nothing more. It was an effort at being friendly. Then he struggled slowly to his feet and shuffled off with his bucket. I hacked into the pork chops and chewed slowly. They had the texture and taste of canvas.

When I had finished, for some idiot reason I ordered the apple cobbler. It was about as good as the pork.

The woman in the booth in front of me turned around to face me. She had just been served a cup of coffee but she had no sugar. She asked if she could borrow mine. She turned her back to me, took two sips of her coffee and then turned around again. In half a minute she had picked up her cup and saucer and slid out of her booth. She came and sat next to me.

I said hello.

"Hi! My name's Gwendoline," she said. "What's yours?"

I told her.

"You're not from around here, are you?"

"Well, not exactly," I said. "But my people come from around here."

I was really stretching it.

"Who are your people?" she asked.

I told her that my last name is Harris.

"Oh, I know some Harrises. There's a lot of Harrises around here. Which ones do you belong to?"

"One Harris is about the same as another," I said. "Somewhere down the line we're all related."

"Somewhere down the line," she agreed, "we are all of us related. It doesn't matter what our last name is."

She sipped her coffee and looked out the window.

"Is that your bike?"

"It is," I said.

"Those things scare me," she said. "You don't ride it too fast, I hope."

I grinned. "Not too fast," I said.

"Where have you been? Where are you going?"

"Just all over," I told her. "Just trying to find out how things are."

She didn't respond to my gambit. She sat for a few silent seconds and looked dreamily out the window.

"So," I said. "How are things?"

Very slowly she turned her face to me. We locked eyes, but she didn't speak. She was studying me.

I was waiting for a bombshell. The way she looked at me, I knew she had secrets to tell. I expected she would explode in a tirade of all the racial injustices she had ever experienced or heard about. I expected that in the next few minutes she would put a human face to all my earlier imaginings and fears. My hatred and dread would be renewed.

I was surprised to learn that what was uppermost in my mind was not what was most important to Gwendoline.

I was still in the throes of the addiction. Once you begin thinking in a certain way, the thinking becomes obsession. Everything explains itself in terms of race.

On one side of the racial fence, there is a racial justification for every negative thought or action, and all you end up seeing is a person's color.

On the other side of the racial fence, it's the same thing. Everything gets based on race. For every failure the excuse is founded on race. You get used to seeing yourself as a victim, you get comfortable with the role, you learn to see the world through the eyes of a victim. If it *can* happen, you tell yourself, it must *be* happening. All the time.

But Gwendoline said nothing about being black. She talked about her health, she talked about her weight, she told me she had been diagnosed as schizophrenic, she told me her husband didn't make her happy. So she gained even more weight.

"I haven't always been this fat," she said. "I used to be very pretty. My doctor says I'm gaining weight to keep my husband from wanting to sleep with me. Maybe he's right."

She had been recently pregnant, she said, and had recently had an abortion—her second.

"I'll be damned if I'm going to have another child with that man," she said. "Not until that man gets his act together. Not at this late date."

She had a twenty-five-year-old daughter who was living in Washington, D.C. She told me I should look her up. She had two other children.

I couldn't tell how old she was, and would have guessed she was in her midfifties at least. She told me she was only forty-two.

"It's the weight," she said. "The weight and all the worries and being unhappy. All that plays on your body just like it plays on your mind. It makes you look older. It makes you feel older."

Gwendoline shifted her weight. She turned once more toward the window and looked out.

"But I'm going to get myself together," she said. "Wait and see."

"I believe you," I said.

She looked up sharply.

"You do?" she said. "Do you really think I will?"

I nodded. She frowned. I don't think she believed me. I don't think she believed it herself. She bit her bottom lip and stared at me. I wanted to change the subject.

"How are the white folks treating you?" I asked her.

"The white folks?" she said. "Haven't you heard what I've been telling you? It's not all about white folks, and it's not all about race. I haven't got time to worry about what the white folks are doing or thinking or saying. This is my life. I've got to get on with it. White folks do not own my happiness and my sorrow. They are not going to make my life any better or any worse. All they can do, if they've got a mind to, is put up little barriers. It's like a game. And all I have to do is find some way around them. And we've been finding ways around them for two hundred years. There's always a way. Believe me, there is always a way."

She smiled a tiny little bit. I started to speak, but she stopped me.

"I know what you're thinking," she said. "All you people in the North think the same thing. Slavery and lynching and toilets for coloreds only."

She saw in my eyes the recognition of her truth. She laughed.

"We've gotten past that now," she said. "There ain't no going back. You maybe will get some flare-ups now and again, but that's just a desperate try by some people to hang on to what's not theirs anyway. There ain't no going back."

"But are we moving forward?" I asked.

"Sugar," she said, "anytime you're not going backwards, you're going forwards. Think about getting caught in a flash flood. All black folks have to do is keep on hanging on. We have to remember where we came from. Maybe we can touch on it from time to time, but that's enough. We got to quit dwelling on the poison of the past. We got to get on with it."

She looked down and away, as if she was about to say something embarrassing or shameful.

"Slavery and lynching, that's what somebody else went through. Maybe they went through it so we could be here, but we can't do anything about what happened a long time ago. We're here now. There's more important things to worry about."

Her sadness had left her. She was having a good time now.

"I'm in control of my own dignity," she said. "No white man and nobody else can take it away from me unless I let him, like I let my husband. All somebody else can do to me is kill me or something like that, take my life, and right about now I'd say that's not a real big deal. Apart from that, nobody owns me. And nobody owes me nothing."

I sat on the edge of my bench. I was waiting for more. But she was all played out.

"Excuse me if I went crazy," she said. "But you know how it is. When you keep that stuff all bottled up inside you, soon as you get a little outlet, it all comes gushing out. I can't talk like that at home. My husband doesn't want to hear my ideas. He thinks I'm crazy."

"You're not crazy," I said. "You ought to tell more people what you think."

"Nobody wants to listen to me," she said quietly.

"You'd be surprised."

She touched my cheek.

"You're sweet," she said.

We sat quietly for a minute or two. Then she asked me if I had a place to sleep for the night.

"I'm just going to ride the countryside tonight," I said. "I want to see what's lying around. And I want to be in Raleigh tomorrow morning. There's a guy I need to see."

"Give a call if you change your mind," she said. "You'll be welcomed."

She wrote her name and her address on a paper napkin and slid it over to me.

"If I'm not there or if my husband answers," she said, "tell him we talked. Tell him who you are. Tell him you're coming on over. He'll give you directions and we'll find room for you."

The crabby waitress brought our bills written on little green pieces of lined paper. She set them down and walked away without a word or a second glance.

"Can I pay for your coffee?" I asked Gwendoline.

"No," she said. "I was going to buy yours."

"I didn't have coffee."

"Then I'm going to pay for your pie or something."

She grabbed for the check but I snatched it away.

"Let me get yours," I said.

"Only if you promise to call me."

I promised, but I knew I never would.

She walked me out to the bike and stood with me while I got ready to leave.

"It's a pretty motorcycle," she said. "You ought to give it a name."

I looked at her and smiled.

"Where are you going first?" she wanted to know.

I thought for a moment. I thought I had avoided the strong pull of sentimental curiosity, but its effect on me was stronger than ever.

"Over to the courthouse, I think. Something you said makes me want to find something."

I didn't tell her what.

"Some family stuff," I said.

"Do you want me to go with you? I know them over there."

"I think this is something I want to do alone," I said. "You understand, don't you?"

She put her arms around me and kissed my cheek.

"In case I don't see you again," she said. "But anyway, you can write to me."

"I will," I said. But I knew I wouldn't. I knew I was a thief. Gwendoline probably knew it too.

I had entered her life. I had knocked on the door and she had invited me in. She had trusted me with her secrets and now I was walking off with them to sell them for profit. I felt like Jean Valjean with the bishop's candlesticks. Gwendoline probably knew she would never see or hear from me again.

I took her hand and squeezed it. When I hugged her, I kissed the soft spot where her neck joins her shoulder. Then I hurried. I got on the bike and rode away. I didn't have to look back to know she was there watching me disappear.

I didn't go far. The courthouse is practically right next door to the restaurant. I pulled into the lot and up the slight hill and I stopped.

It's hard to believe, but the courthouse is the same building Joseph Harris would have known. I stand on this hill and look at it, the same as Joseph might have stood here and looked at it. This same tree might have been here then, maybe even the bell that hangs out front. This is the meaning of history, that we are linked to the deep past in ways both vital and insignificant, often in ways we are not aware of and care nothing about.

This is the fourth (or fifth; they're not quite sure) courthouse building serving the county. But this is the first that has stood on this site. It was built in 1826 by Dabney Cosby, a brick mason who was trained by Thomas Jefferson and who had worked with Jefferson on some of the buildings at the University of Virginia in Charlottesville.

That the building was made of brick at all astounds me. Clapboard would have been more common. A wooden courthouse would have stood a greater risk of burning down. The records I have come to find might no longer exist.

But what really amazes me is the line that runs from me to Joseph to John Harris and through this courthouse to Dabney Cosby and to Thomas Jefferson. In how many ways are the lowest of the low linked, then, to those whose names we praise? In how many ways are we all linked to greatness, and linked to each other?

A simple low brick building. The columns give it stature. It looks a little like a humble classical Greek temple. It looks like a church without a steeple.

Around back, in an extension that certainly was not here a hundred fifty years ago, in a room whose rear wall is covered with shelf after shelf of old record books, I walked in and, with a little help from one of the women who worked there, I found the book and turned to the page that holds the original document. Joseph Harris's deed to freedom.

I certainly do not need a piece of paper to give me legitimacy or to prove that Joseph existed. *I* am living and loving proof that he was here. But something touched me as I touched that page. Joseph's breath fanned my cheek. I think my heart stopped.

When it resumed, it beat at a much slower pace, calmer and quieter. My heart became still and serene.

I had expected more, I think. I had thought I might want to shout, beat my fists upon my chest and howl like a happy dog for an hour. But it was such a peaceful moment, and I don't know why, that I just wanted to run my hand across the page over and over and over.

Something that Joseph had touched, I was now touching. The parched paper that had emancipated Joseph so many years ago was now emancipating me. It could very easily have said: *Know all men that by these presents Eddy L. Harris is hereby manumitted, emancipated and liberated from the shame and degradation of slavery. Joseph, like Jesus, has suffered in your stead. He has borne your shame. You are set free.*

At the same time this deed was fastening me. I was tied now to Joseph in a way that blood could never bind me. I was his debtor.

Because of the way other folks see us I have always been linked to black people. Now I am linked because of how *I* see us. And I see now that being black is not only about slavery. It is about strength and patience, about pain and survival and connectedness. It is about courage. It is about sacrifice and it is about love. Being black is about hope.

Because of all that has been, people of color live in constant danger. Our lives are serious, our talk is serious, our thinking ought to be very serious. We can never assume that the world is one thing or another, nor that the world is all black, nor that it is all white, nor that the world is safe and that everything is rosy. We must not forget that our collective life is a war.

We must never forget how long the road has been. We must never forget that we are still on that road. And we must not forget that if we are ever to arrive at our destination, we are responsible for one another.

When I graduated from high school, the headmaster in his final report urged me to go forth and be a credit to my race. It was one more shred of evidence that who I was and what I did would only be seen in the context of color. At the time I took as an insult the assumption that I could only be a source of pride and honor to black people.

Now I see that I am just a rung on the ladder. As I am seen, others will be seen. What I do matters. As I now stand on the shoulders of those who have gone before, others who come after will stand on mine. I hope my shoulders are somehow broad enough.

I took a deep breath and closed the book containing Joseph Harris's original records. I had found my roots.

What has passed is not entirely gone. It lives within us. The future is born of us. Time is not so rigid as we pretend. I come south to see what lies ahead and I touch the past.

Several weeks later, deeper into spring, I went to an Easter Sunday service in Atlanta.

Looking back on it, the chronology of my journey had taken on the fluidity of memory, the fluidity of a dream.

I had arrived in Atlanta and the delicate scent of lilac flooded my helmet, filled my senses. I had ridden through a patch of heavy shade. The air was cool. Over the road hung clusters of wild lilac bushes, the great clumps of purplish pink flowers dangling from the branches. Their perfume surrounded me and made my Easter Sunday smell like Easter ought to smell.

I had come into Atlanta the night before, come in a driving wind that left me exhausted. When I went to mass the next morning, boring Catholic mass at Immaculate Heart of Mary, I nearly fell asleep. The sermon said nothing to me, did not touch me, did not speak to me, did not rouse me, was not relevant to the world around me.

This was not what I had in mind for Easter.

I wanted some joy, I wanted some noise, I wanted a celebration.

So the idea came to me that I should go to a black church for a second Easter service. And what better church in Atlanta to attend than Ebenezer Baptist Church, the church in which Martin Luther King had been pastor?

But the service that day had been moved to the Martin Luther King International Chapel at Morehouse College, a black school near downtown. I got directions and went, not knowing what to expect.

The place was not a chapel at all, it was an auditorium—huge, impersonal, cold. And it was packed. I felt I was in a theater awaiting some kind of performance.

A big symphony orchestra crowded the stage, strings and brass and tympani drums and a thin man wielding a baton. Behind them was a large choir. A few white faces were sprinkled throughout, but not many: a white lady playing the cello, a white lady violinist, a white lady singing in the choir. Off to one side was the children's choir, a big group of well-mannered boys and girls in white shirts and dresses.

At the front of the stage, in the robes of their office, sat the clergy.

When the music began, trumpeters searched for the right notes, sounding tinny. The strings scraped and grated. The music, European in tradition, was uninspired.

Surely it had been a mistake for me to come.

Lawrence Carter spoke first. "Christianity," he said, "is the only religion in the world with a holiday dedicated to the day death died."

I started to doze.

There were a couple of readings, then the next piece of orchestra music began. When it was over, Assistant Pastor Sharon Austin recognized visiting ministers and out-of-town groups that had made the journey specially to be here. In a minute she was asking for donations.

Then all of a sudden the choir was singing. No orchestra, just an accompanying piano. The music had more emotion. I perked up.

From somewhere in the hall an old woman's voice rang out and started wailing with the music. Sharon Austin invited us all to sing. The people seemed to know the song. I closed my eyes and swayed with the soaring voices. I forgot I was in church. I forgot that the prayers invoked the name of Jesus. And in their place I heard prayers and thanksgivings to my great-grandfather Joseph.

Sharon Austin prayed: "Yet you reminded us this morning, [Great-Grandfather Joseph], that it's all right, that you've fixed it, that you've paid the price."

As she prayed the choir continued to sing, and the congregation clapped hands to keep time.

"It's all right to sing, oh yes," Sharon Austin cried. "We're in worship. Why don't you all stand and give praise this morning?"

And everyone stood, singing, clapping.

Then the music stopped and things quieted for Edward Reynolds.

"I don't know what your circumstances may be today, but on Good Friday there was a man who went to a rugged cross. And even though they put a spear in his side, he said not a mumbling word—because he knew of his purpose in this life."

Joseph again.

"And so it is that we come today and say thank you."

Thank you, Joseph.

"Thank you for allowing us to see another day. It is by your grace that we stand here this morning. Thank you for your love.

"Because you were willing to die, it means now I know I have a right to be here. We can't do it without your spirit. Because you lived, all hurt is gone; because you lived, I know what the future will be; that life is worth living because you lived."

And then a song to remind us in the chorus that *there was no easier way.*

Now it was Pastor Joseph Roberts who stood to speak.

First he thanked the whole world for coming, then he thanked the choir, and the children's choir, the orchestra and the college and anyone else he could think of. Then he mumbled a prayer, invoking the spirit to move him this morning.

Joseph Roberts, middle-aged, balding, metal-rimmed glasses around his eyes, a gray Vandyke around his mouth. From time to time, he stroked the beard or scratched it, took off the glasses and gestured with them. He was what I expected in a black Baptist preacher, starting softly, starting simply—talking about Mary Magdalene and her lowly station and why she was the one to receive the gospel message that Jesus had risen—building nicely, becoming more forceful, more expressive and unrestrained, then bouncing around wildly until he was almost apoplectic, and coming to a violent crescendo.

"When you fall down . . ." he said, and he was still talking about Mary Magdalene's sinful past, but he could have been talking about black people who had been locked in slavery once and were forever disparaged because of it.

"When you fall down, some people will never remember that you were ever up. They'll always remember when you were down."

Mary Magdalene was certainly nothing to us, he said. She was possessed by demons and was an inhabitant of a faraway and unimportant city near the border with gentiles. But perhaps we have missed something about her, some quality which we fail to see and appreciate.

Can you imagine what it must have been like to be demon-possessed—or to be a slave, I thought—forced to live the life of a pariah?

Mary was called worthless and evil because of her wicked lifestyle. She was never loved for herself. And so Mary must have been often depressed and disillusioned.

People never forgot who Mary was, Joseph Roberts said.

"There was a man who was roaming in the tombs and when that person was healed the people said, 'We don't want to have anything to do with him. We are mad because you [Jesus] exorcised the demons and put them in the hogs instead and caused us to have an economic downturn. Get him out of here.'

"And the people remembered who he was, and wouldn't forgive him and wouldn't let him alone."

Then Joseph Roberts quieted down.

"I'm wondering if you know some people this morning," he said, "who have something in their past that they might rightfully be ashamed of, but they're trying to overcome it, they're trying to live beyond it, but you say, 'Oh, that's just so and so.' But you never know who God is going to send to deliver a message to you."

He paused. Then he started to get violent, hollering and gesturing wildly, and the congregation could feel his fire. The hot coal had touched his lips, and the spirit was moving him.

"Don't ever feel that somebody is so low that they can't teach you something," he said. "Maybe it's because they've seen the downside of the mountain that they know more than you do on the upside of the mountain. Always remember where you came from."

His voice took on more energy and force. He was talking about Joseph. And he was talking directly to me.

"Always remember that if it had not been for [men like Joseph] on your side you wouldn't be sitting up here this morning. Always remember that it was [a man like Joseph] who brought you from a mighty long way. And it is especially necessary . . ."

He halted. Sweat was on his brow. He took his glasses off. He made a kind of fist and gesticulated passionately, and he said it again. The crowd was with him, erupting in a frenzy.

"It is especially necessary for those black people who have the opportunity to go to universities."

He was pointing at me, shouting wildly.

"It is especially necessary for the little buppies [black urban professionals] of our race who are finally getting the key to the executive washroom to remember where you came from, to remember that if it had not been for [men like Joseph] on your side, you couldn't be anything."

The crowd went crazy. They were yelling and screaming and applauding with abandon. And so was I.

If this had happened a year ago, or even half a year ago, I might have slumped in my seat or slithered out of there. But this Easter morning I knew that Pastor Roberts was right.

Joseph Harris is nothing to be ashamed of. The millions of

other slaves whose names I will never know are all to be proud of. If not for them and their lessons of love and endurance, I would be nothing at all.

I had indeed found my roots.

I had touched the past, which is one thing. The difficult part is carrying the past into the future, carrying it without pain and without shame, remembering how we came to be here, remembering that without the past there is no present, no future. It is here in the present, in us, that past and future meet.

I understood then that Joseph's emancipation deed is a monument to both past and future. It is a reminder of his responsibility to me, and of mine to my children's children. It is a symbol.

That Joseph was a slave is important. That Joseph was black matters. His courage and his farsightedness underscore my debt to him. And while I cannot celebrate slavery, I can surely celebrate the slave.

I recalled running my hands over the dried, crinkly paper, and a surge of pride flowed through me. There was a lot to be sad about and angry about, but there was a lot be proud of, too. A lot to be joyful for. A lot to celebrate.

I went outside and leaned against a tree that Joseph might have leaned against. I lay on the southern grass. The wind caressed my cheek. I looked up at the cloudless sky and breathed in the cool moist air of afternoon. It smelled like home.

XII

The past is history, the future is perfect.

—Orel Hershieser

 ❧

Somewhere in the South a man is waiting to call me nigger. A man who does not know me. A man, perhaps a woman, perhaps a child. Waiting to reject me without knowing a single thing about me except that I am black, not caring to get to know me, not caring enough even to try. Waiting to hate me, or someone who looks like me—some other man, some woman, some child. Waiting to tell us we don't belong. Waiting to call us nigger.

His mind is already made up.

Evil lives in the world. Always has. Always will. But evil is not all there is.

Before she let me get on my way, Gwendoline told me one last thing. She whispered it, spoke it almost to herself, as her lips grazed my ear in our embrace.

"Racism exists," she said. "It is not the worst thing there is. It can be overcome."

I had wanted to ask what she thought was worse than racism, had wanted to ask how she thought it could be overcome. But I never did. I got on my bike and rode away, rode down a narrow lane until the road ran out. I rode down roads with numbers for names, rode down roads with no names at all. I rode until the heat of day stole my strength, rode until the cool evening air brought it back. I rode until the midnight light was the only light there was, and I was deeper and deeper into the South.

The South had always meant one hateful thing to me. I had never considered the possibility that it would mean anything else.

Suppose, I asked myself now, suppose that somewhere in the South someone is waiting to offer me a cool drink, to invite me home, to be my friend. Suppose someone is waiting to understand me a little. Suppose somewhere in the South the future is taking root, a flower among the weeds. Suppose somewhere someone is sorry.

I did not ask Gwendoline what is worse than racism. I did not ask her how it can be overcome. I think now I know. The answers are simple and intertwined. Worse than the racism itself is believing in racism and affirming it, losing yourself, letting racist ways and racist thinking define who you are and what you think and feel, until instead of acting, you can only react.

There is evil in the world—yes. But evil is not all there is. And yes! Evil can be overcome.

Great-Grandfather Joseph had seen evil, more in a single day probably than I will ever know in a lifetime, more than enough to last several generations. Yet when the time came, he did not let the evil block his way. He loaded his wagon with whatever possessions he owned and carried on down the road deeper into the South. He took his tools and his clothes. He took the name that would not have been his but for slavery and made the best of it, took the life that would not have been his but for slavery and made the best of it, took the circumstances that would not have been his but for slavery and overcame them. And all this without a mumbling word. He had a life to get on with. He had a star to aim for, a star to stand on, a destiny to follow, a fortune to find.

There were men waiting to call him nigger, men waiting to refuse him, men willing to hate him for the color of his skin. But he would not be denied.

There were men waiting to humiliate him, to threaten him for no reason, to lynch him for getting out of line. But they could not take his soul.

He was born here—in this South. He belonged here.

And he had become my hero.

I relaxed in the saddle now and rode on. My heart slowed. My breathing came easily. Stars appeared. The breeze picked up. It was going to be a beautiful night.

That next morning I headed back to Raleigh to find Andrew. There was plenty I wanted to tell him.

Thinking he would come to the train station as he usually did, I went there and waited for him. The afternoon train to Washington and New York came and went. Andrew never showed up.

It didn't matter. I don't know exactly what I would have said to him anyway, but something. I just wondered what had made him break his routine that day; something I had said the last time, perhaps. Or something he had said.

I imagined him sitting in another part of the city, perhaps on a bench near North Carolina State University. Doubtless he was watching the pretty young women sauntering to class, reminding him that there is still beauty in the world. But I preferred to think he had strolled over to the east side of the capitol, to the black side of town, to take in the beauty that was there.

I didn't wait for him. I got on the bike and rode out of town. There was someplace else I wanted to go. And this time, with Joseph's hand on my shoulder to guide me, his guardian eye protecting me, I knew where I was going.

After that, the rest was easy.

It is a three-hour ride from Raleigh to Wilmington on the Atlantic coast. It took me three days.

The wind had shifted. It blew a stiff and steady stream from west to east. I didn't want to head into it, didn't want to fight the wind all day, and I didn't want it hitting me from the side and shoving me back and forth across the road. I thought it would be nice to have the wind at my back for a change and so I made my way east along Highway 64.

Along the eastern shore of North Carolina there is a strip of land—several strips, really, a chain of sand islands called the Outer Banks where the wind blows meanly off the sea. There are few trees and only the bare shrubs to block the wind. The land is flat. Only the dunes that rise seem to offer any variety. The wind blows the sand and deposits it elsewhere. The dunes are forever shifting, but slowly. One hundred years from now a dune that looks as solid as the earth will have moved many feet. Another may have disappeared altogether.

I have walked to the edge of the sea. The wind blows. The sand stings my eyes. The ocean roars. It is the cold gray color of loneliness.

A liquid eeriness hangs in the mist and settles all around.

I walk along the line where the dry sand meets the wet. At the edge of the surf there are footprints, deep impressions in the sand. There is no one else around, but someone has been walking here, a lonely ghost, an unseen companion whose footsteps parallel my own.

The wind blows and a howling sound adds to the desolation. The islands seem almost haunted, barren and scary. A wet chill rips right through the skin and into the marrow of the bone. If this were a castle on the moors, it would be the scene of murderous encounters, a place where restless souls walk the night. Their wailing would awaken the winds. This isolation would be their hell. And these dunes . . . these dunes are the shoulders of giants upon which the next generation must stand.

I would guess that something momentous had happened here—if I didn't already know it.

Here on these dunes, some of which are quite high, a young man and his brother came to encounter destiny. They hauled a contraption up these sand hills again and again and again. And each time they would push the thing off the hill. These dunes and this wind were perfect.

Orville and Wilbur Wright set up shop here at Kitty Hawk. From 1900 to 1902 they built glider after glider and shoved each one off Kill Devil Hills until they had mastered the principles of controlled glider flight.

They were learning to fly.

They affixed a motor to their aeroplane and in mid-December 1903, the Wright brothers became the first to achieve and sustain powered flight.

It wasn't much of a flight. Only twelve seconds. But look where those twelve seconds have brought us.

So it is with a life well lived, all too brief in the grand scheme of things, all too imperfect, but full of consequence.

I have always admired the Wright brothers, not quite as heroes but as men who were told it couldn't be done, as men who then did it. I wanted to be like them. I wanted to fly, to soar—not just in an airplane, but into the magical realm of the barely possible. I wanted to dream and then to turn the dreams into reality and then into myth. I wanted to touch the stars.

I wanted to discover cures to incurable diseases, to invent something, anything. I wanted to rob from the rich and give to the poor, perform miracles, save the world. I wanted to be president.

I, who couldn't then and cannot now turn on a good fastball, wanted to hit sixty homers in a season.

In the same classroom where I used to get myself in trouble sword fighting with pencils against Charles Reynolds, a small hand-painted sign was posted on the wall over the blackboard in the back of the room. AIM FOR THE STARS, it said. And I did.

If I failed the stars and reached the moon—well, better than missing the moon and hitting the dull ground.

When I was a kid, a bookwormish runt, an invalid first with casts and then heavy braces on my legs, I spent my early reading years surrounded by biographies of great men and women. I imagined myself to be Amelia Earhart and Charles Lindbergh, George Washington Carver and Thomas Alva Edison, Jim Thorpe and Jesse Owens, Crazy Horse, Sitting Bull, Joaquin Murietta. I was Orville Wright and Wilbur Wright on alternate days, I was Marie Curie. I was Vasco Nuñez de Balboa, I was Christopher Columbus. A time or two I was even Jesus.

It didn't occur to me to be a great black man, nor even a great American. I just wanted to be great.

I was young and stupid. I did not see limitations because of my race or my sex or my nationality. I didn't see limitations at all. Kids never do until they learn them.

But there are limitations to greatness—even to other people's greatness, tarnished now when seen through my prism of racial obsession, and I wondered if I ought to have any of these men and women as my heroes. I wondered if children ought to have heroes at all. The men and women we worship are as flawed as the men and women we don't.

Think of the indignities, the many nonheroic moments my hero Joseph endured just to survive; think how my father had to play the coward, hang his head and let himself be run out of town by men in sheets. Lives all too marred, yet full of merit.

When Wilbur Wright died of typhoid in 1912, his father honored him with a worshipful eulogy. He did not remember the little boy who played hooky from school, who swiped candy from the general store, who disobeyed and found trouble as easily as any man's son. He remembered Wilbur not entirely as Wilbur was, but with admiring eyes that did not question, that did not see the blemishes. It is the way heroes must always be seen.

The eulogy was this:

A short life, full of consequences. An unfailing intellect, imperturbable temper, great self-reliance and as great modesty. Seeing the right clearly, pursuing it steadily, he lived and died.

It is the way every son dreams of one day being seen by his father. And I have often wished that my own father would finally come to understand and appreciate me with similar words of praise—the way I have finally come to understand and appreciate him.

Seeing the right clearly and pursuing it steadily.

But if Wilbur—or any other hero—had truly seen the right clearly, if he had spent as much time dreaming of justice as he spent dreaming of flight, if Babe Ruth had spent as much time championing Negro baseball as he spent being a champion baseball player, if Henry Ford had hired blacks as something other than janitors, if . . . if . . . if . . .

If our heroes had been truly heroic, had seen the right clearly and pursued it, we wouldn't be in the fix we're in. We could all be a lot farther along the road. If they had only had a little more vision.

I expect too much.

I want more from men than ought to be asked.

I should like my heroes flawless, brave and true and larger than life, and I wonder how a person could reasonably have as his hero someone who had moments of weakness. I wonder how a black man can have as his hero someone who had at his core a racist heart.

A hero is someone you want to emulate. A hero is someone who is heroic. And racism—my main concern for the moment, but not my only concern—is antiheroic.

So it seems we would need to strike from the list of our heroes all those who were imperfect. While we're at it, we might as well strike from the list anyone who doesn't think as we do, who doesn't have as his main concern those things which are most important to us, who doesn't think like us, look like us, or is not like us at all.

Because of the racist language he used, am I forbidden to admire Mark Twain? Because of how they thought and not for what they did, do I ignore Huey Long or George Wallace? Because he did not speak out, because he fought for the wrong side, because he did not do enough, because he did not see the right clearly enough nor pursue it steadily enough—must I refuse to admit and admire the greatness, the genius, the skill, the efforts of . . . of just about anyone you can think of?

Does it matter? Does racism, inadvertent or otherwise, negate everything else a person is or tries or achieves? And can there really be such a thing as inadvertent racism?

Does silent participation in an unjust system turn heroes into cowards instead?

Do time and circumstance and great achievements mitigate? Or should we hold our heroes accountable—or even more than accountable—for all that is and all that has been?

The nation—and the world—could have been a lot farther along if the ones we admire had had the necessary courage, if we all did. But we are, all of us, victims of the times we live in. And none of us is completely innocent. None of us.

Living as they did, when they did, and products of a racist society, isn't it probable the Wright brothers—and their heroic brethren—were racists? Does this spoil, limit, or diminish their achievements?

Even the most heroic among us cannot help but be influenced by the surrounding environment, by the culture that raised him, by the milieu in which he finds himself.

What, then, does this say about me?

Until I came south to awaken these feelings and thoughts of racism, I would have said I was different, that these things have not affected me. Now I see, in the way I think, that I have been as affected as anyone else. And if I had not come south, these feelings may have lain dormant forever.

Environment does influence us—even if we can't see the effect. It makes us who we are.

I am black. I can be nothing else. In this country I am forced—I know now—to see the world not through the eyes of a man or citizen or a human being but through the narrow-focused eyes of a black man. Every thought, every experience is focused through the funnel viewpoint of being black.

At the same time I am American. I can lay claim to no place else. There is no way out for me. I am caught.

But which am I more—black or American?

In 1915 Theodore Roosevelt wrote that there is no room in this country for "hyphenated Americanism." Maybe he had a point. In or out, fish or fowl, be one thing or another, but get off that fence.

"There can be no fifty-fifty Americanism in this country," he said. *"There is room here for only 100 percent Americanism, only for those who are Americans and nothing else."*

This is the land that made me. Its history and its heritage are mine. Its various cultures live within me. Each achievement is mine. I own every dream. Each fulfillment belongs to me. And I am responsible for every promise that has not been kept.

We all bear that responsibility. None of us is blameless. None of us.

The trouble is, too many of us attempt to exclude instead of include. We narrow the definition of what it means to be American, or what it takes to be black, and we want to leave out the rest, especially those who are different from us, whose thinking, whose experience varies from our own. We limit our families carefully.

All men are not created equal.

"Goddamn it! I was born in this country! My children were born in this country! What the hell does someone have to do to become an American?"

—Joseph Kennedy.

All men are not created equal, not even rich powerful ones. Joseph Kennedy had turned his family into a political and financial dynasty. It was not enough. Even Joseph Kennedy felt the sting of discrimination. He was a Catholic.

"As a nation we began by declaring that all men are created equal. We now practically read it: All men are created equal except Negroes. Soon it will read: All men are created equal except Negroes and foreigners and Catholics."

—Abraham Lincoln.

If Thomas Jefferson or Robert E. Lee, Babe Ruth or Wilbur Wright had as their excuse that they were victims of the times in which they lived, what excuse for racism do we have in our more enlightened age?

It's simple: we have no excuse. We ought to know better.

I spent the night on the beach near Kitty Hawk. I woke up stiff. The early morning air was chilling, so I tossed on the Confederate soldier's cap I had bought at Gettysburg and walked across the highway to a small restaurant for breakfast. I had taken my cap off when I went in, but now I put it back on. I sat at a table next to a burly fellow wearing a baseball cap. The emblem sewn onto the crown of his cap was a rebel flag.

I clenched my fists and shoved them into my pockets. I resisted my impulse to smack him or tell him off. It was enough that I made him uncomfortable.

He sneered at me. I sneered back. He looked away and every time his eyes sneaked back around for a glance at me, I was still there, staring at him. I hoped he would get up and say something to me. I was trying to provoke him into provoking me. But all he did was stare.

He didn't like that I sat near him. He didn't like that I was there at all. But what he hated more than anything else was that I was wearing a symbol of the old Confederacy on my head. After all, Benvisti had said, *"Symbols are indivisible. If it's mine, it can't be yours."*

I was co-opting this man's symbol and corrupting it, defiling it.

He stared at me as if to let me know I didn't belong. I stared at him to let him know I did. I sat back and relaxed. I stuck my long legs out. And then I smirked at him. He seethed.

My breakfast that morning, country ham and two eggs on toast, tasted especially fine. I wondered how his food tasted.

❧

In a little while the sun came up. The morning mist and fog drifted out to sea and hung in a thick indecisive line until quite suddenly it vanished. One minute it was there, the next minute, after I had given full attention to the road, the fog was gone. I was riding south toward Hatteras on Highway 12. The wind was gusting and sand had blown across the road. I was picking my way carefully.

The islands are very narrow. The ocean is almost always in view. And there is no protection from the wind. When it blows, you feel it. The bike leans into the wind to compensate. But still every now and again the bike slides sideways. When you hit a patch of sand, the bike skids and for a second or two you lose control.

But the sun is full on your face and warm. The wind is alive and cooling. The day is streaked with color.

At Cape Hatteras the road bends sharply to the west. In a few minutes the road abruptly ends. There is no more island.

A ferry takes you to the next one, Ocracoke, a short ride in a small boat.

At the far end of Ocracoke there is a little village where the next ferry waits. On the edge of the village there is an inn owned by Jacob, a young man who rode the ferry with me, and his younger brother, Peter. Jacob had been admiring my bike, and as we talked and I told him where I was going, he offered me a room for the night.

"The house is completely booked up," he told me. "But you can be our guest." He was telling me I wouldn't have to pay.

"You may have to pitch your tent in the yard," he said, "but we'll find a place for you. In the attic or in the yard, but somewhere. If anybody cancels, we'll give you the nicest room."

When the ferry landed, I followed Jacob to the house that sits across the road from the general store. Clapboard, white, built from the timbers of a wrecked sailing ship, the old two-story house sits deep in the yard. The driveway is unpaved and covered with big rocks. I left my bike close to the road and walked. Jacob got out of his car, Peter came from the house. They both received me as warmly as if they knew me. Peter went to fetch cool drinks. Jacob gave me a tour of the place, upstairs and down, and out back to the garage that was big enough to be a barn. Then we sat in the rocking chairs in the shade of the front porch and lingered a long time there, sipping iced tea, munching on snacks and talking.

But in the end I didn't stay the night. I don't know why. It wasn't at all like me to decline a kindness or refuse hospitality. But something seemed to beckon. It might have been the way the late afternoon sun caught the tips of waves in the sound and streaked them silver, sparkling on the water. The sea breeze smelled of exotic worlds, foreign ports. It carried aloft excitement and the promise of something new, some magic on the other side of the horizon. I wanted to travel on. I had the urge to ride in the cool of the evening and deep into the night.

I caught the last ferry to Cedar Island and rode until darkness slipped around me. Then night fell with the suddenness of fatigue. In Morehead City I quit for the evening and carried on the next morning.

I will never know what I missed by not staying the night with Jacob and Peter. But I know that the slightest wind can blow a ship drastically off course. The history of the world has been formed by the seemingly insignificant decisions as well by the important ones. The future is decided by every little thing we do. Everything that happens, each moment well spent, each wasted minute, every smile or hello, becomes a paving stone on the path. Change one thing and you change the shape of tomorrow.

I chose to ride on that night. And that would make all the difference.

In the morning I got on the road early. I was in a tremendous hurry—I realize it now—but told myself I merely wanted to beat the heat. I wanted to ride as long as possible in the continuation of yesterday, but the cool that lingered since evening was warming rapidly. The sun had come up quickly. The blue had been scorched from the sky. The soft morning mist thickened into haze. It was going to be a hot day.

My haste, however, had nothing to do with heat.

Looking back now I see that not only was I eager to reach Charleston, my next significant destination, but I was impatient to reach my rendezvous with the evil in the haze. The evil spirit of the South. It was out there—somewhere—dressed in white, streaked with red, covered with blood, waiting for me. And I wanted to find it. I wanted to see it for myself, wanted to feel it. I did not know if my sword would fall from my hand and I might turn coward. Or I might turn violent. Though it might easily kill me, I doubted I could kill it. But I had to find the evil, confront it and spit in its eye. If ever I was going to put it fully behind me, I had to touch it, admit it was there, and move past it.

It was a Saturday morning. I was headed toward Wrightsville Beach, a place that people from Raleigh and Greensboro and Fayetteville flock to on warm weekends. Traffic was heavy. To escape it, I drove like a maniac from Morehead City to Jacksonville. From there I slowed down and took my time.

It was a nice morning to be out riding on a bike. I was not the only one who thought so. I passed several bikers coming from the opposite direction. Each one in turn threw up his hand to wave.

There is a special camaraderie among motorcyclists. You are part of a family. You will be waved at each time you pass. You will be talked to about your bike. You will be offered help when you need it. The kinship crosses the barriers we normally erect. You are a motorcyclist whether man or woman, black or white or brown, local or foreign. You pass a cyclist and he will wave. You stop nearby and he will have a chat.

I never gave a second thought to the motorcyclists who waved; only to the ones who didn't.

Then I noticed that more than motorcyclists were waving at me. Drivers in oncoming lanes were throwing up their hands to me, often when I was not expecting it. I would see the hand fly up and think the driver was scratching his nose. When I realized it was a wave, it was too late to wave back. We had already passed.

Not everybody waved, of course, but enough to make me wonder if it was some kind of signal. Was there a cop ahead? Were they telling me to slow down?

I slowed. And it gave me more time to react to the waving. And it was infectious. I started waving first.

And then I wondered why they were waving back. Could they not see that I was black? With my arms covered by the sleeves of my jacket and my face partly hidden by the visor of my helmet, maybe they couldn't tell.

I leaned to the side to look at myself in the mirror. I thought maybe only my eyes and nose could be seen, but the mask is big enough that you can see almost the whole face. Nothing was hidden. They were waving at me anyway. And not only people on the road.

I passed through Hampstead. An elderly man with no shirt on was mowing his lawn. He walked deliberately, almost frailly. He pushed the mower carefully. When the car in front of me passed him, the old man stopped mowing. He took one hand off the mower handle and waved. When I got close enough, he did the same to me.

If he waved at everyone who passed, it would take him all day to cut his grass.

I wondered if this is what Great-Grandfather Joseph would have found.

When Virginia started enforcing laws requiring freed blacks to leave the state, Joseph almost certainly would have come into North Carolina. I don't know if he would have made his way along the coast, but having been a slave who had never seen the sea, it would have been on his mind. The whole wide world would have been on his mind. He would have wanted to explore it.

He was thirty-seven years old when he gained his freedom. There was so much that he had missed. So much that he would never get a chance to do. So many people he would never meet. So many places he would never see. Not knowing when he might die, he would have wanted to see and do it all. Even if it meant his sampling of the world would be brief and his exposure limited. A little of a lot would have suited him fine.

Perhaps his mission was like mine: to get out and about, see the lay of the land, meet some folks, and put the evil behind him.

The heat caught up with me in Wrightsville Beach and I pulled into the parking lot of a little strip mall to rest. I thought I might find a cold drink here. But it was too early. The shops were still closed. I got off the bike and found a narrow band of shade. I leaned against the wall and slid down to sit on the pavement. No one else was around. No other cars were in the parking lot. The bike was alone, its blue skin gleaming in the bright sun. And I was all alone, sitting, pondering, wondering, dreaming. I took out my notebook and started to write but felt lazy. I took a little nap.

When I awoke, a teenaged boy was standing over me. The shops were open and he had just come out of the video store. He was leaning on his bicycle.

"Is that your motorcycle?" he said.

He was standing against the bright sky. I squinted up at him and couldn't make him out, but I could see that he pointed and I followed the line of his arm out to the parking lot where my bike sat. Another young man, older than this one, was walking around the bike and looking it over carefully.

"It's a beauty," the kid said. He introduced himself and told me his name. Joseph.

The guy walking around my bike had my attention now. I shook Joseph's hand, but only halfheartedly.

"What are you doing?"

"I was taking a nap," I said.

"No," he said. "What are you doing here? You don't live around here, do you?"

"Just passing through."

Joseph leaned his bicycle against the wall. He sat down beside me.

The guy inspecting my motorcycle came over now.

"That's a great-looking machine," he said. "I never saw one like it before."

Then he sat down on the curb near me.

"My name is Jack."

We shook hands.

Jack was a young man about twenty-three years old. He was tall and strong-looking, blond and tan. He looked like a sailor, or at the very least a surfer. He worked at the end of the mall in a shop that sold small sailboats and beach gear.

We fell into a chat about riding around the country on a bike, and he told me he wished he could be doing the same thing. It seems every man I've met has at one time or another dreamed of it. "To be free as the wind," he said.

We talked a little about the South. We did not talk about race. We talked about where I had been and where I was going. We did not talk about why.

"You must be very tired," he said.

"And hot," I added.

He nodded. "It's going to be a scorcher today," he said. "It's not even ten o'clock yet."

He had to work all day, he said, but if I wanted a place to nap for a few hours, or maybe a cold beer, he told me I could use his house. He gave me directions.

"It's on the peninsula," he said. "Close to the beach, in fact almost right on it. And the front of the house faces the estuary. You can watch the boats going in and out of the harbor. When a cool breeze blows and when the sun goes down in the late afternoon there's no better spot than on our balcony."

He had a roommate.

"He should still be there," he said. "But if he's not, just go on up the steps to the second floor and make yourself at home. We usually leave the door unlocked."

Just then his roommate pulled up in a white sporty car. He parked in front of the boat shop, saw us, and came down to where we were sitting.

He was about the same age as Jack, a little taller, less muscular, not quite as blond. When Jack explained that he had just opened the doors of their home to me, Greg did not look immediately pleased.

"Actually," he said, "I have some things to do."

"That's okay," Jack said. He turned to me. "Look, the door's open, there are beers in the fridge, there's a hammock swinging on the balcony. Just go and make yourself at home. One of us will be along later this afternoon to check on you, to see if you need anything."

Greg and I looked at each other. I was wondering what was going on. Greg was probably wondering the same. He studied me, wondering perhaps what his response should be. It took him a moment to see the rightness of Jack's invitation. Finally he gave in.

"I don't know how many beers there are," he said. "I could go to the store and buy some more. What kind do you like?"

"Beer is beer," I said. "Any wildly expensive imported dark beer from Germany will do."

Greg smiled and frowned at the same time. Jack laughed. Greg said, "I'll see what I can find."

Jack went back to work, arranging the sailboats in the parking lot and then hosing them down, hoisting the sails and making everything look neat and new and desirable. Greg and I watched him for a few minutes. We talked a little more. Then, satisfied, I suppose, that I was not a murderer or a thief, Greg got up to run his errands. He invited me to go along with him. He tried to be casual. He didn't want the invitation to look like he didn't want to leave me alone in his house. I turned him down.

"Okay, then," he said. "I'll see you later."

Slowly he walked to the car. He stuck his head inside the boat shop and said something to Jack. Then he got into his car and drove away.

Joseph just sat quietly through it all. He was looking dreamily at me and at the bike. Finally, now that we were alone, he spoke.

We talked about the bike a little, but that wasn't what he really wanted to talk about. He was doing badly in school. His parents were divorced. He didn't get along well with his mother's new boyfriend. His father had moved away. He just wanted to spend some time talking to an adult male.

"I don't get to do it much," he said.

He wanted to get some things off his chest. It didn't matter that he was white and I was black.

We talked about a minister he had gotten close to. Joseph said he liked the guy but wasn't sure why. The minister was helping to keep him out of trouble.

We talked about how much he hated school. I told him I had always hated school too.

"It's not just that," he said. "I'm beginning to wonder if I'm really stupid. People are always telling me that. I'm beginning to believe it."

"Well, don't," I said. "That just gives you an excuse to fail. When you start to believe it, you'll always have an easy reason for why things aren't working. Pretty cowardly, don't you think?"

He thought for a long moment, then nodded.

He told me about a book his grandmother had given him.

"It's about a man who canoed down the Mississippi River," he said. I raised my eyebrows.

"It was his big dream," he told me. "His friends told him it was a stupid idea. Nobody believed he could do it. But he did it anyway."

"That sounds pretty interesting," I said. "Is it any good?"

"I haven't started it yet. My grandmother liked it a lot, though. She thought I should read it. She said it might inspire me to try harder and do better and not give up and all that stuff. Sometimes it's very easy to give up, you know."

"Yeah, sometimes," I said.

I could feel myself beginning to frown. I stared out at my shiny blue bike. I looked at Joseph. He was smiling vaguely. I wondered where this boy had come from and who was counseling whom.

Many were the ways in which I myself had given up. It is so

much easier to believe in racist ways of thinking. I could see how through my surrender I had come to affirm and legitimize racism. I had lost myself to its addiction. I had let myself be controlled by it, defined by it. I was no longer acting, only reacting.

I changed the subject.

"What are you going to do all day?" I asked.

"There's nothing to do," he said. "Maybe I'll go home and read that book."

For the next two minutes Joseph sat quietly staring at me. Finally I asked him if anything was wrong.

"Nothing," he said. "It's just that you look sort of familiar. Not like I've seen you before or anything. But just kind of familiar."

He tightened his lips and shook his head.

"I don't know," he said.

He got up.

"I guess I'd better go," he said. "But I'll see you later. I know where they live. Maybe I'll come by."

I sat for a few minutes after Joseph had left and wondered what to do. I wondered what was going on. Something out of my control, something warm and surprising.

I know what Joseph meant when he said I looked somehow familiar. But maybe on a deeper level, a level Joseph had not touched yet, I looked familiar to other southerners too. A prodigal son returned home, recognized and made welcome. Was that why people were waving at me all the time?

Suddenly I knew why I had not stayed the night on Ocracoke with Peter and Jacob.

The South had always meant only one miserable thing to me. The possibility of anything else had never been entertained. My mind had already been made up and I had not wanted to be shown another way of seeing. I had not been willing to give the South a chance. I wanted to hate it still.

It's easier when you have an enemy, something to blame for the way things are, something to galvanize your disparate fears and inadequacies. You get so mired in a way of thinking that you lose all sight. The deeper you sink the darker it is, the easier on the eyes. The darkness becomes familiar, comfortable. It hides you, and you are safe. You can't see, but neither can you be seen. The darkness is your protector.

The South hated me, this I was sure of; and I hated the South doubly. Even after my outrageous eruption of joy at a sense of belonging here, even as serenity washed over me and I recognized the South as home, and even as I had come home to make peace, still I was looking for reasons to hate the place. I had been looking for coon hunters and Klansmen. I should have been looking for angels of mercy.

I had asked myself, Suppose that somewhere in the South someone was waiting to offer me a cool drink, to invite me home, to be my friend? Well, there they were, Peter and Jacob, and I had turned my back to them. And now here they were again, Jack and Greg and Joseph. I would not let it happen again.

Evil still lives in the world, it's true, but evil is not all there is. And evil can be overcome by better angels. Coon hunters and Klansmen have not been able to destroy us in all this time. There are angels among us, heroes in matters that seem so small. It is they who keep the devils at bay. But you've got to give them a chance.

If Great-Grandfather Joseph would not have been denied by anything so trivial as a mind made up, neither would I. I would accept every kindness as if I had earned it, and I would offer kindness in return. For a simple kindness shown may bring about a change of heart.

I stayed three days with Jack and Greg in Wrightsville Beach.

The house they lived in was a gray clapboard, two-story building facing the estuary. Steps from the street led to the second-floor balcony. Someone else lived on the first floor.

That first afternoon, before I knew I was going to be invited to stay the night, I left my gear on the bike, went up, and lay in the hammock until Greg returned. He had not yet bought the beer.

I folded one arm for a pillow behind my head. The other arm I laid across my chest. I could feel my heart beating against my palm, slowly, calmly, surely. I kicked off my shoes and pulled off my socks. I wiggled my toes.

One leg dangled over the side of the hammock. My foot could

just barely reach the floor, just enough that I could give a little push, and the hammock started to swing slowly from side to side.

A breeze fanned my face, but still the sun was very hot on it. Morning slid into noon. The sun climbed high and crossed the sky, blazed white hot, and crowded the afternoon with light. A glare like a fireball bounced off the water and I had to squint to watch the sailboats and the big cruisers passing through the channel on their way to freedom and the open sea.

My bike was sitting patiently down below. The sun hit against the bright blue and sparkled. It made me think of a horse, lathered up with sweat, glistening in the sun, loaded down with gear, and waiting patiently while some lonesome cowboy stops off in a saloon to have a drink, happy to have these moments of rest before hitting the dusty trail once again. And like the cowboy inside, I was reluctant to move on and impatient at the same time. I had found an uneasy peace.

The hammock swayed. The cool salt-scented breeze crowded the air. The sun beat gently, warmly on my face and arms. I could hardly keep my eyes open. Blindingly bright patches of light reflected off the water. I could not see the boats drifting in the inlet. When they entered the bright patches, they were swallowed up by the light.

I could not keep my eyes open. I wanted to sleep, I wanted to lose myself in the land of dreams, the great dark void where peace and rage do battle while time stands still. If peace wins, it is almost like death. I surrendered to the peace. I closed my eyes and slept.

It was a hallucinating sleep, at once fitful and deep, troubling and confused. The rage that had been stored inside me came pouring out like poison vomited after a long night's debauchery.

It was like some hideous malarial nightmare. I was hot and cold at the same time, wet and clammy. I tossed in the hammock and could not get comfortable. Finally I fell into a noisy sleep. Eventually my snoring wakened me. When I awoke, drool coated the corners of my mouth and dripped into my beard.

The South had done this to me, turned me into some kind of paranoid schizophrenic, outraged one minute and at peace the next, forever questioning motives, ever on the lookout for evil directed at me and then finding it, real or imagined, behind every tree, suspicious of every good turn, reminded by every person I talked to and by everything I saw and did and felt that I am black, and that I am hated for it.

This is not how I wanted to live my life, not how I had lived it up till now. Maybe that's why I had to come. I needed to be reminded. I could no more have stayed away than I could have run rings around the moon. From all sides the South had been tugging at me.

Nor could I long continue to live a kind of raceless existence, and I see now why certain themes are not only expected from black writers, but why black writers themselves feel compelled to explore them. Because no one else explores those themes. And no one else but a black man knows their contours. It doesn't have to be, but a black man's point of view—a black writer's point of view—is different precisely because he *is* black. And like every black person in this country, when he wakes up each day, being black is on his mind in ways that being white is never on a white person's mind.

And yet in focusing on this race thing, I have missed the life and world around me. I have seen it, but I have not seen it, have not held the crystal orb up to the light and watched the sparkles dance. I have not appreciated it. I have tasted the world vaguely, never knowing what I was eating. I could have been eating anything at all.

This is not the journey I had planned to make. Even after the road had led me—had almost forced me—into the South, this journey was not at all what I intended. But it was the journey, I suppose, I had to make.

I don't know what I did intend, if it was anything more than just an excursion on my new toy. I had thought learning to ride would give me an added expertise, and thought I would best learn to ride by putting in hour after hour on the open road— superhighways, back roads, and country lanes. The people I met, the birds and the trees, the earth I smelled and the towns I visited, the flavor of the country I tasted—these, I thought, would make my story. By focusing on them I would find and see and maybe even touch the soul of the South.

What I have found instead has been my own black soul. I have learned in some small way what it is to be black, what it is to live in this cocoon of insecurity. The journey has been all inside my head and in my soul, hardly on the road at all. I have traveled my black self, but I have missed the South.

Before my tour of the South is over, I will have seen much that I won't remember. I will have zigzagged countless miles and endless times back and forth across the South, but I will have lost the South in an addict's dreams, and in the telling of the story.

If I came to learn about the South, to know it, to understand it, then I have failed. I have not explored the nooks and crannies where the South gets its lore and color and charm. I have not crept into any backwoods hollows, have not been to any hillbilly bars. "King" Oliver, Basin Street, the blues and jazz seem far away and unattainable. I will have to leave those flavors for another trip—or another traveler.

You cannot see every tree in a forest. Even if you see every tree you cannot remember each one or describe each one, but only those trees that somehow strike you, that have meaning, trees that mark the path into the deep wood and out again, trees that bear fruit for you to eat, trees especially beautiful, exceptionally deformed, trees whose leaves you already know. In fact certain trees you won't even see, no matter if they stand right in front of you.

And so it is with the road. You cannot go everywhere, see everything, talk to everyone. And you cannot tell every detail of what you have seen and done. You pick your route and your stories of the road—or they pick you, it seems—by the way they add color and fill in detail to the tableau being painted inside your frame of mind. (I never saw so many motorcycles on the road, for example, until I bought one; now I see them everywhere.)

You seek to prove your assumptions, at all cost if you are a propagandist, or to disprove them. But have them you will, and everything you see and do will seem to pertain directly to what has been going on in your head and what for the moment at least is important. It is nearly impossible to just go, to be an observer only.

So when the road passed me like a relay baton from one place to the next, one person to the next, it was with a purpose.

In South Carolina, I did not see the coastal swamps or the beach resorts.

In Charleston, I nearly ignored the lady squatting on the sidewalk in her floppy red hat.

In Andersonville, Georgia, I hardly heard Willie Ann Towns when she told me she liked to eat dirt.

The simple stories that people like to tell to strangers and that make traveling such a joy were hidden behind the veil of my racist agenda.

I saw everything in terms of race. (Perhaps for a little while longer it will still be necessary to see the world this way.) And I was drawn to people for whom race was an issue and who at least were willing to talk about it.

᠕᠍᠊

Eleanor Tate writes children's books whose central characters are always black. Her goal seems to be giving black kids a positive self-image.

"Because it's necessary," she said. "They're not getting much from anywhere else these days."

She was about my age, wore a very close-cut Afro. She was thin, almost petite. I met her on a street corner in Myrtle Beach, South Carolina. We talked for a minute and then she decided to show me around. I climbed into her car and we toured the black neighborhood where she lived. It is not a very pretty place, dusty streets with no sidewalks. The grass at the edge of the roads has been worn completely away. Broken bottles in the streets, debris in the yards, trash strewn all over. Too many broken-down cars, bars on the windows of houses, people hanging around with no place to go and nothing to do, their loud voices and laughter trying to hide the despair in their eyes.

"Drugs have taken over here the same as they have taken over everywhere else. People steal, people get drunk, people hurt other people. It's what we have come to be," she said.

But it wasn't always like that. Her eyes lit up briefly while she remembered.

"Maybe it could be that way again," she said. "But we need to remember what we used to have, the way we used to be."

She told me to go back to North Myrtle Beach and have a look at a little town nestled along the oceanfront.

"It used to be a big black resort," she said. "Now it's all decay. That's what we have allowed to happen to ourselves."

Atlantic Beach has been hit by hard times. Its rich history has been eroded, forgotten by all but the few who care.

In the 1930s a black man named George Tyson bought the land but couldn't hold on to it. He sold some of it, mortgaged the rest, and when he couldn't make payments on the mortgage, a group of black doctors, lawyers, and teachers purchased the land and formed the Atlantic Beach Company to save the area and develop the property. They subdivided it into lots and sold them. In 1966 Atlantic Beach elected a mayor and a town council and was issued a charter by the state of South Carolina. It was a comfortable little black community.

But there's more to it than that. Time and circumstance allowed Atlantic Beach to prosper. It became a beach resort for black people.

Blacks were prohibited by law from setting foot on practically every beach in the state. South Carolina was viciously segregated, and any amenity that catered to whites—hotels, housing, public schools, even the ocean—was by and large off-limits to blacks, except those who served whites in some capacity or other.

Atlantic Beach became their haven. When they wanted a day at the beach, they could come here and enjoy the ocean and the beach without being arrested. They could relax and vacation without insult or racial harassment.

From the 1940s to the 1970s and the end of rigid segregation, Atlantic Beach drew blacks from all over the country: professionals on vacation lived in relative luxury, nationally known entertainers performed, locals needing a day in the sun and a dip in the ocean basked in the glory of black wealth.

Atlantic Beach thrived.

But now the roads are rutted. The houses look more like shacks. Shop windows are boarded up. The area looks almost bombed out, deserted except for a few out-of-work men loitering in the shade.

This is what integration has done. As soon as it was all right to go to the white hotels, who could be bothered with the black ones? White people wouldn't patronize black establishments, and blacks no longer had to. Black businesses and areas dried up. Money left the black community, and with the money went those who could get out. White businesses and white communities got richer. Black communities went into decline. Only the poor were left behind—for the most part.

Eleanor might not be rich—I couldn't tell and didn't ask—but she had accomplished plenty. Five books published and numerous awards, for starters. She has been a newspaper editor and a reporter, has sat on the board of a black storytellers association, helped found the South Carolina Academy of Authors, and was a director of a national festival for black storytelling.

I asked Eleanor why she still lived here. She was insulted by the question—and rightly so.

"It's my home," she said. "What would you rather I did, move to some white neighborhood where I won't be welcomed anyway? There is no reason to leave here. I have my house and my friends. And I like being around black people. I just wish I could do something to uplift them so they could all be better off, spiritually and physically."

I told her she sounded heroic.

"There are no heroes," she said. "You are what you are and you do what you do. If you're lucky enough and you live right, who you are and what you do become heroic. But that's all. I just do what I can."

It is easy to forget the strength and tender love that exists among black people. We see the violent images on the television and we forget that all is not selfishness, drugs, death and despair. We forget about the caring that goes on and the gentle hope that holds people together. We forget the sacrifice of those who could save themselves if they were not trying to save others. We forget the real heroes. We forget the angels.

XIII

For bigotry, which is unreasoning, can be cured only in death. Yet fear, if honest, can be erased by truth.

—Theodore L. White

A feeling of complete and utter dread fell over me as I drove south into Charleston. I was terrified, nearly shaking with fright, and I didn't know why.

The next day I would be just as completely, just as utterly redeemed, and then again two days later, and then again later, and later still.

But this night found me on a dark and nearly deserted road. I had taken sort of a wrong turn—only sort of a wrong turn because when you don't know where you're headed and you don't really care, when you're just going, with no place to be and no itinerary, it doesn't matter much what road you find yourself on. But I had veered off the main road to Charleston.

I was looking for a place to camp, an isolated meadow amid the trees where I could pull off the road and pitch my tent. I had been taking my time, had been searching for the perfect spot, but darkness had slipped swiftly down around me and caught me unawares. In the heat of the day I had removed my jacket, but the sun's warmth was no more and I was getting cold. I tried to speed up to end the search sooner, but that only made the wind around me move faster. I grew colder. I had to slow down. The search seemed endless.

Finally I found a spot that looked perfect. I passed it, checked out the surrounding area, and then went back to it.

It was far enough off the road that passing cars wouldn't see me. It was in a clearing within a grove of palmettos. The earth was soft and sandy. I wanted to turn the bike around to face out in case I needed to make a speedy exit, but I had trouble in the sand. I got stuck for a moment and made an awful racket trying to get the bike on to more solid ground. It was then that a strange dread swept over me.

I had started to remove my camping gear from the bike. Suddenly everything around me went still. The wind stopped. There was no noise. The air was cool. A shadow passed overhead. I was sure an evil spirit was lurking here, some restless ghost; or that something horrible had happened here, or was about to, some blood-curdling, bone-chilling act of violence.

In the woods a twig snapped. My heart skipped a beat.

I held my breath to listen. I didn't move. I didn't want to make a sound, didn't want to reveal my presence. If someone hiding in these trees suddenly appeared toting a shotgun, I was defenseless.

My heart began to pound. I felt my hands tremble and my legs shake.

I'm sure it was nothing, sure it was just the darkness and the quiet and the isolation—simply my imagination running away with me. But I got on my bike and got out of there anyway. I went to find a hotel.

All the way down the road I laughed at my panic. But even as I laughed, I imagined some goon sneaking out in the night. He carried, of course, a long-bladed hunting knife, or a big axe, or maybe a chainsaw. And without even bothering to knock on my tent flap to see who was at home, he started hacking into the tent and into me. He lived in those trees, hiding—from the law, from the world, from the future. I was an intruder he did not trust, a trespasser he wanted gone, and killing me was the only way he knew.

I don't know where such thoughts came from, but I had the distinct feeling that something horrible had happened in that grove. I wondered if maybe Joseph had been there, or someplace near, and had experienced some pain. I wondered if he was warning me somehow.

I put those thoughts out of my mind, found a hotel on the outskirts of Charleston, and went to sleep.

I slept well, had no bad dreams, and rose late.

The next afternoon, on my way into town, I pulled into a parking lot where a man sitting beside a cart was selling boiled peanuts. A big hand-painted sign lay against the side of the cart. I had seen similar signs all along South Carolina roads but before I came south I had never heard of such a thing as boiled peanuts. I pulled into the lot to grab a bag.

The old man swished around in a huge vat and dug up a ladle-ful of peanuts. He strained them and dumped them into a brown paper bag. I started eating them right away.

"I've never had these before," I said.

"Where you been?" said he laughing. "Out of the country? Or you just don't know good eating."

"Both, I guess. I'm not from around here."

"Buddy, I can see that," he said. He shook my hand.

His old hands were long and bony. His face was taut, his legs thin. His trousers were torn. His left shoe had split along one side. He looked frail, almost as if he were ill, but he had a mouthful of healthy teeth, yellowed from tobacco, but all there. He smiled broadly.

"I'm going to let you have those," he said.

"No," I said. "I want to pay for them."

"Man, one bag of goobers ain't going to break me. You take those peanuts and have a good time. Suck on them before you crack them open, suck all the juice out of them. It's kind of salty but sweet at the same time. You eat a mess of them and they'll really fill you up. Good for you too."

I cracked a few shells. They were soft. The juice, water they had been boiled in, spilled out of each one. The nuts inside were soft too, salty like the juice, and very different from roasted peanuts. And they were hot.

"This is how we eat them around here," he told me. "Boiled, not roasted. They're better, don't you think?"

I didn't get a chance to answer.

As we were gabbing, a little red car skidded up and two young men got out to buy peanuts from this old man. They were engrossed in conversation.

"You should have seen it," one fellow said. "This Filipino bumped into my car and then wasn't going to stop. I had to speed up and cut him off. He pretended he didn't see me, and you know how they drive, like they can't see. And this poor white boy beside him was looking all indignant. Can you believe it? A Filipino and a cracker. Now I seen everything. I let them know right away that this warn't no ignorant nigger they were dealing with. I took care of them real good."

"Hey," the other fellow said, "did you hear about that big crash up on 17-A?"

"What? Last night?"

"Yeah," he said. "Not a crash, really. This big semitruck ran off the road into a clearing, smashed into some palmetto trees, and got stuck in the sand."

"Whereabouts?"

"About an hour out of town."

An hour out of town, Highway 17-A. Somewhere in the vicinity of where I had almost pitched my tent.

I took my boiled goobers and rode in a trance toward town. Sitting on the curb at the corner of Cumberland and King streets, I put them in my mouth, one by one.

I was wearing an old torn T-shirt that I had bought the year I graduated from the university. My favorite. On the front was the Stanford University logo, on the back a cartoonish design that commemorated my graduating class—1977. There were holes in it back and front, the sleeves were frayed, the collar had almost separated from the body of the shirt.

Now all of a sudden, I no longer wanted to wear it. I was no longer the young man who had bought it, no longer the man I had been even a few months ago.

When I finished eating the peanuts, I went to my bike and took off the shirt. I put on a different shirt and threw the past away. I wanted no link with it.

When I explored Charleston it was with new eyes. I believe now in ghosts. I believe now that we carry the past with us, not just a personal past but the deep past as well. I believe we have two lives, the one we live for ourselves, and the one we live for others. And perhaps the measure of a man's worth is the smallness of the gap between the two.

I'm sure Great-Grandfather Joseph would have passed this way, if only to see Charleston, then as well as now one of the most beautiful and charming cities in the country. If he was at all like me, he would have come here to touch the past and then to put it behind him, to remind himself of what he had escaped and what he was no longer, to remind himself that the line between good and bad fortune is thinly drawn, to remind himself that he could never really escape, that he would never be free, that no man ever is.

We are parties to our own lack of freedom, and no matter which side of the gate we are on we are all of us prisoners.

Once again slavery takes center stage, and we see slave and slaver both as prisoners mired in deceit and self-deception: the lies about inferiority and over-sexed savagery, the myths about the inability to learn, the lack of a work ethic, and about the docile, happy-go-lucky slave, the southern falsehood too that whites and blacks cannot live together, that they have been and must remain strangers to one another. Against these lies in particular Charleston gives beautiful and expert testimony.

Charleston was the capital of slavery in America, the country's primary slave port. Half the city was black, and more whites owned slaves here than in any other city. The beauty of the city, its wealth and its economy were built on slave labor, and on the labor of free blacks. Black men and women worked here, slave and free, and are on the record as butchers and fishermen, seamstresses, laundresses, nurses and midwives, tailors and cap makers, blacksmiths, porters, masons, printers, cabinetmakers, coach makers, shoemakers, locksmiths, sailors, barbers, book-binders and barrel makers, painters and plasterers. They were a decidedly industrious lot. They did everything that needed doing.

And yet the image passed down is of a docile slave idling in the shade, loitering with nothing to do, without a thought in his head, an image that was comforting to the white population, no doubt. Whites, then as now, were afraid of uncontrolled blacks. Racial stereotypes of lazy blacks were promoted to maintain the myths of superiority and the need for subordination, but if the image had been a true picture, there would have been no need to control blacks so severely.

Remember that Denmark Vesey lived in Charleston. He had won a $1,500 lottery prize and with part of that money he bought his freedom. He educated himself, began preaching to other blacks, and urged them to fight for deliverance. A slave revolt was planned for June 16, 1822. It failed but not before many whites were killed.

So much for the docile black who did not resist his captivity.

And so much for the image of lazy trifling blacks. Black labor built this city, and yet there is no monument to their efforts, certainly no monument to slavery, no reminders at all.

It is as if the city in its guilt or shame is trying to pretend that slavery never existed. But here in Charleston of all places there ought to be some kind of shrine.

"Here was a thin neck in the hourglass of the Afro-American past, a place where individual grains from all along the West African coast had been funneled together, only to be fanned out across the American landscape with the passage of time."
—Peter H. Wood.

Nearly all the slaves brought into the country from Africa and the West Indies, if they did not come through New Orleans, came through Charleston. In the same way that European immigrants to America were quarantined at Ellis Island in New York, newly arrived slaves were quarantined at Sullivan Island just north of the city. Sullivan Island now is a mostly black community, a quiet place where people live and not much else. If you didn't already know the history, you'd never know it. There is no Ellis Island–type museum. There are no reminders.

On the corner of Meeting Street and St. Michael's Alley, in the shade of St. Michael's Episcopal Church, an old woman in a red floppy hat squats on the pavement. She has but a few teeth in her head, she never smiles. But in her hands and in her face are centuries of patience and hard work. Her name is Miss Stokes and she sits here all day every day, she said, and weaves baskets. Palm fronds, they looked like to me, but she said they were blades of sweetgrass.

"Hard work?"

"What isn't?" she replied. "A lot of work, a lot of patience."

I almost missed her. I actually ignored her at first, passed her by and came back to her, this link to the deep past. She was a Gullah woman, she said, a vestige of African culture kept alive. She weaves baskets, she speaks another language, one that I cannot understand—a mixture of English, American and Creole. She sits all day doing what her ancestors did. She is a monument to slavery.

I walked over to Chalmers Street where the old slave market used to be. The market is closed now, all boarded up. For a time it was a tourist attraction. People came to see where and how slave auctions took place. Now it's nothing but an empty shell of memories, a low brick building, twice as long as it is wide, not many windows, and no way for air to circulate. It's dark inside, must have seemed even darker in 1820 when it was built. It must have been hot. In summer it must have been an inferno.

The city is crawling with tourists. But they do not come to the old slave market. They have nothing to do with it; it has nothing to do with them. They are on holiday, after all.

Instead they take expensive carriage rides along the old streets. They spend hours on the USS *Yorktown,* a permanently moored aircraft carrier that sits in the harbor. They ride the ferries out into the harbor where the Cooper River flows into the sea and Fort Sumter rises above the waves. The Civil War officially began here with the bombardment of Sumter. Those were painful days in American history, but they were days of honor, glorious days, romantic. The tourists don't seem to mind being reminded of it.

Along the north face of Washington Square there is a little monument to General Pierre Gustave Beauregard, the Confederate brigadier who ordered the assault on Sumter.

In the center of the square there is a large marble obelisk, another monument to the war. The names of great battles and campaigns are etched on its sides: Richmond, Petersburg, Drury's Bluff, Sumter, Manassas, Battery Wagner. Shrines to the effort to keep blacks enslaved.

But nowhere in the city is there a shrine to any effort to free the slaves, or even to the contribution blacks have made to the city.

When I walked out of the square and turned up Queen Street, a young woman approached. As we walked toward each other, very subtly she removed her purse from the shoulder nearest me and put it over her other arm. She clutched it close.

I wanted to scream at her for her stupidity.

"Lady, do you think I couldn't have that thing if I wanted it, the purse and you too?"

But there was no rage inside. I just laughed. This is the monument to black people I have been looking for, her attitude and her behavior.

On one side of Calhoun Street, the houses are old and beautiful. On the other side of Calhoun Street the houses are old and falling down. There is a black side of town, of course, and the people who live here seem to have missed out on the prosperity boom in the main part of town. Their front porches are collapsing. Paint peels off the walls. Young people sit on the front stoops and drink liquor concealed in brown paper bags.

This is another monument to black people.

I walked among the old magnificent homes. Some had been preserved, others restored. Hundreds of houses remain from the early 1800s, dozens more are even older. They are beautiful houses. It's a beautiful city. The shady tree-lined streets, the old churches, these houses—the entire town is a link to the past. And I realized that none of this would be here if not for the labor of black women and men.

A crew was rehabbing one of the homes, and at the top of a ladder a black man was perched. In his hands he held hammer and chisel. He waved down at me as I passed. I made a fist and gave him a black power salute. He looked at me like he didn't understand, like I was crazy. He went back to work.

I told this to a man named Phillip Carter as we stood waiting in line for ice cream cones at one of the food shops in the old market, now another tourist trap full of junk food and souvenirs. The market runs all the way from Meeting to East Bay Street.

"I get sick watching these out-of-towners eating all this silly stuff," he said. But he was about to eat an ice cream just the same.

We talked awhile and when I told him about the worker on the ladder, Phillip shook his head. I thought he was as incredulous as I was. I was wrong.

"Fists waving in the air and fancy handshakes," he said. "These things we do not need. We need to find a way to get on with it. We need to know what's important and what's not."

Women like Miss Stokes know, he said. He didn't know her, didn't call her by name, but he knew that women like her sat near the church and weaved baskets.

"They live down on the islands," he said. "They are keepers of the past for us."

We took our cones outside. Tourists crowded the streets. They stopped traffic to take pictures. They hurried on to the next site.

"To these tourists the past is just a place to visit," he said. "But it lives inside those old basket weavers. They are our monuments. These beautiful homes are our monuments. None of this would be here if not for us. Not the city, not the whole damned country. We have a lot to be proud of. No matter what you or anybody else can do, we are here. And we have been here. And we are going to be here. None of that stuff that happened a hundred years ago, two hundred years ago is going to stop us or help us, but we shouldn't forget it. If anything, we need longer memories. We've been measuring ourselves by how far we've advanced since slavery, and how far from it we are, how many generations and all that. But me, I wish I were closer to it. I wish my grandfather had been a slave. I want to be able to feel it, to hear his old stories and know how it was. What's happened has happened and we shouldn't be ashamed of it. We need to touch it from time to time, then set it aside and just get on with it. We owe it to ourselves; nobody else owes us a damned thing."

Now it was my turn to shake my head—not at what he was saying, but that he was saying it at all.

I wanted to ask him one more question, but I never did. I wanted to know why he was here.

Eleanor Tate had already given me the answer. Ron White tomorrow would give me the answer again. And then a man named Gopher.

Ron White is a retired Marine Corps sergeant who put his life savings into an empty building just outside Beaufort, South Carolina. He turned the building into a restaurant. A Marine Corps flag waves in the wind. The sign out front says: REAL HOME COOKING. I stopped there for lunch on my way south toward the coastal islands and Gullah country.

Inside, the place was packed. Black men, white men, not many women. Soldiers from the base across the road. Two local policemen. A table crowded with men whose bellies were so big they could not see their feet. I pointed to one as he was leaving.

"That guy was skinny when he came in here," I said. "You're going to kill these white people. You're feeding them too much."

Fried chicken, greens, black-eyed peas, corn bread, grits, stew, barbecue. And massive portions. And oh it was good. These are things I used to eat when I was a kid. My childhood came flooding back to me in wave after wave of soul food delight.

I had a plate piled high with just about everything. It's a wonder my belly wasn't as huge as the other men's when I left. The only disappointment was the pie. It was pecan. They didn't have coconut.

Sergeant White came from Memphis, was stationed here by the Marines and decided to stay.

"And it's been all right?"

"It seems to work," he said. "I stay busy, and that's what it's all about. Trying to do what I can to get on with it. If you're not moving forward you're standing still. And that's the same as going backwards."

He left me to talk to another ex-Marine and his wife, and to a colonel from the base. He had to get on with it, had to keep busy.

≈●

Spanish moss covers the trees in Carolina, hanging from the branches of the oak trees and creating canopies of shade. Every tree becomes a weeping willow, every lawn invites a picnic.

Closer to the sea, the tall marsh grass hides meandering backwaters, deadens the sound, quiets the world. This is the low country.

I had followed Highway 21 through Beaufort, across St. Helena Sound, over a series of islands to one called Fripp, and the end—or beginning—of the road.

Fripp Island is a private island. It used to be a vacation resort, but now the developers are selling homes for year-round living. There is a guard posted at the gate and you cannot get in without prior invitation. I tried, was refused, and ended up in the sales office. I wanted to have a look around. It was no place I'd want to live anyway—too sterile, too safe, too private. But worst of all it gave me a sense of sudden loss.

I met Gopher on my way back. He was fishing off a bridge, said he hadn't caught anything all day. I had stopped to ask him what had happened with the developers.

"I thought this was all Gullah country," I said.

"It is," he said. "But it's changing. We've been discovered. And somebody has decided this part of the world is valuable real estate."

He wore clothes that made him look like a vagrant. He didn't sound like one.

He spent the long days fishing, he said, and that gave him plenty of time to think. There wasn't much else to do. I asked him why he hadn't left, why he still lived here. In this backwater country, in the South, in the middle of nothing to do.

"Why not?" he said. "People always sound surprised that a black man either stays in the South or leaves and comes back. This is home, man. It's not a bad place to be, better than some."

But home was under siege.

"You know," he said, "General Sherman gave this land to

black people after the Civil War. He took it from the former slave owners and gave it to the former slaves. It took them almost a hundred fifty years, but now they're winning it back. Buying out the ones who'll sell, taking it from the ones who won't."

"Taking it? They can't just take your land."

"They have their ways," he said. "They would prefer you to sell it but they ain't going to try and make you. All they have to do is find a couple people whose kids don't want to stay here and have no reason to hang on to the property. You get a few people to sell, start developing the land around, and pretty soon property values are up. The tax assessor man says the land around is worth more too so you have to pay more in taxes than you can afford. It's not long before you either sell out or the state comes to take your land for the back taxes you owe. The developer gets it on the auction block and probably at a cheaper price than he offered you in the first place. Land that has been in your family for a hundred years gets turned into private estates and golf courses that they'll shoot you for trying to cross. And maybe when all is said and done, you've got a pocketful of money, but that's not going to last you long. And you can't buy anything like you just lost. It wouldn't be that much money. So you go from owning your own home and your own land to being poor and begging. It just ain't fair."

"And you can't see it coming, can you?" I said.

He looked up and gave me a wry smile.

"Oh, we saw it coming," he said. "We always knew the white man would get us sooner or later. If he wants you, one way or another he'll get you. But we hold out as long as we can. That's why I'm here. Trying to hold out."

He squinted up into the sun and took a deep breath to fill his head with the smell of the marsh. He seemed a little sadder now.

"The difference between poor black people and poor white people," he said, "is that poor white people think that because they're white they have an advantage over us. And sometimes they do, but mostly they don't. The game is all about rich against poor. They can't see it because the color game blinds them. They ought to be on our side but they think the rule of law is in their favor, and that's a false hope, believe me."

*" . . . wonder whether we do not rest our hopes too much upon
constitutions, upon laws and upon courts. These are false hopes,
believe me, these are false hopes."*

—Learned Hand.

I looked carefully at Gopher, at his sun-darkened young face
and at his strong gnarly hands. He looked poor. He wasn't.

As I rode south along the coast, through Savannah and deeper
into Georgia, I tried to remember why I had come to the South
in the first place, what I had expected to find. White people
shooting at me. Black people bitching and moaning. A reason
to hate this place. Or was I looking for a reason to love this
place? I didn't really know anymore. But the South was surprising
me. The South was a contradiction, always had been.

Many if not most of the country's greatest forefathers were
slave-holding southerners preaching liberty and the rights of
man. James Oglethorpe, who founded Georgia, was vehemently
against slavery.

A southern state—Virginia—elected the first black governor
in the U.S. More blacks were hired on to state payrolls during
the reign of George Wallace—"Segregation now, segregation
forever"—than ever before. And while Mississippi is synony-
mous with racial hatred, there are more elected black officials
in Mississippi than in any other state.

I no longer knew what to make of anything.

I walked the dark streets of Savannah and breathed in the night
air. A street called Bull cuts through the center of town. Quiet
neighborhoods extend on either side of it. The houses are old,
some are large, most are lovely. Every few blocks there is a little
square. A little to the east, the pavement is chipped and the yards
are weeds if anything green, but mostly dirt. The houses are not
in good shape. You can always tell when you reach the poor black
neighborhood. But there is a street sign that read E. HARRIS, and
that made me smile.

I rode on like some lonesome cowboy looking for a place to
call home. But the dusty roads keep calling him, something keeps

beckoning him. One more place to see, one more stranger to talk to. He rides restlessly from town to town, has a look around, then rides on again.

Somewhere near Valdosta, Georgia, I stopped for gas. Then I pulled my bike over to the edge of the parking lot and lay in the grass. Three men approached me. They were dressed alike, all three, in blue jeans and light blue shirts and bright orange safety vests. They had been working on the road. A bus was waiting for them, and beside the bus a man stood holding a shotgun. This was part of a prison chain gang.

They had come over to talk about the bike. They looked it over and praised it, and then I said, "So how are the white folks treating you all down here?"

Right away two of them left, as if it was some trap and there might be trouble. But the third stayed and talked until he got the signal from the guard that it was time to move on.

The light in his eyes flashed. He was like a little boy about to say something naughty and delighting in it. He laughed boisterously.

"About like white folks treat niggers anyplace else," he said. "You know how they are."

The light in his eyes dimmed while he thought. His broad smile of crooked teeth relaxed and reformed itself, tensing again in a pursing of his lips. First his eyes narrowed into a frown of thoughtfulness, then into one of anger. The light that had been a twinkle in his eyes now became like fire.

"It's a good thing I'm in jail," he said. "If I had stayed in Detroit, where I'm from, I think I'd be dead by now, killed either by some junkie or killed by the police. If I had stayed in Detroit I'd have been stealing and robbing and killing folks just to get by."

"What have you been doing down here?"

"Stealing and robbing just to get by," he said. "But not killing, anyway." He laughed.

He had come south to be with his family.

"There ain't nothing left in Detroit. There ain't nothing nowhere else in this country either for black people. No jobs. No way to get no money. Nothing in the cities but dope killers and angry white people who don't want you around nohow. They got the whole loaf and they got the nerve to hate you 'cause you're asking for a few crumbs. At least here I got me some family."

"Is it different? The South, I mean."

"Oh, it's different," he said. "But it ain't better. White folks is white folks, that's all there is to it. But you know what I mean. My people went up north fifty, sixty years ago, and here I am coming back south to the same old shit they were trying to get away from. Not much has changed. When a white man looks at you, he still ain't really looking at you. He might be trying to be your friend, he might even be your friend, I mean really think he's your friend, but when he looks at you he's looking right past you at something else. He don't see you. He sees some make-believe image of you. He sees how you fit in with what he thinks black people are or how we ought to be. He's built up such a mind thing about black people that he thinks he knows all about you and your whole damned family before you say word one. And deep down inside, he hates you. He wants to know why you can't settle down and be a good little nigger and be happy with his leavings, the shit work he's going let you do, the little shack he's going let you live in. He'd be a damned sight happier if you just disappeared and quit wasting time and taking up space on HIS land, in HIS country that he stole fair and square. You ain't never going to mean nothing to him. You don't mean nothing to anybody white. And it don't matter if you're up north or down here somewhere. Our life is a war, man. You hear what I'm saying?"

He slapped me on the shoulder and went back to the bus. He was whistling as he walked, happy to have had an audience.

I thought back to Greg and Jack, how we had sat and talked on their verandah overlooking the sea, how they had opened their home to me, and invited me to stay as long as I liked. They are young, so young in fact that when Greg and I finally went to buy beer, he pulled out his driver's license to show he was over twenty-one.

I asked Greg why he had done it, pulled his ID before the salesgirl asked for it.

He said, "I didn't want to put her on the spot. I'm over twenty-one, but I look young. I didn't want her to feel embarrassed that she had asked me for the ID, and didn't want her wondering if she should have asked for it. Just a courtesy."

I understood. And later that evening when we talked, I asked why that same courtesy wasn't applied with rebel flags. "If you know it might make somebody uncomfortable," I said, "why not put it aside for the sake of someone else?"

We talked about affirmative action.

"It's not the best answer, maybe not even the right answer," I said. "But if you know the playing field is not level, why not make the sacrifice for the good of the country? Otherwise these problems we have will never go away."

We talked deep into the night, those youths and I; it was the same conversation I had had at the cocktail party in Connecticut, but with a difference.

"If a man as confident and capable as I think I am can be made to feel this way," I said, "how do you think the less confident and able might be feeling?"

"I never thought about it that way," they said.

Greg and Jack were young enough, their minds not yet made up, and they were willing to listen and to think.

And there was another difference.

I had calmed down. I was making peace.

I slept on their sofa, snored resoundingly. When I awoke, peace was all over me, in my beard and in my eyes, it covered the front of my shirt and bathed all of me.

XIV

The time has come for men to turn into gods or perish.

—Alan Harrington

🙶

I don't know when I started to like the South—and I mean really to like the place as opposed to simply not disliking it— but I did. Then I fell in love.

On one of my approaches to Atlanta I stopped for gas at one of those superstations that sell gasoline and groceries and auto parts; it even had a delicatessen inside. It's the kind of gas station where travelers in a hurry like to stop because they can fill up with gas, let the kids run around, stretch their legs, have lunch, buy snacks, even shower if they need to, and then be back on the road within minutes.

The building was modern, lots of windows, dozens of shoppers inside, and cars parked all around. In one of the cars, old and heavily loaded down with clothes and boxes and a few lamps, a young couple obviously on the move were rearranging their belongings. Another car, similarly loaded, was sitting beside a gasoline pump. The hose from the pump to the car's gas tank hung loosely, the nozzle was about to fall out. The young man filling his car was more interested in my bike than in paying attention to what he was doing. I filled my tank and rode over to the building to pay. The young man followed me.

"That's a real nice bike," he said.

I smiled and went on inside.

When I came back out, the two old cars were sitting side by side, both of them next to the bike. The two young couples were leaning on the hood of one of the cars. They were studying a road map. I sat in the shade, drank the apple juice I had bought, and ate the potato chips.

When they had finished with the map, the two young men came over to admire the bike. They must have been older, but they didn't look more than nineteen or twenty. The two women with them looked even younger. But even at such a young age they had about them a haggard aspect, already worn down by life. They had been on the road many days and showed it. They looked tired. They looked poor. They might easily have been migrant farm workers, fruit and vegetable pickers. In an earlier time they might have been hippies.

They had come from Michigan, they said, and were on their way first to Atlanta, then to who knows where. One of them, Mike, said he had an uncle in Atlanta. They were all going to stay with the uncle until he got tired of them. By then they hoped to have found a different situation. They were looking for work, they wanted to find a new start, a new life.

"And if he gets tired of us or we can't find nothing to do," Mike said, "we'll pack up the cars and move on again. Anyway, it's got to be better than Michigan. There's nothing left in Michigan. No jobs, no future. No life." He pulled out a pack of cigarettes and lit one.

"You can say that again," said the other. He took the cigarette from Mike and with it lit one of his own.

"Cities are falling apart," he said. "And they're getting more and more dangerous all the time. There's nothing left up there.

So when Mike says he's going to give it a try in Atlanta, I asked him if I could come along."

"What are you going to do?" I asked.

"Jim here is going to keep on going to school at night. I'm a pretty fair mechanic. I think I can find a job."

"And I'm going to work days," Jim said. "I don't know what, but I'll find something."

"What are they going to do?" I asked, looking at the two young women.

"School. Jobs. Same as us. We'll figure something out."

"Good luck," I said.

"Thanks."

Jim turned to Mike and asked if he wanted anything from the store. He asked the two women, and they went in with him.

Mike was frowning when I looked back at him.

"To tell you the truth," he said. "We didn't give this a whole lot of thought. I just knew I had to get out of there. It's bad and it's getting worse. Jobs and tension and general decay. It's just hopeless up there."

"And you think it'll be better down here?"

"One thing's for damned sure," he said. "It won't be any worse. And that's good enough for me."

The four piled into the cars and drove away. I waved them out of sight.

As I watched them disappear, I wondered if they had any idea what lay ahead, if they had any notion of the history of the South, what the South had been and what it had meant, what it still means. They were so young. I wondered if they had given any thought to it at all.

Perhaps they didn't need to. Perhaps the South for these young ones would be different from what it had been for those older. I could hope anyway.

I needed a new visor for my helmet. Mine was old and scuffed up, and I could no longer see very clearly out of it. Rocks kicked up by passing trucks, bits of gravel and ten thousand insects had slammed into the visor and scarred it. The bug juice had dried so hard that I had to scrape it off. The paper towels and coarse cloths I used had scratched the visor further. Now the glaring sun made it nearly impossible to see.

On the way out of Atlanta there was a cycle shop, far on the southern outskirts of town. I stopped there.

It was a cluttered space. The air smelled of grease. The concrete floor was coated with a layer of something slippery.

The man who owned the place took his time about coming to wait on me. He was as friendly as could be with another man. At me he barely glanced. Without a word, without a nod or a smile, with nothing so much as, "I'll be with you in a second," he just ignored me until the other man left.

When my turn came he was still gruff. He never smiled, was never pleasant, never called me sir, but he thanked me, even gave me directions out of town. And there was something about him, his grease-stained shirt, his overhanging belly, his big hammy hands—something about him that told where I was, that told where we had been together, this man and I.

How can you know where you need to get *to* unless you know what you need to get away *from*?

That evening when I stopped for the night at the Colonial Motel in North Thomaston, the innkeeper was a man from India or Pakistan. I thought nothing of it at first but there was something so incongruous about his being in that dark, lonely town that when I checked in, I had to ask.

"What in the world are you doing here, in the middle of racist redneck Georgia, of all places?" I asked. If I were Asian or African or anything else, this would not be my first choice of places to live.

He frowned at me. "There is an opportunity here," he said warily. "I and my family have taken it. We will try to make a good living."

Then I explained.

"The racist South has not only directed its venom against blacks," I said. "From time to time Jews and Catholics and foreigners of all kinds have been targets of southern hatred."

"It is the same in many places," he said. "People hate people, people kill people. One place is very often as bad as another." Then he added, "Or as good."

This last made me stop and think.

"But why here?" I asked.

"Hope," he said. "What else is there?"

What indeed!

I drove south full of hope that next morning. I wanted very much for the innkeeper and for Jim and Mike and their girlfriends to find happiness and peace here. I hoped, as I rode in the cool air toward Americus, for them.

I passed the factory that makes mobile homes, passed the mobile home at the side of the road, clutter in the yard, the big picture of Elvis Presley in the window, the rebel flag hanging.

At the next junction I turned off the main road and headed toward Andersonville and Camp Sumter, largest of the Confederacy's military prisons. Once more to touch the past.

There is a cemetery near the prison. The headstones are white and arranged neatly in rows like soldiers on parade. You walk between the rows and an old sad song plays in your head. Maybe the song is "Dixie," the song of the South, played as lament on guitar, not as a march, not as celebration. And it makes you want to cry—for what has been, but mostly for what could have been. The beauty of the landscape, the green and well-manicured slopes of softly rolling hills, the trees and the cool forgiving shade these trees bring to a hot afternoon, do not help you to forget that 13,000 men died here in about a year's time, mostly from disease and malnutrition, exposure to the heat and cold and poor sanitation. It doesn't even try to make you forget. If anything it reminds us what we are capable of, that we fought and why we fought, and what we have done to one another.

The new South and the old South are never very far removed. The South is rooted in the past, and that may not be a bad thing, to be reminded of what we once were, what we are and what we are not, what we are trying to get away from, what we are trying to get to.

It was here in Andersonville that Willie Ann Towns told me she likes to eat dirt.

I had cruised slowly through the old part of the town, parked, and went inside the old general store, went inside the old railroad station now turned into a museum. When I finished looking around at things of interest to someone else, I crossed the tracks and entered a residential neighborhood where all the houses were small and made of brick and looked exactly alike. Willie Ann Towns was sitting on the front steps of her house.

I stopped, pretending I was lost, and asked for directions.

"How y'all doing?" I asked.

Slowly Willie Ann got up and came down to the curb.

"That's a pretty bike," she said. "Where you going on it?"

"Just going," I said. "Do you live here?"

She nodded. She said it was a housing project.

There weren't very many houses, six or seven in a row leading down a short street. You don't expect to see housing projects out in the middle of nowhere. You think of housing projects and welfare as products of the city. But the countryside has its poor as well.

"What's it like inside?" I wanted to know. I wanted to know everything about being poor and black in a little backwater place like Andersonville.

Willie Ann told me about the smallness of the little two-room houses that looked a bit like slave quarters on some plantation. The only difference was the bricks, the indoor plumbing and heat.

We talked for a good long time about nothing to do when suddenly she told me that she likes to eat dirt.

I hardly heard her, but asked her why.

"It tastes good," she said. "Dirt and chalk too. But you have to be careful about the chalk."

I was too tunnel-visioned to hear. I wanted her to tell me about the South, about how it was living here, and I missed what she was telling me, that it's the same as it's always been, that some people still eat dirt.

And then at a café in Americus where I stopped to get a hot dog and a bowl of chili, the South fooled me again.

It was a bright, very clean little place in a row of shops facing the square. I sat at the lunch counter. A black man was sitting next to me. Two white men were sitting in the far corner. They were leaning against the wall and reading the news. They looked like they owned the place.

I asked the man next to me, "What's with those two white guys in the corner?"

He looked at me, looked at them, then bent back over his lunch and kept eating.

"How the hell should I know?" he said. "I don't even know what they're doing in here. They don't like to get too close to us nohow."

"Sounds like nothing has changed in all these years," I said.

He looked up and gave a twisted smile.

"Oh, some things change," he said. "I remember when we couldn't sit at the lunch counter with them. Now we do. Now we own the place."

The black woman behind the counter heard us. She was frantically busy, filling orders, answering the phone, quietly calling orders to someone in the kitchen, taking money and making change. But she stopped for a minute. I think she just wanted to smile at me. She was beautiful and when I paid my bill, I told her so.

"That's the owner," the fellow beside me said. "We still got the white folks who like to sit in the corner away from us, but their money's good." He slapped me on the shoulder. "And we'll take it," he said, as if he owned the place himself.

In a way, I guess he did.

He walked away happy, and so did I.

How eagerly I had anticipated evil at every turn, expected it, longed for the horrors to visit me. I almost wanted it to happen, wanted to find nothing changed, wanted to hate the place. I was no better than the racist who on seeing me has his mind already made up. I wanted the South to prove the stereotypes carefully harbored in my mind.

How easy it is to insist that it is all about race, about black and white, about the past. Then you never have to think about the future.

I am glad for the man in the cycle shop, glad for the two white men sitting in the corner at the café in Americus, for they remind us of what we—I hope *we*—are trying to leave behind. At the same time they tell how far we are from where we are trying to go.

I began to look at the people who waved at me. I had been waving back all along, but as reflex. Now I looked each man in the face—only rarely would a woman wave—and I waved in return. There is nothing very grand about a wave. But it's those little things that can make all the difference in the world.

I made my way to Fort Walton Beach in the Florida panhandle. My bike needed a routine service and I called Forte Cycle Center for an appointment. They were booked solid. I explained that I was traveling through. They told me to come in and they would see what they could do.

"It might be a long wait," the service manager said when I finally arrived. "But we'll get you in."

I sat in the shade and read. Someone brought me a cold soda. An old man who used to ride motorcycles but could not any longer came to talk to me. We sat on the ground together. I had lunch at Mary's Kitchen up the road and the waitress called me sugar, brought me pie, made me feel at home.

When I finally went back to the shop, it was closed but they had stayed on to finish the bike for me. It was a family operation, everybody seemed to be there to see me off. They asked where I was headed. I said, "North, I think." And they told me where to stay the night. They even called ahead for me and arranged for a cheaper rate than I would have gotten on my own. I don't know why they did this.

I spent the night in a hotel called Americano, in a town called Niceville.

The morning brought with it brightest sunshine and gladness. I was wickedly happy as I rode into the heat. I took off my jacket and wrapped a damp bandanna around my throat. I flew past every car on my side of the road, waved to every driver coming toward me. I was cool and cocky, a little too much at ease.

The knot in the bandanna came loose. The bandanna flew from my neck. I tried to grab it as it slipped off but was too slow. Immediately I looked for a place to turn around and pulled off on the left side of the road. The pavement there had ended. I was on gravel and dirt and going too fast. The bike skidded out from under me. At the last instant, I jumped. I fell.

The bike tottered and finally fell as well. The engine had not shut off and the rear wheel was spinning round and round. I walked over to it and switched off the motor. Then I sat on the ground and laughed.

The bike wasn't damaged. I walked back in the road and got my bandanna. Then I waited for someone to help me lift the bike.

It was a young kid from up the road in Florala, he said. He had seen the bike on its side when he passed and came back to see if I needed help.

"Florala," I said. "That's in Alabama, right? How is it there?"

"Boring," he said. "I hate it."

"Do you have any black friends?"

"Yeah, a few," he said. "And they hate it too."

"And there's no tension?"

"Some," he said. "There are people who don't like black people. Sure. But there are people who do. And mostly we get along fine. At least my friends and I do."

I wondered if there was something going on that I didn't know anything about. I kept riding and I kept waving until I passed through a little town called Opp. I followed the road into town, made a right at the light, and drove through a residential neighborhood. A man about to get into a pickup truck waved. I waved and rode on.

But this final waving nagged at me and so I slowed the bike and turned around. I went around the block and found the man. He was writing something in a notebook, and when he heard me, he looked up and waved again.

I pulled in front of him and got off the bike. He got out of the truck.

"What's the matter?" he said. "Are you lost?"

"No, I'm not lost," I said. "I'm just trying to figure out why everybody keeps waving at me."

He laughed. "You're in South Alabama," he said.

"That's what I mean," I said. "This is Alabama."

"Alabama is a very friendly place," he said.

He offered me his hand, told me his name—James Anderman.

"Alabama scares the hell out of me," I said. "It hasn't exactly been what you'd call a very friendly place to black people. In fact just the opposite."

"Well, South Alabama has always been different," he said. He got on his soapbox and started preaching to me.

"But Alabama in general has changed a lot, you know. The whole of the South has changed a lot. Haven't you seen it? You'll find this is the friendliest part of the country. And I know you're thinking about what goes on between blacks and whites down here, but I tell you it's not like that anymore. Not entirely. It's not entirely disappeared either, of course, but even when it was bad—well, I can't say it wasn't as bad as you probably heard, but still it was different. White people in the South have always been friendly toward black people, friendlier than in the North. The difference is that in the North white people claim they love black people but they don't know any. They can pass their whole lives without knowing any. It ain't that way down here. That could never happen without a whole lot of effort. So up north they want equality for black people as a race but not as individuals. Down here, even when things were bad and blacks were despised and thoroughly mistreated, and I admit it, you were severely mistreated, but we never disliked the black people we knew. We hated the race, you could say, but loved the people."

"I hope you don't think that makes a bad situation better," I said.

"Not better," he said. "But different. The South is not a bad place. I just can't allow myself to believe that it is. That would make everybody who lives here bad. And me too. And I don't think I'm bad. We've done some bad things, that's true, but who hasn't? There's good people here too. I've got a lot of friends who are southerners who have done a lot of good things. I can't believe this is a bad place full of bad people. Don't you like it here? Be honest. Don't you like it just a little?"

I admitted that the South was growing on me. And I wished out loud that the past had not been so ugly, wished that my trip could have been all about food and fun, running from place to place on my bike and smelling the seasons change, talking to people about their lives, hearing their stories, listening to their laughter. Then I'm sure I would love the South. But the shadow covers me too.

"I think it *is* better down here," he said. "And I mean better for black people. We know black people. We understand them better than they do up north, because we've been through the fire together down here. Right here in this very state we did some of the meanest things you can ever imagine. Horrible inhuman things. And I don't think anybody is proud of it. Oh, maybe a few crazy people, but I don't think anybody really wants to see those days again. They were too painful—for all of us—and too wrong. We've come a long way together. We've shared a great deal of suffering and shame and pain together. We have felt, and some of us—black and white—still feel passions of rage and hate. And this binds us. We think about this problem every day of our lives. Our memories won't let us forget. But if we're lucky and we raise our children right, then maybe their children's children will be different. If there's hope for this country, I think it's right here in the battlefield, right here in the South. We'll find a way because everywhere you look the memories stare us right in the face. What we have done and what we do affect how the rest of the country and the rest of the world sees us. On some deep level they even affect how we see ourselves. We have to find a way."

He took a deep breath and was going to start again. He really wanted to convince or convert me. He wanted, I think, to convince himself. But I stopped him.

We talked on for a long time anyway, talked about his father and how his father had raised him to try and be fair. He told me about the part of town they called the nigger quarters and about the black men who lived there, black men his father considered friends.

"Did he ever invite them home for dinner?" I asked.

"Black people came to our house many times," he said. "They were always around."

"To sit down and have dinner?"

James looked away. His face was ashamed and sad.

"No," he said. "And my father never went to their homes to eat either. But those were different days. And I know you think that's not a good excuse, but my father was a good man. A lot of white people never had dinner in our house either."

"But those men weren't his friends, were they?" I said. "And the blacks were."

"All I can say is they were different times," he said. "And maybe he couldn't invite them home, I guess."

James ran his fingers through his hair. He was visibly pained.

"Tell me this one thing," he said. "You've been traveling all over on that thing. Has anybody mistreated you, been really malicious to you? I mean once you got to talking so he could know you weren't going to cause him any harm."

I shook my head.

"You see," he said. "It's an individual thing. Some people will treat you good, some bad, but most when they get to know you one on one will be kind to you. At least in the South we're not afraid to get to know black people."

There was something in what he said.

I turned off the road I was on and headed up toward Tuskegee, where the famous institute is.

By tradition an all-black college. Started in 1881 when Lewis Adams, a former slave, and George Campbell, a former slave owner, persuaded the state of Alabama that a college for blacks would be a good thing. Tuskegee Institute illustrates the paradox of the South. A former slave working with a former slave owner. The state of Alabama giving $2,000 for teachers' salaries but nothing for land or buildings or equipment.

A falling-down church and an old wooden shack were the school until the treasurer of another black college, Hampton Institute in Virginia, made a personal loan of $200 to Tuskegee with which the school was able to buy a hundred acres of abandoned farm-land. There are 268 acres now and 161 buildings. From 30 students in the first class the school has grown into an academic community of 5,000—students, faculty, and staff. The campus is a national historic site administered by the U.S. National Park Service. It is a monument, a living museum.

For many of the old buildings on campus the bricks were made by students, and the buildings themselves were built by students. It was the philosophy of the school and its founder, Booker T.

Washington, that young blacks receive a practical education as well as a theoretical and creative one. To Booker T., who had been born a slave and who had worked his way through college as a janitor, graduating with honors, education was a total experience, meant to take place in the classroom and the workshop, but also in the dormitories and the dining halls. He wanted Tuskegee to be what he called a civilizing agent.

So the school taught agriculture, and the students ate the produce from the school farm. Students made bricks and built buildings. And when they graduated, many students became educators, not only in the classroom. They went back, many of them, to the plantation areas to show people there how to put new energy and new ideas into farming and into life itself.

The buildings are old, some in need of repair; many wooden ones could use a coat of paint. And as I walked through the campus and into the buildings I felt nothing so much as the paradox of black/white life in America.

If not for donations from benefactors like Andrew Carnegie and John D. Rockefeller, Tuskegee would not exist. If not for segregation and the two societies, Tuskegee would not need to exist. And who knows if the Carnegies and the Rockefellers and the Huntingtons were so generous only as a way to keep blacks in schools for blacks and away from schools for whites?

The whole thing was making me crazy, giving me a headache, making me want to examine everyone's motives, everything's reasons. I went a mile or so down the road to the center of town and sat in the very center of a noisy little restaurant just off the town's main square. The sign read: PIERCE'S RESTAURANT. COUNTRY COOKING.

I talked to no one, just sat and watched the black people laughing and talking loud and loading down the country food. My spirits were lifted. I got an order of fried chicken, a side order of greens and one of black-eyed peas, some macaroni and cheese, and I ate until I couldn't eat any more.

The place was owned by a black man. The ladies behind the counter were black. Most of the customers were black as well, but not all. There were many white people, farmers in overalls, laborers in blue jeans and dirty shirts, county bureaucrats in suits and ties. There were no private tables, you sat where you found a space. White people and black people sat shoulder to shoulder in this dusty southern town and ate greens and ham and sweet potatoes together. I don't know how close they sat—or even if they talked—once they left this two-room restaurant and the thousands of places like it in the South, but as James Anderman had said, in many ways blacks and whites are familiar with each other here. They may not be best friends, may not invite one another home for dinner, but they know each other. They are comfortable around each other in ways that they are not in the North. I cannot imagine a white lady sitting alone in a black restaurant in Cleveland or in St. Louis. That woman in Saratoga Springs couldn't even walk on the same street with me without panicking. And yet here in the racist South, a lone white woman sits and reads a book and eats her lunch.

Lunch hour for most was over. All the white people had left by the time she arrived. But she came in and sat and ate.

She was a nurse, dressed all in white. Her hair was so gray, even it was white. Her name—so the tag pinned to her dress said—was Grace Comer. I did not talk to her. I didn't need to. I just watched her and I think she must have felt me watching, for she looked up from her book and smiled at me.

James Anderman thinks that if there's hope for this country, it's right here, right here in the South. And I begin to wonder.

There is plenty to remind you that evil still lives in the world. And so we leap at the little flickers of hope, as if we were moths and the flickers bright flames. A smile, a wave, a moment's kindness. Enough flickers and there will be flame, and the flame will become blaze.

I was falling in love with this place. I took the hour's ride from Tuskegee to Montgomery without the dread and rage that perhaps rightly ought to have been within me. So much had happened in Montgomery, so much started here, that it is easy to think the entire struggle for human rights began here. Let's not forget Booker T. and George Washington Carver, Sojourner Truth and Denmark Vesey and Harriet Tubman and Nat Turner and Ida Wells. These are the names we know. Let us not forget Rosa Parks, an ordinary woman, somebody's seamstress. She was simply tired one day—so the story goes—and refused to give up her seat to a white man. It was 1955. It wasn't that blacks had to sit at the back of the bus, as if there were a special section for them. It was simply that no black person was allowed to sit in front of a white person no matter where he sat. Rosa Parks was arrested for not surrendering her seat.

Some say she was just tired. Others claim the whole affair was planned. I am proud of her either way, proud of the blacks in Montgomery who refused to ride the buses as long as seating remained segregated. They made the necessary sacrifice. They walked to work and the buses ran empty for eleven months.

We like to think of them as ordinary people: Rosa and the black men and women who boycotted the buses; the college students in Greensboro and Nashville who sat at segregated lunch counters and endured the cursings and the beatings until the lunch counters were integrated; the men and women who marched peacefully for the right to vote; Elizabeth Eckford and eight black schoolmates who silently walked through a crowd of angry whites spitting at them, cursing them, hating them that first day blacks were allowed to go to Little Rock High School, and maybe every day afterwards.

They were not ordinary people but strong and brave, and we must never forget them and what they did for us.

Men like my father who hung his head in fear and shame to live and proudly tell the story. These are our heroes. Quiet heroes like Great-Grandfather Joseph and the many like him, men and women, whom we should remember if for no other reason than that they endured and that they survived and that they carried us one step farther, one step closer.

And while we are remembering, let us remember too the whites who believed in racial equality and were cursed and beaten, arrested and killed alongside the blacks.

Let us never forget.

And let us lift every voice in praise.

XV

This is not the end. It is not even the beginning of the end. But it is, perhaps, the end of the beginning.

—Winston Churchill

F rom the Ohio River south to the Gulf of Mexico. From the Atlantic to the Mississippi and a little beyond. More than half a million square miles—not counting Texas—and still only 14 percent of the country. Yet the South is the nation's linchpin, it seems. The South holds the key to our salvation. Always has, always will—until salvation comes.

Over the entire expanse at once, as if over all the earth, clouds of darkness have tangled together and threaten rain. The shadows cast are long and grotesque. They expand—the shadows on the earth, the clouds in the sky. They block the sun's rays, absorb them, and steal the light until all that remain are the shadows on the ground.

Our good fortunes and our joys, our triumphs may bring us relief and lightness, but only temporarily, it seems; it is our defeats, failure and sorrow that cast the shadows that darken our days as long as we live.

But through the gaps in the clouds a little light falls. And perhaps this is enough—a beginning. New shapes begin to form, and in these new shapes there is some peace, some tranquillity, some small reason to be calm.

I cannot help but wonder if Joseph passed this way, and wonder too what he might have felt in passing. There is no way to know, of course, no way but to imagine his route and what he might have gone through, how white he might have had to become in order to get by, only then to discover how black he truly was.

There was no way to know which route he might have taken, but I knew I was following in Joseph's footsteps. I knew now where I was going.

Before I arrived there, before it was all over, I would finally find the men who had been waiting to call me nigger, tempting me to violence. They were but two men out of the many hating me before they knew me. And they brought to mind all the pain of an old wound that has never healed. But by the time I found them, my rage had already been tempered.

My first night in Montgomery I slept the sleep of the drunk, a night of motion and crazy dreams. I woke up not knowing where I was.

I was at the Riverfront Inn, a very nice hotel on the corner of Coosa and Tallapoosa, the street names doubtless adding to my crazy dreams. I had checked in because I felt I had to. I checked in expecting—I don't know why—to be turned away, at the very least to be looked at askance and made to feel unwelcome. I wasn't. I sat in the hotel restaurant and ate a grilled steak for dinner. I made myself as conspicuous as possible. I moved to the hotel bar and stayed a couple of hours drinking alone. I waited for someone to suggest that I might not belong there. But no one ever did.

Cocktail waitresses flirted and called me sir. Hotel staff asked if everything was all right. Other guests smiled and said hello. It isn't much, but after all that has been, it's something.

I ended up watching the ball game at the bar and listening to the bartender's predictions for the rest of the season.

I stayed longer than I needed to, drank more than I should have, found my room eventually and went to sleep until voices I did not recognize were shouting in the hallway and half-awakened me.

"This place is full of racists," the one angrily said to the other. "And their racism is real, so real you can touch it."

"But what can you do?" the other one said in such a way that I could almost see him throw up his hands. "You cannot let it hold you back or stop you from getting where you need to be."

"You cannot ignore it," the first one said.

"You cannot ignore it, that is true. But when it rains you put up an umbrella. When it snows you wear rubber boots. Racism exists, yes. But it is not the worst thing there is."

"Tell me what is worse," the first one said.

"Being afraid to confront your fears is worse," the other one answered him. "You must not be afraid to face them. Your fears must never control you. You must learn to surrender what you do not need and move forward. This is what we have always done. Remember, you must not be like the men who hate you. In order for you not to hate, you must be able to forget."

"But in order to know who I am, I must remember."

I drifted deeper into sleep with their words ringing inside my head. When I awoke I knew that this little journey would end up either costing me my life, or somehow saving it. Perhaps both.

I knew I had come to the South to face my fears and to surrender them, to forget the many things it is best to forget, and to remember what is essential to remember. Until I did these, the South would own my anger and my sanity, my dignity, my pride, my sense of self.

"You northern blacks have given up the fight," a man on a street corner told me. "You ran away like cowards from the real struggle and got sucked into the battle about being able to join the country club."

He was a policeman. He had been standing on the corner of Hull and Jefferson, acting as a crossing guard for the children and the tourists who this morning were wandering in this part of the city they call Old Alabama Town, a historic area with old homes open for touring.

I had approached him after looking into an old house with what must have been slave quarters attached, and I asked him quite casually, "How are the white folks treating you?" He looked at me and sneered.

"This is Alabama, son," he said, though he seemed younger than I. "How do you think they're treating us?"

He had come from Birmingham, he told me, and couldn't wait to get back there. His name was Bell.

"This place is too tame," he said.

"So what are you doing here?"

"When I got out of the service, they were looking for cops in Montgomery," he said. "When there's an opening in Birmingham, I'll go back home."

I asked if he had ever thought about moving out of the South. He looked at me as if I were pathetically stupid.

"The front line is here," he said. "You blacks in the North are fighting a rearguard action to keep from losing ground—to keep from losing your material gains, actually, what little you've really gained. We're down here fighting the real fight, the quiet fight for dignity."

"Are we winning?"

"Inch by inch," he said. "The governor of Virginia is a black man. We got black mayors and black chiefs of police in places you never would have dreamed possible. And over in Mississippi—in Mississippi, of all God's places!—there are more elected blacks than anywhere."

"So you're optimistic about the future?"

"No," he said flatly. "I would have to be a damned fool or very naive to be optimistic. White folks is white folks, as they say. How can I be optimistic? It's the optimists that get us into all this trouble. They look for a few things going right and take great cheer from it. They forget about everything else that's still going wrong. They never see what's really happening because they can't see through those thick rose-colored glasses they wear. When they see things get a little bit better they think all of a sudden that everything is going to motor on fine and dandy all by itself. I know that ain't so. I'm no optimist. We've got a long hard fight on our hands, and I'm staying here to do some of the fighting."

It seems very often that blacks in the North feel themselves superior to blacks in the South because they think blacks in the South were simple-minded enough to stay and suffer the worst of the horrors and indignities. Southern blacks too often are called " 'Bamas" and country niggers, and are seen as backward and uneducated. This man Bell was telling me the opposite, that blacks in the South look down on blacks in the North.

"They're up there killing each other, doing the white man's work," he said. "They escaped to the Promised Land and got handed a bunch of lies. Now they don't know what to do. But we're down here like we've always been, suffering, enduring, hanging on. We'll win this thing just by hanging on. Like all those black folks who suffered a whole lot more than you and me ever will. The white man beat us with sticks and clubs, shot us and lynched us, pitched us in the river. But here we are, still here. Eventually the white man's going to get tired and he's going to quit. Eventually they're going to see that it's taking two of them to hold one of us down, and they'll see that they're not getting anywhere either."

"So you are an optimist," I said.

"No," he said emphatically. "An optimist thinks the white man is going to realize what a fool he's been and how he's been wasting all his time and money and energy holding us in a ditch, and that he's going to reach down and pull us up and hand in hand we'll all walk off into the happy sunset together. That's an optimist. But me, all I want is for the white man to leave us alone. He doesn't have to help us. I just want him to stop blocking the way. And that's why I say this battle is really about dignity. If they would stop trying to deny us that, we could make it on our own."

A group of kids came toward us, primary school kids, black and white and I think I saw an Asian face. They were walking two by two, holding hands to keep together. I looked at Bell and he was smiling.

He had to leave me now to stop what little traffic there was and help them cross the street.

"We're here," he said. "And we're going to be here. We in the South know it hasn't been easy and that's why we fight so hard, the one side against the other, the one side with the other. You all in the North seem to have forgotten what we in the South will never forget. Every day we face the reminders of what we've been through. Here in the South we could never forget. None of us. Black or white."

Four blocks from where Bell and I stood, on the corner of Dexter and Decatur, is the Dexter Avenue Baptist Church. It was Martin Luther King's first parish. When you call the Montgomery Chamber of Commerce, some old white lady will answer the phone. If you ask her, as I did, to tell you if the Dexter Avenue Church has any historical significance, she will answer indignantly and say to you, as she said to me with a hint of pride in her voice:

"My heavens, yes. That was Dr. Martin Luther King's church."

She will make it clear that she thinks everyone ought to know the history of her town and country.

And when you ask her about the Sixteenth Street Baptist Church where Addie Mae Collins, Denise McNair, Carole Robertson, and Cynthia Wesley were blown up one Sunday morning when a bomb was tossed through the window, the Chamber of Commerce lady will tell you without skipping a beat:

"Mister, that church is in Birmingham."

As if you should know that too.

This history, she seems to be saying, is her history, the pain of the past, her pain as well, and we all ought to know it and never forget any part of it.

There is a street in Montgomery named Jefferson Davis, of course, but there is also one named for Rosa Parks, of all people. They intersect. Mostly Rosa Parks Avenue runs through a black section of town, the same as every Martin Luther King Drive, Street, or Avenue in the country does. But wouldn't it say something wonderful if Rosa Parks and Martin King were recognized in white neighborhoods as well for what they did? Maybe one day.

But in the center of the business district, only three streets away from the first White House of the Confederacy and in the shadow of the state capitol with its rebel battle flag flying, a Civil Rights Memorial has been built. Businessmen and politicians and tourists and others—black, white, and all colors—pass it daily, and there it sits as reminder of the struggle that has not been won, that is not yet over, that goes on and on everywhere and forever.

The monument is a curved wall of black granite, smooth and cool, and on it are inscribed the words of Martin Luther King. "[We will not be satisfied] . . . *until justice rolls down like waters and righteousness like a mighty stream."*

In front of the wall, from the center of a circular black granite table, water spouts up and flows over the table's flat surface. On the tabletop, beneath the thin sheet of cool flowing water, are engraved as if burning the dates of important events in the battle for human rights in this country, and with those dates, the names of important men, women, and children who sacrificed for the future.

It was a violent struggle. Of the fifty-two dates inscribed there, thirty-two of them mention death; four others involved less lethal violence.

Some of the people who died in the struggle knew what they were doing, others did not. Some are household names, most are the quiet heroes we never hear about unless we search for them. But they are there. They have always been with us. They are extraordinary people, and we must never forget them and what they did for us—for all of us—that we might live in harmony, not in dominance or in servility, in peace and not in fear.

George Lee murdered for urging blacks to vote.

Lamar Smith murdered for the same thing.

Emmett Till murdered for flirting with a white woman.

John Reese killed when white men shot through the windows of the café where he was dancing.

Willie Edwards, Jr., forced by Klansmen to jump into the Alabama River where he drowned.

Mack Charles Parker taken by a mob from his jail cell and lynched.

Herbert Lee murdered by a state legislator for registering blacks to vote.

Cpl. Roman Ducksworth, Jr., murdered by a police officer.

Paul Guihard, a French news reporter killed by gunfire from a white mob.

William Lewis Moore murdered as he tried to deliver to the governor of Mississippi a letter urging tolerance.

Medgar Evers murdered at home by a sniper.

Addie Mae Collins, Denise McNair, Carole Robertson, Cynthia Wesley murdered for being black, for being young, for being in church one Sunday morning, the wrong place at the wrong time.

Virgil Lamar Ware murdered by white teenagers for being black, for being young, for being on the street with his brother, the wrong place at the wrong time.

Louis Allen murdered for witnessing the murder of Herbert Lee.

Rev. Bruce Klunder murdered for protesting the building of a segregated school. A bulldozer crushed him.

Henry Hezekiah and *Charles Eddie* Moore murdered by Klansmen.

James Earl Chaney, Andrew Goodman, Michael Henry Schwerner arrested by the sheriff, handed over to Klansmen, murdered, and buried in an earthen dam.

Lt. Col. Lemuel Penn murdered by Klansmen shooting from a passing car.

Jimmie Lee Jackson beaten and shot by Alabama state police as he tried to protect his grandfather from a police attack.

Rev. James Reeb beaten to death as he walked down a street in Selma.

Viola Gregg Liuzzo murdered by Klansmen shooting from a passing car.

Oneal Moore killed by a shotgun blast from a passing car.

Willie Brewster murdered by members of the National States Rights Party, a group responsible for church bombings.

Jonathan Myrick Daniels arrested for helping blacks register to vote, released suddenly, murdered moments later.

Samuel Leamon Younge, Jr., murdered at a gas station for arguing about segregated restrooms.

Vernon Ferdinand Dahmer burned to death after he offered to pay the poll taxes for those who couldn't afford the fee.

Ben Chester White murdered by Klansmen.

Clarence Triggs murdered for attending civil rights meetings.

Wharlest Jackson murdered for taking a job previously reserved for whites.

Benjamin Brown killed by police who fired into a crowd.

Samuel Ephesians Hammond, Jr., Delano Herman Middleton, Henry Ezekial Smith killed by police firing on student protesters.

Dr. Martin Luther King, Jr., assassinated for wanting a better world.

These are merely the ones whose names we know, the ones we recognize. There have been and are still many many others, many others whose sacrifice will never be known, many others whose names have been lost, the ones who died, and the ones who suffered the torture of a living hell. But one day we will know who they are, these silent heroes, we will see them all around us.

> *"One day the South will recognize its real heroes."*
> —Martin Luther King, Jr.

By the time I found the men waiting to call me nigger, I had been to this Civil Rights Memorial and sat in the cool shade. The late afternoon sun could not reach the place where I sat, where I meditated. I cooled my bottom on the pavement and rested. The tall shadow of people I had never met fell over me. I felt a deep sense of peace.

The Civil Rights Memorial fronts a modern office building that houses the Southern Poverty Law Center. The man who started the center, Morris Dees, is a lawyer who made a fortune publishing a cookbook. For some godly reason he turned his back on the security of business. He got involved instead in the right fight and on the right side. I wanted to meet him. I wanted to ask him why. Morris Dees is a white man.

When the Sixteenth Street Baptist Church was bombed in Birmingham, Dees was a part-time minister at a white church. From the pulpit he asked members of his parish to donate money to help rebuild the church. He asked them to pray for the families of the four little girls who were killed. His congregation of Christians walked out on him.

Five years later Dees was devoted full-time to civil rights law.

Lawyers from Washington had come to the South to put into motion the legal workings of the Civil Rights Act of 1964 and the Voting Rights Act of 1965. When those structures were set up, the northern lawyers went home. Dees got involved with the lawsuits that would make the real gains possible. He made a lot of enemies. Ku Klux Klan graffiti were painted on his office walls. His office was flooded. The hate mail started.

In the 1980s Dees took on the Klan itself when Klansmen lynched a nineteen-year-old black kid named Michael Donald. Dees and the Law Center sued in civil court on behalf of Donald's mother and won a seven-million-dollar judgment against the United Klans of America. This particular branch of the Klan was essentially put out of business, bankrupt.

Dees became something of a marked man. Hate mail increased, death threats were not uncommon. No wonder then that I could not get into his office. I had to have an appointment and no amount of persuasion could gain me access. They didn't know me and they were not going to let me in.

I left Montgomery and came back, I made connections with politicians in Mississippi and tried to get to Dees through them, I called the Law Center and said I wanted to interview Mr. Dees for a book I was writing, but nothing I tried got me past the voice on the intercom system or past the women who juggled me from one to another on the telephone.

I only wanted to ask one question. I simply wanted to know why he did what he did. I wanted to hear it from Dees, but I already knew what he would say.

As I sat on the steps at the memorial I ran scenario after scenario in my head. I imagined Dees' soft drawl, his paunch, and the tired sadness beneath his eyes. I imagined the fire within them. He didn't look like a lawyer. He certainly didn't look like a cookbook salesman. He just looked like a southern white man.

Why I do what I do? I imagined him saying. Because I love your people and I love my people. Well, they are the same people. I do what I do because I love my country. And this is what my country stands for. It stands for justice. I do what I do because I love the South and I do not want to see the South ruined again, and the only way to avoid such destruction is to redeem the past. This is the only way I know how. I do what I do because no one else would do it. I do what I do because of a debt I owe to those who will come after. I do what I do because it's right and it's good and it needs doing. I do what I do because I have no choice.

"Some things you must always be unable to bear. Some things you must never stop refusing to bear. Injustice and outrage and dishonor and shame. No matter how young you are or how old you have got. Not for kudos and not for cash; your picture in the paper nor money in the bank either. Just refuse to bear them."

—William Faulkner.

Suddenly, mysteriously, miraculously, I found myself loving the South. Fear and loathing vanished. My eyes opened all at once and I saw the South for what it truly is, in all of its contradiction and confusion, a swirl of strangeness and strain.

The South is a wounded old dog.

How it longs for its glory days when it was the most savage beast on the block, how it longs for its youth. How it growls and snarls, ferociously barking its bravado while craving a gentle word, a little understanding, the kind touch of a friendly hand. The South is old and tired.

The South is as afraid of me as I had been of it.

I pulled into the gravel parking lot of a roadside café near Philadelphia, Mississippi. A hot day, the sun beat down brightly. I was in my leather jacket and sweltering. I peeled it off, then took off the helmet. I was frowning from the heat, from the effort. My hair was matted, my beard overgrown and wild. I must have looked mean, angry, and dangerous.

A man was watching me from the window. He stared hard and I stared hard back. I frowned even more. We locked eyes and I would not back down, would not give an inch. Unmoving, un-flinching, I glowered fiercely at him. He looked away.

On the side of the building there was a window where you could get cold drinks and ice cream. That's all I wanted, a cold drink. I didn't want to go inside. I only wanted a moment to stretch my legs. I had been on the bike a long time that day, doing more miles in a few hours than Great-Grandfather Joseph, on foot or in a wagon, could have done in weeks. Perhaps that is why, at the end of his journey, knowing firsthand the slow difficulty of each long day's journey toward frontier and future, he sank his bucket where he was and dug his well, and started a stagecoach line.

In those days, Mississippi was the far West, new country, the distant frontier and the end of the line. As a nation we have always looked west to find the future, west to the setting sun, west to paradise, to unspoiled and uncrowded lands, wide open spaces, freedom. Joseph would have been no different from any other American in his expectations, desires, and concerns. Only in one concern was his outlook different: He went west to escape, went west until the great river blocked his way.

There he settled, in Tennessee, and there he established his line.

Others would come behind him, others would cross the river and push on farther west. From somewhere to the river they would need transportation. Joseph, with one eye surely on the past and the other eye squarely on the future, supplied travelers with speedier transport and so found his own future.

I wonder what they called Joseph. *Mister? Sir? Uncle Joe?* I wonder if they knew he was black. I wonder if it would have mattered. Instead of riding a creaky old wagon over a rutted road, they could ride a stagecoach and drastically shorten their travel time. Efficiency, that's all that mattered. Time saved was money earned. They were in a hurry. Even then Americans were always in a hurry.

Despite the speed of stagecoach and railroad, however, they could not do in a month what I on the bike could do in a day. I was in a hurry too, putting miles between me and the past, in a hurry to taste as much of the South as I could, flying with not much rhyme or reason, other than to ride on. On and on. This day, I had ridden forever.

Now with a cold soda I washed the heat and dust from my mouth. I strolled to stretch my legs. I crunched ice as I walked. I went back to the bike and suited up.

The man in the window was still there, not moving, still staring.

He raised his eyebrows. I smiled. And then, once broken, I couldn't help myself. I grinned. The tough guy laughed.

Quickly then he came running out.

"If you hadn't smiled," he said, "I never would have come out."

I wanted to tell him he was the one who had prompted my smile. I kept it to myself.

"But then you laughed," he said. "Then I knew it was all right to come out and talk to you. I wanted to see your bike."

Always the bike.

We talked. He invited me to his little farm. He had a room where I could take a nap, he said. I could spend some days there if I wanted to. I told him I was in a hurry, but I could use the nap, I said. I followed him home. His girlfriend made iced tea. I took a five-minute nap. That was enough. The rest of my time there I spent walking with him—his name was Bob—down by the river and making promises that I would return one day and that we'd go fishing together.

I don't even remember where Bob lives. I was just on the road somewhere and a stranger offered me a spot in his shade. How could I have refused?

"I found Christ when I was ten," he said. "That has made all the difference. Now I'm color-blind."

"I don't know if that's such a good thing," I said. "It takes more than blindness. It takes awareness. We don't have to stop seeing our differences. We shouldn't have to stop being different, shouldn't even have to worry about it. We just have to stop making it a crime to be different."

"I'm doing my best," he said. "I'm trying to raise my kid right, anyway. It starts at home, the good and the bad, don't you think? Even so, you never know what's going to influence somebody."

He told me the story of his young son in school.

"There is a new kid in class, a black kid," he said. "All the kids in class have been calling him nigger. Every time they talked about him they called him nigger. My son had never heard that word before. He thought nigger was the boy's name. He went up to this new kid and introduced himself, just as the teacher was coming over to where they were. 'Hello, Nigger,' my son said. The teacher heard him and he was in big trouble. Now he's confused. He's only six. He's in trouble at school for trying to be friendly to a black kid. I wonder what all this will do to him, now that he's eaten from the tree—if you know what I mean."

He picked up a long branch and pretended to fish with it.

"What do I tell him?" he asked. "What do we do?"

I shrugged.

"Kids learn to be heartless and hateful at home," he said.

"But then it quickly spreads," I said. "A kid hears his father say something, the kid passes it to another kid, pretty soon all the kids have picked up some evil idea. It's like a disease. It's infectious."

"Maybe the good can be too," he said. "My father was prejudiced and I was raised to be prejudiced. But my father had a change of heart. He was in the hospital and all his best nurses were black. That opened his eyes. But even before that, he worked with black men and had black friends. It's funny. He was a racist but there were black men he trusted more than white ones."

"Did the black men ever come to his house?"

"Yes," he said. "He invited them home. But I'm sure around his white friends he said things and acted just like they did, just like he was supposed to do. But something good must have happened. It rubbed off on me, I think. Maybe it will rub off on somebody else. Maybe we can all have a change of heart."

Maybe, I said. But with all this goodness rubbing off, why has it taken so long?

❧

"Don't ask me," George Brett told me. This was at a roadside hamburger bar in Demopolis, Alabama. It was raining. I had stopped to grab something to eat while I waited for the roads to dry. I sat at a splintery picnic table beneath the shelter and ate a greasy grilled chicken sandwich. There were other tables, plenty of places George could have chosen to sit. But he sat next to me.

He didn't sit beside me for any reason. He didn't start talking to me, didn't mention the bike, didn't even say hello. He nodded at me, but that was all. He wasn't sitting with me so much as he simply wasn't avoiding me. I was sitting near the walk-up window where he had placed his order and paid for it. Now that he had gotten his burger he sat beside me to eat it. I felt compelled to speak to him.

"I'm not a good one to ask," he said. "We couldn't afford none of that being prejudiced stuff. My daddy was a school principal. It just never made any sense in my house."

≥❧

The South was trying hard, reaching out to me in such simple, subtle ways, offering me friendship's hand, showing me its prettiest face.

Its pretty faces are lovely to look at, sweet and inviting. But the South has an ugly face too. And its ugly face is the face of a nightmare.

Greg Davis was a nightmare. My path crossed his at a gasoline station in northeast Tennessee. I had filled my tank and absent-mindedly took my time moving away from the pump. The car behind me started honking.

Way back near Sopchoppy, Florida, a car had started honking behind me. I had been taking my time that day too, driving at the speed limit for a change, not racing like a maniac. The car behind was trying to get around me. The driver was in an awful hurry. Oncoming traffic wouldn't let him pass. And I wouldn't let him get around me. I wouldn't speed up either. He started weaving in the lane to get my attention. He never stopped blowing his horn.

He got my attention all right. I slowed down even more. When he moved left in the lane, I moved left. When he moved to the right, so did I. I made him pay for his impatience.

About a mile down the road we approached the entrance to a hospital. I went past it. The frantic man behind me turned in. I felt miserable. Beside him in the car a woman seemed to be in agony. Maybe she had had a heart attack. Maybe she was having a baby. Who knows, but I swore I would try to see the other fellow's point of view and be more considerate.

But not today. Today in Tennessee I was up to my old tricks.

This crazy man wanted me to move at his pace. I forced him to move at mine.

"Are you going to get that thing out of my way?" he shouted. "Or am I going to have to knock it over?"

"And me with it, I presume."

"Get the hell out of the way."

Slowly, very slowly I put on the jacket. Then the gloves. Even in this heat, I dug the gloves out of my gear and put them on. Then my sunglasses. Finally I grabbed the helmet and started to put it on, but first I had to wipe off the visor. The man behind me was burning with rage.

"What's your problem?" I said.

"You're my fucking problem," he screamed. "Now get out of my way."

"No," I said gently. "What's your real problem?"

"You want me to say it," the man said to me. "All right, then, I'll say it. I don't like niggers."

"Simple as that, is it?" I stayed cool and calm.

"Simple as that. You're a nigger, and I don't like you."

I waited for him to get out of his car.

He was about my size, a little heavier maybe, stockier and surely stronger. I couldn't tell if he was older or younger. But he drove an old car that had a few dents in the door and was beginning to rust around the edges; soon it would need a new muffler. The door creaked when it was opened and closed.

I thought of all the ways in my life I had deflected racist attacks—subtle and unconscious racism, or overt racism of the most dangerous kind—and how I had protected myself sometimes with laughter, sometimes with kindness, once with a gun. But this time I wasn't sure I wanted to deflect it. I had been through too much to try to avoid it—too many miles, too many emotions, remembrances, and discoveries. His pride was on the line, and now so was my own.

"You don't even know me, mister . . . mister . . . What's your name?"

He stood up taller.

"Davis," he said, as if he were proud of it, as if I should know who he was. "Greg Davis."

Funny what people will tell you, even information that can be used against them. No wonder common crooks so often get caught.

"Well, Greg Davis, you don't even know me," I said. "You don't know anything about me. How can you not like me?"

"I know enough about you," he said. "I know all I need to know. You're a nigger and that's enough for me."

If he had said this to me two weeks ago I would have popped him in the mouth, six weeks ago I would have broken his arm, four months ago and I would be telling this story to my death-row prison mates. Today all I could do was laugh at him.

All of a crazy sudden, my fear and loathing and most of my rage escaped from me, and the only response I had for Greg Davis was laughter.

The South is a little child wanting approval, a scared and con-fused little orphan hiding its self-doubt behind a wall of bluster and self-righteousness.

But then the South has always been very righteous about its wrongness.

In Greenwood, Mississippi, Martha Gabler had told me about her mother whose church refused to be integrated. Someone asked the old woman what Jesus would have done in a similar situation. "Wouldn't Jesus let those black people into his church?" she was asked. She thought for a good while.

"Of course he would," she said. Then she thought a little more.

"But Jesus would have been wrong," she said.

That was the old old South, Martha told me. She wanted me to know things were changing.

This same Martha Gabler who had been raised by a woman who could not see the rightness of acting as Jesus would have done, the living God she prayed to; this same Martha Gabler who was rich and white, the same as her mother; this same Martha Gabler whose household like her mother's was tended to by an old black woman who washed the clothes, made the beds, scrubbed the floors, and minded the children—this same Martha Gabler invited me to stay in her home, sleep in her guest bedroom, and make myself totally and remarkably at home.

The next day she organized a luncheon for me to meet her

friends and to discuss, I suppose, changes they had all seen in the South over the years. But some things never change. I asked them to notice that the waiters and waitresses in this restaurant, as in many many others, were white. The kitchen help was black.

"Why?" I asked.

One lady offered the country's poor economy as an answer.

"Whites have been forced out of the good jobs," she said. "They've had to take jobs black people would normally do. Blacks get forced down even lower."

But Martha—dear Martha—was truly astounded.

"I never honestly paid attention before. To tell you the truth," she said, "I never even thought about who was a waiter and who always worked in the kitchen. I will from now on."

And that was enough for me.

We spent more than two hours at lunch. We talked about many things, important things, I'm sure. But what I remember most was her promise to watch the world a little more carefully.

"If we are ever really going to change," she said, "if things are ever going to get better, we need to look at a lot of things more carefully."

Martha Gabler is the South to me. She represents the glorious generosity that all people are capable of.

Greg Davis is just a throwback to the past, clinging to it the way an old dog clings to life even as it goes into the woods to find a quiet private place to die.

I looked at Greg Davis with pity. He made a fist. I just laughed at him some more. He looked absurd.

He watched me quizzically, as if I was crazy. He took half a step back. I thought he was going to get into his car and drive away. I didn't want that. I had been through too much to let him off that easily.

I had swung south and now was making my way up through Louisiana, winding my way through Cajun country, listening to a language I could not make heads or tails of. I had crossed the great river at Baton Rouge, headed for Natchitoches. I had heard there was a statue called the Good Negro in the town square, hat in hand, head bowed. I wanted to see the shameful thing. Touch the past.

That Sunday morning I passed along Jackson Street in Alexandria, passed Emmanuel Baptist Church. All the churchgoers on their way to the service were white. Every single one. Two blocks down the street, the same street, the same side of the road, Good Hope Baptist Church was receiving its black congregation. Nothing, it seemed, had changed in a hundred years.

I went to a Catholic mass on the other side of the Cape River. As usual I was not paying attention. My mind wandered during readings. *What were these people thinking of me, the only black face in their church this morning?* But something suddenly caught my ear. I knew, of course, I could not have heard what I thought I had heard.

". . . you must lay aside your former way of life and the old South . . ."

I knew he could not have, but I would have sworn he had said "old South." I picked up my missal and found the chapter in Ephesians the lector had been reading from. It said "old self," but that was close enough.

When I left mass that morning, twenty, thirty people greeted me in the friendliest fashion and shook my hand hello.

Some things do change.

Some things never do.

Bernie Moreland stopped me outside a convenience store where I was drinking juice and eating a doughnut.

"Man, it sure is good to see you," he said.

I thought he had mistaken me for somebody else.

"It's good to see a black man standing tall and proud," he said. "These black people in the South are all hangdog tired. I have just got to get out of here."

He was a musician from Kansas City. His wife, who was from Alexandria, had dragged him here to live.

"Not even for love can I take much more of this," he said.

"It's not changing?"

"Not fast enough for me," he said. "Not fast enough, not far enough. You be careful on that bike. This is still the South, you know."

As Greg Davis was at this moment making very clear.

But other places, other people were making other gestures, other signs that things were indeed very different.

The Good Negro had been removed from the square in Natchitoches. In the place where it used to stand, flowers now grow.

The South was growing on me, little by little, showing me the tiny ways it was trying to make peace. With the past, perhaps. Perhaps with me.

On my way out of Natchitoches I was flying along the narrow roads at my customary eighty-five, ninety miles an hour, up through the back country, heading toward Arkansas. Just before Winnfield and the left turn that would take me north, I saw a cop far in the distance ahead of me. I tried to slow down, but at that speed, with him coming toward me, there was no way. As soon as he got close, the red lights were on, the siren squealed for half a moment to get my attention. The police car skidded into a U-turn in the middle of the road. I slowed immediately and stopped.

The Louisiana trooper who pulled himself from the car was tall and thin. He walked slow. He took long careful strides. As he walked toward me, he started speaking. His drawl was as slow as his walk.

"How y'all doing today?" he said.

I just laughed. What else could I do? He had me red-handed.

"I don't know yet," I said. "I'll tell you in a minute."

But already he was talking. He even smiled. The cop in North Carolina who had given me the speeding ticket had not been pleasant. Why should this man be?

I took out my license and handed it to him. He went back to the car and talked into the radio a minute. Then he came back.

"That's a nice-looking bike," he said. "But you ought to drive it a little slower."

"You're right," I said. I was perfectly willing to grovel my way out of a speeding ticket. I would have tried in North Carolina, but that cop wanted nothing friendly to pass between us.

"We got some nice scenery down here," he said. "You ought to slow down and take a look at some of it. Stop and go fishing or something. You're too young to be in a hurry."

He handed back the license.

"I'm not going to give you a ticket," he said. "Just promise me you'll slow it up a little bit."

"I promise," I said. "That's it?"

"That's it," he said.

I tried to read his name tag, Ponthiaux, I think, but he had turned already and was climbing back into his car. He made another U-turn and went on down the road.

I thought once more of the cop in North Carolina who had given me a ticket, the difference in their ways. I just shook my head. I put him out of my mind, far away. I wanted to remember Ponthiaux.

And I wanted to remember Doug Elms, a cop in Little Rock two days later. He came up to me as I was getting on my bike. He was on a bike of his own, had been riding as part of a funeral motorcade. He stopped me, we chatted, he asked if he could take my bike for a spin.

"You can ride mine," he said.

I declined. He insisted. We traded bikes and I followed him.

"I wanted you to see the difference," he said. "Your sweet machine and this old clunker."

We rode out to a café. He bought me lunch. That evening he told me I could go with him when he was on patrol.

"Not on bikes, though," he said. "In a police car."

I was simply astounded.

I did not know what to make of any of this. Maybe some conspiracy was afoot to make me love the South and report back to the real world how everything was right and getting better.

But then there was Greg Davis. And there was Michael Grissom, a failed songwriter turned author in Nashville, Tennessee.

I had ridden up the Natchez Trace from Jackson, where I had met the governor of Mississippi.

Oh yes! I met Ray Mabus, governor of Mississippi. Martha Gabler somehow arranged it. And though I was not very excited about it I went, left Martha's house just after breakfast, and sped south to Jackson. I had to be there at 11:30. The governor, I was warned, was a busy man.

At faster-than-normal speeds it would have been more than a

two-hour trip. I had less time than that. I drove like a maniac, thinking I could explain my speed by saying to any cop who stopped me, "I have a date with the governor. Radio ahead if you don't believe me."

I didn't find out until later that the Mississippi State Patrol are not great supporters of the governor.

Luckily, I was not stopped.

The meeting lasted all of thirty seconds. It was a waste of time for me, nothing but a photo opportunity for Mabus.

Anne Sapp, the governor's director of policy management, tried to console me.

"What was that all about?" I asked. "I thought I was going to get an interview. Does he think I came all this way just to shake his hand and get my picture taken? Believe me, it's not that big a deal to say I was in the capitol with the governor of Mississippi."

"Well," she said. "There was a time when it would have been a very big deal indeed for a black person just to set foot inside this building. Let alone get photographed with the governor."

We went to a black neighborhood, she and I, for a huge lunch of greens and ham and beans and corn bread and sweet potatoes. The place was packed. No wonder there were no cops on the highway to stop me. They were all in here. Black cops sitting with white cops.

"Not long ago," Anne said, "there were no black state troopers. We're inching along in Mississippi. It's not a bad place."

But I couldn't stay. I had made a date to meet Michael Grissom the next afternoon in Nashville. I rode through the night and all the next morning to find him. It started to rain. I stopped for a few hours. I continued on. I really wanted to meet him.

I knew him only as the author of a book that had grabbed my attention one day. The cover of the book is white, with blue letters, all bordered in red. In the center, the thing that caught my eye was the red-white-and-blue battle flag of the Confederacy. The man in whose shop I found the book was embarrassed even to carry the thing, he said. But it was selling like crazy, he admitted, and this too embarrassed him.

Southern by the Grace of God. I didn't want to read it. But I wanted to talk to the man who wrote it.

I found Grissom through his publisher, phoned him, and made the date. I did not tell him I was black, and he was startled, frightened, in fact, when I crept up behind him and introduced myself. His face, gaunt and ghostly, fell. He had assumed I was a fan. Now he feared I had come to do him harm.

I let him squirm a minute, then put him at ease.

"Boy howdy!" he kept saying, as if he couldn't get over the shock. "You sure didn't sound black over the phone."

"What does black sound like?" I asked.

"Boy howdy!" he said again.

We sat in a booth in a fast-food restaurant across from Music Row in the heart of Nashville. And we talked for an hour.

Here was a man who believed in strict segregation. He had written a book that celebrates, he said, the lasting legacy of being a southerner.

"That means racist to me," I said.

"It isn't racist to want nothing to do with black people," he said. "I don't want to harm them in any way. I just don't want to be forced to socialize with them. I don't want to have to do business with them. I wouldn't want to have to go to school with them or anything else."

Which may explain why there is hardly any mention in his book of any black contribution to the South, even very little mention of slavery, except in passing.

"Slavery was not a bad thing," he said. "We took a savage race and introduced them to our culture. They were much better off as slaves than they would have been if we had left them in Africa."

"Do you really believe that?" I asked. "Do you think it's a good thing to steal people from their homes and subject them to pain and anguish? Do you think the South should still have slavery?"

"It would sure solve the unemployment problem among blacks," he said. "And most slaves you will find if you look into it were not treated bad. Slaves were valuable property. Nobody wants his property messed up. Yes, I do wish those idyllic days could come back. It was a much more civilized time, chivalrous and honorable."

There was a time, and not so long ago, when I would have wanted to grab Grissom by the throat and thrash the life out of him. Now I just wanted to laugh.

I lie. I did want to hurt him. I wanted to slap him silly, wanted to take hold of his arm and break it, wanted to strangle him by his skinny neck. There was a time, not so long ago, when I would have done it. But now I felt sorry for this man who yearned for what used to be, for a past not even as it really was, but as he wished it had been. I felt sorry that his life was so wretched that he had to live deeply in an imagined past. I sat on my hands and pitied him.

Grissom embodied for me all that the old South stands for, the way it clings to the past and wallows in it, revels in it, and wears blinders to block out the truth. He was the South that refuses to see its guilty hand, and in that refusal holds us back, locks us in the past.

Grissom was the man I most wanted to hate, his the face I wanted to spit upon, the body I most wanted to kick, stab, wound mortally, the neck I most wanted to break. If I needed a face to hang upon the ogres of my nightmares, his was it. In the end there was no hate, only a bemused kind of sadness. It would have been like flogging a child.

In the old South it was the Negro who was looked upon as a child, helpless in the ways of the world, needing protection from himself. How utterly strange.

Grissom even looked like a child. He sat there grinning at me.

I was fleeing Grissom and the violent things I was tempted to do to him when I stopped for gas somewhere east of Knoxville. I had gotten onto the interstate highway and zoomed south toward Chattanooga, then north into the mountains where the air was cool and saving.

I thought I would head back north into Kentucky, go east over those mountains into coal mining country and watch men move mountains.

They do that there. They dismantle mountains to get at the coal. Then they miraculously rebuild them. If you did not know exactly how it had once been, you would never know.

I was drawn there, to see this miracle, to make a certain peace with a place I had left in an uneasy state of mind. I got off the Blue Ridge Parkway and retraced my route through Hampton and Elizabethton, Johnson City and Morristown, Tazewell and up toward the Cumberland Gap. There in the mountains, before I crossed up into Kentucky, Greg Davis came up behind me.

"So what's it going to be?" I said. "A battle of wits? You haven't got a chance."

He started to frown, took a step forward.

"Or are we just going to fight?" I asked. "I am old, my back is tired from spending too much time on that bike, I'm probably not as strong you. But I have been through too much to let you beat me."

I didn't really want to fight him. But I would if I had to, fight him until one of us died, if necessary.

"You're a hardheaded nigger," he said. "You don't know when to leave well enough alone. We have ways of dealing with the likes of you."

"Sounds like the Klan talking," I said. "You better call all your friends. Because no way would I let a man like you beat me at anything."

"You talk tough," he said.

"I'm not tough," I said. "I only know there's no way you can win this fight. There's nothing you can do that will make you better than me. Nothing you can do that can make me afraid of you. You can get a gun and wave it in front of my face, any child can do that. You can blow my brains out, you can get your pals and beat me senseless, maybe you can beat me senseless all by yourself. I doubt it. Anyway in the end it's your loss. I feel sorry for you. You can't see how you're cheating yourself. You think you're holding me back, but you're only hurting yourself. At home you're preparing your children to deal with a white world, but I'm in the world. Black people are here. We've been here and we're going to be here. And if you can't deal with that— after all we've been through together, you and me and all of us— then you're just a poor dumb son of a bitch and I hope you do try to hurt me so I can kill your stupid ass and save somebody else the trouble."

He didn't know what to say. Neither did I.

A small crowd had gathered. They watched and listened in utter silence.

By now my legs had started to shake. I hoped no one could tell.

There was more I could have said, maybe more I should have said, but he hesitated, and while he was thinking I guessed it might be a good time to clear out.

I hopped on the bike and didn't look back.

ॐ

Up over the mountains to Kentucky, back through Pineville and Barbourville, through Corbin and all the way back to the crossroads, where at last the road I had wanted to travel and the road I had found myself on, roads which up to now had diverged, became the same road. I was led no longer by the voice of addiction nor by the soft whispering voices of travel muses or the ghosts of those who had gone before, but this time by my own volition and desire.

I was on my way home.

I returned to this crossroads near London, Kentucky, where my path had turned, to this same small restaurant on the south side of the road. I entered the parking lot. There were only two cars in the lot. I stopped the bike and looked around. It was the same place, still made of brick and wood, still attached to a small hotel, still without charm. But something was different.

I was full of misgivings this second time around. If those same two women were here this day, I knew I would seem a fool to them. They would still be standing at the front counter, no doubt still gabbing about Cliff. Although they had made me feel invisible the last time, they would recognize me today and laugh. They would know that they had driven me out, that their discourtesy had been my ruin. They would feel they had won some small battle. I was looking for an excuse not to have to go in, but couldn't find one. Same as before, the hunger in my belly led the way.

There were a couple of chain restaurants nearby I noticed, but that hardly mattered. There was an entire town just down the road, but that didn't matter either. This was the place I had to come to. This was the place where I wanted to eat.

I pulled open the door slowly, apprehensively, wondering as I walked inside if my treatment would be the same, or if it would be worse.

Right away I noticed that the place seemed redecorated. It was much brighter than before. The glass counter wasn't there. A big buffet wagon stood in the middle of the dining room. I hadn't noticed that before. I wondered if it was the same restaurant.

A harried waitress working alone hustled up to seat me. Her name was Alice, and she smiled at me. She called me sugar. I was in the South all right, and suddenly once more, it really and truly felt like home.

"They've got me working like a six-legged mule," she said. "I'm slow but I won't forget you."

"Take your time," I said. "I'm not in a hurry."

"Thanks, sugar. What can I bring you to drink? Cold glass of iced tea?"

She pulled a pencil from her hair and scratched her head with it.

"Yeah," I said. "Something cool. Iced tea will be fine."

She was about to dash away but something stopped her. She turned back, and stared at me just for a second.

"You know what, sugar? I've got a feeling I know you from somewhere. You got people around here? Maybe I know some of your people."

Yeah. The South. It felt like home.

"You never know," I said. "You never know."

About the Author

Eddy Harris graduated from Stanford University in 1977. He went on to study in London and write for an English-language newspaper in Paris. Mr. Harris is the author of two critically acclaimed travel books, *Mississippi Solo* and *Native Stranger*. He calls St. Louis, Missouri, home.